The KGB Lawsuits

by

Brian Crozier

**Foreword
by
Sir James Goldsmith**

The Claridge Press

First published in Great Britain 1995

by The Claridge Press
33 Canonbury Park South
London N1 2JW
Copyright © Brian Crozier

Printed by
Antony Rowe Limited
Chippenham

CIP data for this title is available from the British Library

ISBN 1-870626-02-8

Politics

Contents

Foreword

Since the fall of the Berlin wall, part of the files of Soviet Bloc Intelligence has become available. This has confirmed the massive campaign of spying, disinformation and other 'active measures', and terrorism which was orchestrated in Eastern Europe. In West Germany alone, East Germany's State Security Service, better known as the STASI, maintained a network of agents estimated at between 3,000 and 5,000, ranging from office cleaners to ministers. Some 50,000 telephones, including government offices, were tapped. All important centres of power, including of course the media, had been infiltrated. No one now denies that Communist Intelligence had operated networks throughout the Western world.

It is amazing, is it not, that those in the West who could see this at the time were mocked, ridiculed and became the targets of widespread media campaigns in their own countries. But Lenin understood the West and appreciated the value of those he described as the 'useful idiots' who pullulate among us.

Brian Crozier was one of the few who also understood.

James Goldsmith

Author's Note

Everybody has heard of the KGB; few would know what the initials FIS stand for. Yet the FIS is simply a new incarnation of the First Chief Directorate of the KGB, which was responsible for its foreign operations. The new initials stand for 'Foreign Intelligence Service', in plain English, whereas KGB stands for three words meaning 'Committee of State Security'.

I am not saying that nothing has changed since the collapse of the Soviet system at the end of 1991, simply that Russian espionage continues where Soviet spying stopped. Anybody naive enough to think otherwise would have had to wake up when the Ames case burst into the headlines in February 1994.[1]

This book, however, is not about espionage as such: it is about one of the main activities of the old KGB, known as 'Active Measures'. Essentially, Active Measures is a euphemism for 'dirty tricks', such as the deliberate planting of falsehoods (known as 'disinformation'), the use of 'agents of influence' (whose job or commitment was to influence Western policies in a pro-Soviet sense), forgeries of documents, and the use of Soviet fronts (such as the World Peace Council, whose remit was to spread the Soviet view of 'peace', meaning disarmament of the Western powers). In sum, Active Measures were at the heart of the Cold War, which the Soviet side used to define as 'peaceful co-existence'.

And in that domain, I have to say that, as far as one can judge, there has been a considerable change since the collapse of the Soviet Union and the 'end of the Cold War'. Whereas Active Measures continued throughout the reign of Mikhail Gorbachev, there is little evidence that they continued once Boris Yeltsin took over from Gorbachev.[2]

One of the most subtle and effective of Soviet Active Measures was the manipulation of Western — and especially British — libel laws in the interest of Soviet objectives. I write 'especially British' because the British laws of defamation are notoriously weighted in favour of the plaintiff, and therefore against the defendant. Whereas those accused of crimes, including murder, are considered innocent until proved guilty, defendants in libel cases are assumed to be guilty unless they can prove their innocence.

I should know, for in the 1980s, I was involved in several libel cases. In one of these, I was the defendant; in others I was on the side of the defendant or defendants, either on contract to find the evidence that would prove the innocence of those accused, or willing and able to help them. In all the cases, there was a demonstrable KGB involvement. Hence the title, 'The KGB Lawsuits'. I stress, however, that the accusers (legally known as 'plaintiffs') were not necessarily aware of a KGB connection. Indeed, it was clearly in the KGB's interests that the plaintiff should not be aware of any such link; just as the ultimate subtlety of an 'agent of influence' is that the person concerned should be 'unconscious' (or as the Americans put it, 'unwitting'): in other words, unaware of a KGB interest in the views he or she might propagate.

The story of the first of the cases examined in this book, in which Sir James Goldsmith was the defendant, has been told elsewhere: by Chapman Pincher in *The Secret Offensive* (1985) and by Ivan Fallon in *Billionaire* (1992), his biography of James Goldsmith, each on the basis of material evidence provided by myself with Goldsmith's approval. Before the Goldsmith case was over, I was sued by Richard Barnet, a co-founder of the American Institute for Policy Studies. I was then involved, though not so directly, in several cases revolving around a Greek newspaper called *To Ethnos* ('The Nation').

I summarised all these cases in a chapter entitled 'The KGB Lawsuits', in *FREE AGENT*, my autobiography (Harper Collins, 1993). Why, then, have I written this book-length account of the same cases? The answer is simply that, in my view, the interest of them lies not only in the bare facts of these sometimes traumatic clashes, but at least as much in the details of the dogged search for documentary evidence, and especially for the elusive but mandatory 'smoking gun' witnesses, in the face of a myriad obstacles and of the sheer perversity of Britain's laws of libel.

Here, then, is the first full account of the KGB lawsuits in which I was involved, and of the Active Counter-Measures that were necessary to contain them.

Notes

1.　Aldrich Ames had headed the CIA's Counter-Intelligence for nine years. He was arrested on 21 February 1994, with his wife Maria, and charged with having spied for the KGB since his appointment in 1985. He had, allegedly, been paid the equivalent of £1.5 million for his services. On 28 April he was sentenced to life imprisonment with no prospect of parole. He had pleaded guilty after prosecutors had agreed to bring lesser charges against his wife. The plea bargain spared the CIA a lengthy and potentially embarrassing trial.

2.　Details of post-Soviet Active Measures are given by Herbert Romerstein, a leading American authority, in a booklet published in German in 1993: *DIENST A: "Aktive Massnahmen" in der rüssichen Aussenpolitik* (Presdock AG, Zurich).

Prologue:

The Battles Begin

It was a bleak day in early January 1981. I was idly looking at Nelson's statue from my office window in Grand Buildings, Trafalgar Square, when the telephone brought me back to reality. It was Sir James Goldsmith. As always (the rule seems invariable), his voice was warm and friendly, in contrast to the snow that was settling on the victor of Trafalgar.

'Brian? I've been asked to address the Media Committee of the Conservative Party in the House of Commons. I've done the draft, while I was in America, but something you said in your interview with Strauss in *Now!* the other day caught my eye. I wonder, could you tell me a bit more about it?'

I knew exactly what Sir James meant. 'The other day' was nearly a year ago. My interview with the Bavarian leader, Dr. Franz Josef Strauss, had appeared in Goldsmith's newsmagazine, *Now!*, in the issue dated 15 February 1980. In it, I had described the extraordinary smear campaign to discredit Strauss, referring in particular to the *Der Spiegel* affair of 1962, which had wrecked his chances — at that time rated very highly — of succeeding the aged Dr. Konrad Adenauer as Federal Chancellor (Prime Minister) of West Germany. A meteoric career had been halted at a critical stage. My article had indeed referred to the KGB's role in the affair, quoting the Czechoslovak defector, General Sejna, as the source.

'Of course, Jimmy. What exactly is the subject of your talk?'

'Subversion in the media.'

'Sounds up my street. What can I tell you that you don't already know?'

'Your reference to the KGB's role in the *Spiegel* affair. Are you sure that's true? Can you give me further details?'

'I'm as sure of the facts as one can be in such matters. But first, could you let me see your draft?'

The text came by special messenger. Even as it stood, it was explosive. But it would be all the more so if he included a reference to the *Spiegel* affair, one of the most astonishing examples of a Soviet success in manipulating Western media. Apart from this, I had few comments to offer on the draft.

Sir James invited me to the large office of Cavenham Communications in the City, from which he had launched *Now!*. For some months, I had been writing a fortnightly column there, covering and analysing world affairs.

It was, I think, our third meeting. I was struck, as always, by the extraordinary charisma of the Anglo-French financier. Six feet four, but slightly stooped, broad-shouldered, piercing blue eyes and a radiant smile.

He asked me to remind him of the details of the *Spiegel* affair.

I did: Jimmy's thinning silver hair was deceptive. I had to remind myself that he was 15 years younger than I: 47 to my 62. In 1962, I was commenting on such affairs for *The Economist* and the BBC. James Goldsmith was in the early stages of his extraordinary career as a gambler of genius, only distantly interested in the West German political scandal.

'This defector from Czechoslovakia, General Sejna — how reliable would you say he is?'

'The point, really, is that he was in a position to know, as a leading figure in his party. He was head of the Defence Committee, or some such function, and he would have had access to top secret information from the Soviets, who wanted to involve the Czech secret service in the operation to discredit Strauss.'

Sir James was pensive. 'Tell me, are you the only writer to have mentioned Sejna's revelations?'

I gave him a reassuring smile. 'Good Lord, no! Bill Buckley mentioned it, and Walter Hahn, among others.'

Jimmy Goldsmith, of course, knew William F. Buckley Jr., Editor of the conservative New York magazine, *National Review*, but asked me who Walter Hahn was.

'He's very well known in defence circles, especially in America. Edits a quarterly called *Strategic Review*. He's a good friend of mine, by the way. If I remember rightly, it was Hahn who first revealed what Sejna said about *Der Spiegel*. Let's go over the draft together, shall we?'

On 21 January 1981, Sir James Goldsmith delivered his talk to the Conservative Party's Media Committee. The title, appropriately, was "The Communist Propaganda Apparatus and other Threats to the Media". The key passage, as we had drafted it, came out in the following words:

> General Sejna, the high-ranking Czech intelligence defector, admitted that the campaign by the German news magazine *Der Spiegel* to discredit Franz-Josef Strauss was orchestrated by the KGB.

Although neither of us realised it at the time, with these few words the die had been cast.

Sir James's father, Major Frank Goldsmith, though German-born, had been elected a Member of Parliament, until hounded out in the wave of anti-German spy hysteria that followed the outbreak of the Great War in 1914. Sir James, however, had never stood for Parliament. His statement, though made in a committee room of the House of Commons, was not privileged.

In the issue of *Now!* dated 7 February 1981, his Media Committee speech was reproduced in full. On 6 March, solicitors acting for Rudolf Augstein, owner and publisher of *Der Spiegel*, issued a writ for libel. They demanded a retraction and an apology, with costs and damages.

We next met in the comfort of Sir James's English home, Ormeley Lodge, on the southern border of Richmond Park. He showed me the writ.

'What are you going to do?' I asked.

'Fight it, of course. All the way.'

Some people have a taste, a feel, for litigation. I am not one of them. Sir James Goldsmith emphatically is. His lawsuits against the satirical weekly, *Private Eye*, have become legendary. The *Spiegel* battle, now beginning, however, would be a titanic one, relegating the earlier battles to mere skirmishes in comparison.

From start to finish, I was deeply involved in it.

Before it ended, more than three years later, my own turn had come.

1. The Wounding of Strauss

I first met the late Franz Josef Strauss in October 1958.

I had been invited to West Germany by the Federal Press Office (*Bundespresseamt*). At the Bonn end of the tour, I had requested an interview with Strauss, at that time Defence Minister in Dr Adenauer's conservative government. His reputation as a dynamic and innovative politician was growing fast, he was seen as a potential successor to 'the Old Man' and I knew he would give me a story for *The Economist*'s confidential weekly bulletin, *Foreign Report*, which I edited.

He did indeed, but he had kept me waiting for 20 minutes, and only half an hour had been allocated for the interview. My next appointment was a press conference at the British embassy with Britain's Prime Minister, Harold Macmillan.

Strauss apologised for keeping me waiting and offered to prolong our talk. I chose Macmillan. A mistake of which I later repented at leisure.

At that time Strauss was Leader of the Bavarian-based Christian Social Union (CSU), junior partners to Chancellor Adenauer's Christian Democratic Union (CDU). Of no one could it more truly be said that the man inside was not the man you saw in the flesh. Built like a bull, he looked like the son of a master butcher, which he was. But he had a mind of rare subtlety and brilliance. (Years later, during an audience with Pope John-Paul II, the common tongue they chose was Latin.)

In 1958, hardly a shadow — other than the envy of those less gifted — disturbed the bright political future that beckoned him. At 82, Adenauer seemed immortal as well as immovable. But death would come in due course, and Strauss (at that time only 43) could fulfil his apparent destiny.

On that trip, with the Cold War at its height, I went to Berlin, East as well as West, and talked with some of the 28,000 refugees pouring across the demarcation line every month. Three years later, the Berlin Wall went up and in the following year, 1962, the 'Spiegel affair' wrecked Franz Josef Strauss's career.

'Die Spiegel Affäre': the story was enacted in the glare of world publicity. But 'the story behind the story' only came to light many years later, and it was when Jimmy Goldsmith referred to it that 'the KGB lawsuits' began.

'Fallex 62' was the code name of a secret NATO exercise. The 'secrecy' was shattered in a sensational article in *Der Spiegel* of 10 October 1962, under the suggestive title of 'Limited Defence Readiness' (*bedingt Abwehrbereit*). What was a top official secret doing in the public pages of a German newsmagazine? Not only were the details correct, but so was the secret NATO analysis of the exercise which *Der Spiegel* also published.

The exercise had been staged in Western Europe in September. It was the first of its kind, based on the assumption that the Soviet forces had started a Third World War by attacking Germany with nuclear weapons. Large parts of West Germany and Britain were assumed to have been reduced to radioactive rubble, with 15 million killed. In the ensuing exchange, the US had sustained still larger casualties.

Having revealed the unrevealable, *Der Spiegel* had taken an anti-Strauss line. There was praise for the line taken by President John F. Kennedy, who was advocating a suitable build-up of NATO's conventional forces so that the use of nuclear weapons could be delayed, or even abandoned. This was not Strauss's view. He argued that if it became known that the Allies were not going to use the nuclear arm, its deterrent effect would be lost. Chancellor Adenauer agreed with his Defence Minister.

It was clear from the article that the German Army commanders went along with Kennedy's view. In other words, they favoured a rapid build-up of conventional forces, whereas the Luftwaffe chiefs supported Strauss in calling for a pre-emptive NATO strike capability, arguing that if the Soviets knew that NATO had this capability, and the will to use it, they would never launch a Warsaw Pact offensive. The popular version of what happened next was that Dr. Strauss exploded when he read the offending article, which he saw as a glaring and unprecedented breach of official security; that he ordered the arrest of all concerned, and in so doing usurped the functions of the Minister of Justice and rode roughshod over the rights of those arrested. In a speech on 2 November 1962, Strauss proclaimed his innocence of such charges, but hardly anybody believed him at the time. Years later, the facts that came to light fully vindicated him, but the vindication came too late to save his career.

In fact, all the relevant decisions were taken by Chancellor Adenauer who, on the evidence, was politically happy that the blame should fall on his Defence Minister.

The Federal Criminal Police (*Bundeskriminalamt*) raided the offices of *Der Spiegel* in Hamburg and Bonn, which they thoroughly searched and sealed off from prying eyes. Rudolf Augstein, the publisher, was arrested. So were the acting Editor, Hans-Detlev Becker, Managing Editor Klaus Jacobi and one of the senior journalists, Hans Schmelz. The Editor, Konrad Ahlers, who had written the offending article, was on holiday in Spain. He was arrested on his return to Germany.

All those arrested were committed to prison to await trial on charges of treason and lesser counts. Several other arrests followed. One of those detained was a Colonel Alfred Martin, at that time a Defence Ministry official. Another was Colonel Adolf Wichts of the Federal Intelligence Service (the famous General Gehlen's *Bundesnachrichtendienst* or BND). It was alleged that it was Martin who had passed military secrets to the magazine, and Wichts who had tipped off Augstein and Ahlers that a raid was about to be ordered, thus enabling them to remove other secret documents from the premises.

According to the Federal Prosecutor-General, a copy of the secret minutes of the Parliamentary Committee of the West German Bundestag had been found in the offices of *Der Spiegel*. Some of these were 'State secrets of the first importance', but there were also classified photographs of unspecified 'military objects'. Gehlen himself told the Defence Ministry that NATO secret documents were in the possession of Augstein. Strauss later declared that information from his own ministry had been passed on to *Der Spiegel* giving the numbers of American nuclear warheads on German soil, with full details of their explosive power and of selected targets.

Strauss was the victim and scapegoat. Politically, events moved fast; juridically, as always, the pace was funereally slow.

Strauss's critics were quick to point out that he had long been the target for smears and attacks from *Der Spiegel*. What else could be expected from him, they asked, than that he should now seize this opportunity to get his own back? The controlled press east of the Iron Curtain joined in the action with customary gusto and unanimity. In Moscow, the anti-Strauss line was taken by *Pravda* and *Izvestiya*; in East Berlin, by the ruling party's daily, *Neues Deutschland*. The general line was that Strauss, by ordering the arrests, had behaved as the Nazis did when Hitler came to power. The public outcry, in the West German press and in the Bundestag, was that Strauss should go, and that Augstein and his journalists should be freed immediately.

From his prison cell, Augstein wrote an article accusing Strauss of various malpractices. Augstein was a powerful man, even in gaol. His article reached its target and was published in *Der Spiegel* of 14 November, under the telling title: 'Shall the State go to ruin for one man?'

At the time, Dr. Adenauer's governing team was a coalition of the two Christian parties (CDU and CSU) and of the Free Democratic Party (FDP), usually known as the 'Liberals'. The FDP leader, Dr. Erich Mende, called on Adenauer to tell him that the opposition Social Democrats (SDP) appeared to have still more damaging information about Strauss. The coalition was in danger, he insisted, unless Strauss was removed.

Although Adenauer was well aware that the charges and abuse hurled at Strauss were unfounded, he chose the easy way out. On 26 November, the Chancellor told his Defence Minister that he would have to go. A new coalition government of the same parties, but excluding Strauss, was announced on 11 December.

So much for the political crisis. The judicial and personal vindication took much longer.

In May 1963, the Federal Supreme Court in Karlsruhe dropped the charges of treason against Augstein and his journalists, on the ground of insufficient evidence. All were released. On 25 October 1966, charges of breaching official secrets against Colonel Martin, the Defence Ministry official, were also dropped, on the curious ground that they could not be pressed 'without endangering the security of the State'.

At the same time, the Supreme Court decided that the police action against *Der Spiegel* had been lawful and constitutional. More relevantly, it also ruled that Strauss and his Defence Ministry had not, as alleged, played a decisive part in initiating the raid. Indeed, it pointed out that Strauss had been on holiday at the time, and the Defence Ministry's report on the security aspects of the article in *Der Spiegel* had gone straight to the Prosecutor-General without being shown to Strauss.

It was not until nearly six years later that the full extent of Strauss's innocence was revealed, when his former Chief Press Officer at the Defence Ministry, Gerd Schmuckle, told the story. Ironically, and to the belated credit of Rudolf Augstein, he did so in an article in *Der Spiegel* itself, dated 30 August 1982.

Schmuckle had gone to Strauss's holiday retreat in Bavaria to show him the original article about the secret Fallex exercise. Strangely, perhaps out of concern for the relaxation of his boss, he had assured Strauss that the article seemed relatively harmless. So Strauss didn't bother to read it, and went right on relaxing.

One more item deserves mention. The man whose approach to Chancellor Adenauer had led to Strauss's exclusion from the cabinet, Dr. Erich Mende, also made amends years later. In December 1979, by then long retired as leader of the FDP, Mende gave an interview to the magazine *Student*. The title told the story: 'NEW FACTS PROVED: A *Spiegel* Scandal, not a Strauss Affair'.

Mende made it clear that Strauss had had nothing to do with the arrests of Augstein, Ahlers and the others. The whole thing had been handled personally by the Chancellor. Even the Federal Justice Minister, Dr. Wolfgang Stammberger (an FDP member of the Cabinet), had been by-passed. He revealed that the facts had been explained to him by Dr. Adenauer in a conversation on Monday 26 November 1962 — the day Strauss had been sacked. Adenauer had decided to exclude Stammberger from the whole operation because he was suspected of being the source of a series of leaks to *Der Spiegel*. It turned out (according to the Chancellor) that Stammberger had been punished for various offences as a member of the Wehrmacht. 'He had [said Mende] been found guilty of bogus reports, fraud and disloyalty as well as forgery of documents. There were papers concerning these matters in the *Spiegel* archives, and Stammberger knew this.'

The Bavarian leader was a fighter, and in the Federal elections of 1980, he made a determined attempt to come back. The attempt failed, and it was his opponent, the Social Democratic leader, Helmut Schmidt, whose party swept back to power, with Schmidt as Chancellor. Clearly, the long shadow of the Spiegel affair was a major reason why Strauss, and the CDU/CSU partnership he then led, lost the elections.

By the time the election campaign began an entirely new angle had come to light: the whole affair, according to a man in a position to know, had been engineered by the KGB as part of a deliberate attempt to discredit Strauss and wreck his chances of becoming Federal Chancellor.

The man was the Czech defector, Major-General Jan Sejna of the Czechoslovak StB, the highest-ranking defector from any of the Soviet Bloc's secret services. Sejna had defected to the West during the great crisis of 1968, known as 'the Prague Spring'. He told his story in his book, *We Will Bury You* (1982).

For months, Sejna was debriefed by his new masters, the CIA. He had much to say of importance, but for some reason, the CIA was not particularly interested in his revelations about the KGB's hand in the *Spiegel* affair and the defamation of Franz Josef Strauss. It is a general rule of the secret world that defectors find life difficult. Having been 'squeezed dry' by the host service, they are given a chance to adapt to civilian life in their country of refuge. Some succeed, others don't. Sejna was one of the unlucky ones. In the end, his problem was solved when he accepted a senior post on the Defense Intelligence Agency (DIA), the Pentagon's relatively small equivalent to the CIA.

It was through the DIA that the facts came out, but not until 1977 — nine years after Sejna's defection. Dr. Walter Hahn, Austrian-born defence specialist, had referred to Sejna in the quarterly *Strategic Review*, of which he was the Editor. Through a friend in the DIA, he was thereupon invited to a classified briefing of Pentagon officials, given by Sejna.

Dr. Hahn, an old friend of mine, later gave me a copy of his (private) report on this meeting. Here are the key passages:

Sejna gave a run-down, among other things, of Czech intelligence operations in the 1950s and 1960s. Among them, he mentioned Franz Josef Strauss and the *Spiegel* Affair. I could not pursue the matter at the briefing but, several months later, I was tipped off that Sejna was no longer under DIA wraps. I arranged a meeting with him in the early summer of 1978. He told me then what he knew about the *Spiegel* Affair.

According to Sejna, the calculation was that the publication by *Der Spiegel* of NATO documents would have the effect, at the very least, of triggering a scandal which would put Strauss under fire for his failure to prevent leaks from the Defence Ministry. At best, given his volatile nature, Strauss might overreact and thus get himself into deeper difficulties. Sejna said that he was present when the Czech Minister of the Interior, Rudolf Barak, presented the plan for the *Spiegel* operation to the Czech Central Committee. Barak had to get approval at the highest level because it represented a 'strategic operation' involving the transfer of documents.

Sejna told me also of a sequel to the story. In 1965, a meeting of high-level Warsaw Pact officials took place in Prague. The meeting was given a briefing by Vladimir Koucky, the secretary of the Czech Central Committee in charge of foreign affairs. Koucky gave a run-down of Czech covert operations in Western Europe. He bragged at length about the success of the operation against Strauss.[1]

Two years elapsed. On a trip to Munich in October 1979, Walter Hahn met Strauss and told him what Sejna had declared. The story sounded plausible, said Strauss. He too had had indications that outside forces were involved in the *Spiegel* Affair.

Hahn then decided that the time was surely ripe to put Sejna's revelations into the public domain. He discussed the matter with William F. Buckley, the American conservative communicator, who instructed an assistant of his, Richard Brookhiser, to meet Sejna and take down what he said. Sejna's words were incorporated in an article by Mr Buckley, under the title 'The Vindication of Strauss', in *National Review* of 8 February 1980.

The Federal elections were scheduled for October, and already there was much speculation about Strauss's chances of finally reaching the top.

Shortly before the Buckley article appeared, I had gone to Munich to

interview Strauss for Sir James Goldsmith's *Now!* magazine (see Pro-
logue). In the accompanying article, I wrote: 'The high-ranking Czech
defector, General Sejna, revealed to Western intelligence services years
after the event that the *Spiegel* Affair was a KGB exercise to discredit
Strauss'.

It was with those words, only slightly modified, that 'the KGB lawsuits' began. A year later, Sir James Goldsmith, in his address to the
Media Committee of the Conservative Party, put it this way: The
campaign...to discredit Franz Josef Strauss was orchestrated by the
KGB'.

When Augstein's writ was served, we had to prove that what Sir
James (and others) had said about the KGB's involvement in the Spiegel
affair was true. I knew the battle was going to be long and tough. But
I could not have guessed how long and how tough. Only a man with the
financial resources and the determination of a James Goldsmith could
have seen it through.

Somewhere in my chaotic files, I knew, was a relevant statement. I
found it: a Memorandum I wrote to Donald Tyerman, then Editor of
The Economist, on 23 June 1961, about a talk I had had at the Foreign
Office with Sir Frank Roberts, then British Ambassador in Moscow. It
ran:

> Sir Frank had Mikoyan [a well-known Armenian Communist and
> a member of the Politburo, at that time headed by Nikita Khruschchev]
> to dinner recently. Mikoyan argued that the West Germans were get-
> ting stronger, that the present government was all right, but that
> Adenauer was getting older, and who knew what would come after
> him? It would be dreadful if Strauss came to power. In that event
> there really would be a revanchist attitude in West Germany and an
> attempt to unify Germany by force.[2]

To me, this record of a conversation in Moscow, more than a year before the *Spiegel* affair began, was a determining element in that it provided, however unwittingly, evidence of Soviet motivation. The Politburo did want to prevent Strauss from becoming Chancellor of West
Germany.

Notes

1.   This document, one of many I passed on to Mr Chapman Pincher, by arrangement with Sir James Goldsmith, also appears in his book, *The Secret Offensive*, along with some others. I reproduce them here because they are essential to an understanding of the libel suit against Sir James. — BC

2.   Asked about this conversation on my behalf by a former foreign Office colleague, Sir Frank Roberts said he had no recollection of the dinner, or of his conversation with me. There is nothing dishonourable about a lapse of memory more than 20 years after the event. But there is no doubt whatever that I did meet Sir Frank at that time and that this is what he said. It should be noted that the conversation took place some 20 months before the *Spiegel* affair began, which showed that at that time the Soviets were worried enough about the prospect of Strauss as Chancellor to mention the matter to a Western diplomat.   The net effect of the Ambassador's (diplomatic?) lapse of memory, however, was that the statement would not have been admissible as evidence in an English Court of Law, since Sir Frank Roberts would presumably not have felt able to appear as a witness for the Defence and be cross-examined. — BC

2. The Hunt for Sejna

One thing was clear: the key potential witness for our defence was the man who had seen the plan for the *Spiegel* operation before his defection: General Jan Sejna. The question was how to gain access to him. There were grounds for optimism in that the political atmosphere had changed for the better with the departure of President Jimmy Carter, and the advent of President Reagan and his team, many of whom were personal and political friends of mine. The impossible had surely become possible.

What I didn't realise until I tested the atmosphere was that it was still thick with the prohibitive mists of the recent past. I thought I had several easy alternative routes to Sejna, but I was wrong. The road ahead was blocked, and unblocking it was going to take time and ingenuity.

My first choice was the Defense Intelligence Agency. During the dark years of post-Watergate and Carter, I had maintained close links with the DIA, which had come through that period relatively unscathed. For one thing, it was buried much deeper in the Washington bureaucracy. Defence as a government activity was less controversial than foreign and domestic intelligence.

During the dark years, however, the DIA had tried, within limits, to fill at least part of the glaring gap created by the collapse and demoralisation of the CIA, in that it initiated a systematic study and analysis of international communism. There was, however, a specific reason why the DIA seemed a natural channel to the Czech defector. After the hard times I mentioned earlier, a friend had introduced him to that Agency. It didn't take the DIA long to realise how valuable Sejna's detailed inside knowledge of Moscow's East European intelligence apparatus, and strategic insights, were going to be. He was offered, and of course accepted, a post as an analyst.

My friendly contacts included two senior officials of the DIA, one of long years' standing. I put my problem to him. To my surprise, he came back to me next morning to say he was very sorry, but 'the General's under wraps'. He added lamely that Sejna was engaged on highly secret work.

So it was not, after all, going to be an administrative walkover. Next, I tried two non-official channels: Walter Hahn and Joseph Douglass. Hahn and I had first met in England, at a conference in Winchester in 1976. This tall new American from Vienna was not only a leading expert on defence problems, but one of the best American scholarly specialists in the politics of the German-speaking world. And it was he, after all, who had first published Sejna's revelations about *Der Spiegel*.

He gave me a cordial reception, and within days had produced a signed statement for me (from which I quoted in the last chapter). I was well aware that under the English rules of evidence, this was a secondary testimony, carrying more weight, of course, than, say a mere article in a magazine, but less than a statement by the original source of the information. There was no doubt about it: as Bill Buckley had reported, Walter Hahn had indeed interviewed General Sejna and the defector had indeed said what was attributed to him. Unfortunately, he was in no position to arrange a meeting for me with the General himself.

My next port of call was Joe Douglass, whom at that stage I knew only by an already formidable reputation. An engineer and scientist by training, he was much in demand as an independent defence analyst. One of my DIA friends gave me his telephone number, and I invited him to dinner. There was an immediate empathy between us.

Over the years, he had spent, at intervals, months on end with Sejna, debriefing him, extracting the last ounce of knowledge from a clear, reliable memory. He too made a Statement for me, which added valuable and convincing details to what Hahn had already reported. As for access to Sejna, he couldn't help me either, at least for the time being.

The solution now seemed obvious. Although I was aware of the rivalries between the DIA and the CIA, I had to try the Director of Central Intelligence himself, William J. Casey, who happened to be another old friend of mine. I rang his direct line at CIA headquarters at Langley, Virginia, and his senior secretary gave me the bad news: the DCI was on a major foreign tour.

Thus it was that on this first trip to America on the *Spiegel* campaign trail, I returned without my main quarry. Not, however, empty-handed. I had the Hahn and Douglass Statements. Moreover, I had stopped in New York on my way back, dropping in on *National Review*'s rabbit warren of offices. There, I met the very tall, very clever, very young Richard Brookhiser, who had taken down General Sejna's statement for use by his boss, Bill Buckley. Richard gave me another statement, recording how the Sejna meeting had been arranged.

Back in London, I telephoned Jimmy Goldsmith, who couldn't keep the disappointment out of his voice on learning that I had failed to meet Sejna. He said: 'Well, it was a good try. I suppose that's it.'

But this wasn't at all the way I saw it. 'Believe me, Jimmy,' I said, 'this is only a temporary setback. Next time round, I'll get to Sejna, I promise you.'

In the event, it wasn't the next time, but the time after. I have never kept a diary, in the Pepys sense, but I have never discarded the pocket diaries which record whom I met, and where and when.

My 1981 Diary tells me that I made a brief business trip to Puerto Rico on Sunday 29 November, then spent six days in Washington. It was during that week that I caught up with Casey. I rang him on arrival and got straight through.

'Bill,' I said, 'if you can possibly see me, I need to tell you about something really important. It's very urgent. Can you fit me in today?'

I could hear him turning over the pages of his own, doubtless better organised, diary. He mumbled something about an Indonesian delegation. 'How long will it take?' he asked.

'We need about half an hour, so that I can give you the background.'

'Come to my office at 2 p.m..'

'I'll be there.'

Over the years, we had met many times, whether at lunches, dinners or conferences, or just the two of us, in Washington or New York, or London or Paris. A tall, gangling man with plain features, watery blue eyes and little hair, he had a direct manner, occasionally abrasive. He was five years older than I and had an enviable background as a founder-member of the American Office of Strategic Services (OSS), the pre-cursor of the CIA. In that capacity, based in London during the war, he had acquired a reputation as a practitioner of secret operations against the enemy.

Returning to New York after the war, he had built up his law firm, specialising in taxation, and put his name to various text books, mostly researched and written by his staff, under his direction. By the time I met him, he was that American success symbol, the self-made million-aire. Although we differed occasionally on tactics, I considered him a political and ideological ally; and so he proved to be, at a critical time.

The main problem in any relationship with Bill Casey was the blurred indistinctiveness of his speech, which became worse as time went on. Indeed, he was said to cultivate it deliberately, for special use when cross-examined by the Congressional oversight committees which he resented and despised. At one meeting, which I did not attend, Frank Barnett, President of the National Strategy Information Center, of which Casey was a founding member, was in the chair. He introduced Casey, the guest speaker, in these words: 'There is no truth in the story that Bill Casey was known in his London days as "the mumbling Pimpernel".'

In the old — that is, the pre-Watergate — days, no signpost pointed the way to what the 'old pros' of the CIA called the 'leafy glade'. Be-yond Arlington, a suburb of Washington, each wooded hill looked much like the next, with little to distinguish one highway from another. One of them led to the huge low building of the Central Intelligence Agency. The old secrecy was meant to discourage the curious, the sightseers, the 'investigative' journalists, for nobody supposed that the KGB was una-ware of the location of its American rival. Now, in the post-Watergate openness (pre-dating *glasnost*), huge signposts pointed the way to CIA headquarters.

In the old days, security was very strict. During the dark years, parties of media people were taken on guided tours. The new DCI was reverting to the older practice. Indeed, Casey was determined to restore the CIA to its former self as an effective instrument of American and allied foreign policy, no longer crippled by restraints imposed to please groups whose interest in that policy was purely destructive. Such peo-ple, whether in Congress or in the media, were in Bill's view indifferent to the fact that their actions amounted to a free gift to the men who wielded power in Moscow. He had set himself the ambition to frustrate their efforts and reverse the disastrous trends of the past few years.

Adorned with the temporary security pass required by visitors, I was whisked up to the Director's huge rectangular office on the seventh floor (or sixth, by the American reckoning).

Bill was his usual brusquely cordial self, and I lost no time filling in the background. Not for the first time, or the last, I was struck by the disturbing fact that, for all his evident qualifications for the top intelligence job — in early experience, in courage, in native ingenuity and will — William J. Casey was handicapped by a quite serious ignorance of politics other than those of his own country, and perhaps of its Latin neighbours. When it came to the politics of Federal Germany, I had to give him the absolute beginners' course. He had heard of Strauss, and of *Der Spiegel*, and that was about it. Fortunately, he did know about the KGB and its methods, about 'Active Measures' and related phenomena. And, he was a quick learner.

It didn't take him long to grasp the fact that the importance of this case far transcended the level of a possible defamation of one tycoon's character by another tycoon.

'Look, Bill,' I said, 'I'm sorry to bother you with this, but this is something we have to win, and I'm blocked by the DIA's bureaucracy.'

He didn't hesitate. 'I'm having breakfast tomorrow with Frank Carlucci and General Williams,' he said. 'I'll tell them we've just got to find a way.' He had mentioned — respectively — his own deputy[1] and the Director of the DIA, Lt.-Gen. James A. Williams. Casey correctly guessed that Williams was unaware of my request to see Sejna.

Next evening, I had a call from Casey's office. 'The Director asked me to give you the unlisted number of the man you want to see,' said his personal assistant's voice. 'Oh, and the name he uses is Jasper Deighton.'[2]

This was the breakthrough I needed. Unfortunately, it had come too late to follow through on this particular visit, as I had to get back to London for various pressing reasons. Back in my Trafalgar Square office, I tried repeatedly to reach Mr Deighton at the number I had been given, initially without success.

Then the secret of success came to me, belatedly. Although an early riser myself, I could not compete with the American military. Senior staff were expected to be at their desks in the Pentagon by 7 a.m.. Allowing for the time gap, I had been dialling his number each morning after he had left home for his office. I knew he was married and assumed his wife thereupon went back to bed, and either slept through telephone calls or cut the instrument off.

I tried again, this time at 10.30, London time. It was 5.30 where Jasper Deighton was, and a sleepy voice with a vaguely Slavonic accent was at the other end. 'Is that Bertram Ruxton?' he asked, quoting a name he had been given to disguise my own identity. I assured him it was, and asked him to come to the Madison Hotel at 3 p.m. on Wednesday 16 December.

I rang Sir James Goldsmith in his Paris office and told him the good news. Delight in his voice, he said: 'Take Concorde. You'll feel much fresher.'

Usually, I flew over by Jumbo, and came back by Concorde — an economy for a traveller flying back via New York and wishing to avoid a night flight and a hotel bill. But this was a special mission, and I took Jimmy's advice.

At 2.45 p.m., East Coast time, lunched and refreshed, I sat in the lobby of the Madison, looking out for a once high-ranking Czech defector. Neither of us knew what the other looked like. I saw two potential candidates and approached them only to learn that neither was my man. I had caught sight of a pale, thin little man with a high forehead and blond hair, dressed unseasonably in a pale summer suit and looking like a minor businessman from the backwoods. After several minutes of mutual consideration, we introduced ourselves.

For psychological reasons, I had booked a suite instead of a single room. We spent the afternoon talking in the drawing room. He confirmed all that I had learned from Walter Hahn and Joe Douglass about his knowledge of the *Spiegel* affair. As Chief of Staff to the Czech Defence Minister and Assistant Secretary to the Defence Council, many secret papers crossed his desk. Among them, at the relevant time, were instructions from the KGB to the Czech StB to handle agents in West Germany charged with obtaining secret NATO documents with the object of using them to create a public scandal calculated to discredit Franz Josef Strauss.

I asked Sejna whether he would be willing to come to London and testify in court, should Augstein's lawsuit come to trial. He hesitated, muttering reservations about his physical security and about the restrictions placed upon him by his employers at the Pentagon. I didn't insist. At that time, these were distant possibilities. There would be time enough to return to them.

A more urgent question was whether he was prepared to make a formal Statement, an Affidavit that would constitute legally acceptable evidence. His reply was that as far as he was concerned, there was no problem, but he could only do so with the approval of his employers. The man was clearly nervous. I wanted him to relax and consider me a friend, as indeed I was prepared to be. I had heard that since arriving in the US, he had married a second time. I invited him and Mrs. Sejna to dinner with me that evening.

The Washington élite tend to gather at the Madison, especially at meal times, and I wanted, if possible, to avoid prying eyes, friendly or otherwise. I therefore ordered a carefully chosen dinner for the stated hour, to be served in the drawing-room of my suite. I should have allowed for possible delays. By the time the Sejnas turned up, about half an hour late, dinner had been served, and was getting cold.

My diary entry for 16 December 1981, transcribed from my private shorthand, simply says: 'Meeting with Sejna. No Americans know.'

Notes

1.   Carlucci went on to become National Security Adviser in succession to Admiral John Poindexter, and later still Defense Secretary, succeeding Caspar Weinberger.
2.   This is not the actual name she gave me, which I withhold for security reasons.

3. The Team in Action

The investigation I conducted on behalf of Sir James Goldsmith broke new ground in various ways. It was essentially journalistic and political in character. Without it, the legal effort would have been rudderless, and inevitably abortive. On the other hand, we needed the expert guidance of the lawyers, whose expertise was different in kind: they knew what would constitute 'evidence' in the eyes of an English judge.

Their problem was that, politically, they started from absolute zero, knowing nothing at all of the background to the case. This applied in particular to the man actually handling it for Allen and Overy, the well-known firm of solicitors retained by Sir James Goldsmith. His name was Graeme Hall, and his real interest, in private life, was rowing. He had rowed for Cambridge University and England, and was official coach to the British Olympics team. A tall, fair young man, Hall had at times a curiously detached attitude towards the whole affair, almost as though it was a matter of indifference to him whether we won or lost. He did, however, willingly accept guidance from me, amounting almost to a beginners' course, on the political and ideological background, including the personalities of the many contacts that had to be made.

There was thus a curious, symbiotic relationship between us (the research team), and them (the lawyers). We told them what it was about, found the witnesses, obtained Statements. They then took over, obtaining more formal Statements in the light of legal requirements of which we had only secondary knowledge. With good will on both sides, it worked.

About half way through the protracted process, Jimmy Goldsmith told me that if the case came to trial, he planned to launch a daily newspaper, 'for the duration', to give a verbatim account of the proceedings. He was prepared to spend £18 million on it, printing it in London and distributing it in many countries. There is no doubt in my mind that this is what he would have done, had things gone that far: a measure of the man's determination.

The hard core of the team, apart from myself, in my London office were 'the two Ronnies' as they became known. One, Ronald W. Baxter, I had first met in mid-1953 when I joined the *Straits Times* in Singapore as Features Editor. Ron Baxter was Editor of the Sunday edition.

He had had a varied career, serving first in the old Colonial Office, then the Foreign and Commonwealth Office. We had renewed acquaintance in the 1970s, when he was Information Officer for Ontario Province, and had come to see me in my office when I was Director of the Institute for the Study of Conflict. He had gone on to be the FCO spokesman, in turn, for two contrasting Foreign Secretaries: Dr. David Owen for Labour, and Lord Carrington for the Conservatives.

A trained journalist, Ron Baxter was exceptionally quick off the mark. With a huge range of contacts, especially in Whitehall, but also in the newspaper world on both sides of the Atlantic, he was adept at obtaining information, often before I would have thought it possible.

The other 'Ronnie' was an operator of a very different kind. A career officer of the Diplomatic Service, Ronald Scrivener had the qualities and defects of his background and training: Westminster and Cambridge; many posts overseas, culminating in service as HM Ambassador in Panama and in Czechoslovakia. He had one qualification, above all, which was indispensable for the *Spiegel* case: fluent and idiomatic German, absorbed in his 'teens at school in Vienna.

It was Scrivener's assignment to find German contacts with special knowledge of the *Spiegel* affair and of the workings of the newsmagazine and its publisher. This he did, with great flair and competence.

In the United States, I had my own network, built up over many years. But it was soon supplemented by a new network Ron Baxter built up, and not least by Sir James Goldsmith's own contacts.

Then there were 'the witnesses' and 'the experts'. Although the two categories were distinct, sometimes they overlapped, in that the witnesses had special knowledge to add to the growing store of information.

The biggest problem, in this as in the later cases I was involved in, was the known or predictable barrier of ignorance which, somehow, had to be pierced or dissolved. It stood to reason that if educated men, including barristers as well as solicitors, had no knowledge of the political background, then such knowledge could not be assumed on the part of the judge (whoever he might be), and (save a miraculous exception) total ignorance on the part of the random citizens picked for the jury had to be presumed. And this was the optimistic presumption. The pessimistic possibility was that one or more members of the jury could turn out to be Marxists of one kind or another: that is, ideological enemies.

In these circumstances, it was obviously part of my assignment to find specialists of renown whose testimony would be acceptable to the uninitiated. Since our concern was with the secret machinations of the KGB and satellite services, this was a relatively easy task for me. Many of the leading international specialists on communism and specifically on the Soviet secret agencies were known to me, some of them friends of long standing, others readily accessible to me or to members of the team.

Those who were happy to help, and who wrote erudite background papers, included:

> John Barron, of the *Reader's Digest*, author of two widely read and authentic books on the KGB;
>
> Robert Conquest, distinguished British scholar on Soviet history, author of *The Great Terror*, on Stalin's purges;
>
> Donald J. Jameson, lately retired after many years' service as the CIA's top expert on Soviet affairs;
>
> His equivalent in the British Secret Intelligence Service (MI-6);
>
> Reed Irvine, an ex-member of the Communist Party USA, now President of *AIM* (Accuracy in Media), a monitoring organisation in Washington, DC;
>
> Peter Worthington, the distinguished Canadian journalist, at that time Editor of the *Toronto Sun* and at one time Moscow bureau chief of the *Toronto Telegram*;
>
> Roy S. Godson and Richard Shultz, joint authors of a short but authoritative book on Soviet disinformation techniques, *Dezinformatsia*; and of course the helpful American specialists named earlier, Walter Hahn and Joseph Douglass.

Among the defectors who contributed papers, or sage advice and relevant background, were: the ex-KGB officers, Yuri Bezmenov (writing as Tomas D. Schuman) and Stanislav Levchenko; and the former Czechoslovak StB (State Secret Security) men Josef Frolik and Ladislaw Bittman. Two Iron Curtain dissidents were enormously helpful: the well-known former Czechoslovak anti-Communist, Josef Josten — of whom, more later — and the ex-Soviet journalist, Leonid Finkelstein.

Other authorities we consulted included the distinguished Harvard historian, Richard Pipes, who was just returning to academic life after two years as Special Adviser on Soviet affairs on the American National Security Council; and Iain Elliot, at that time the very knowledgeable Editor of the London-based bulletin, *Soviet Analyst*.

Inevitably, the investigation yielded an enormous volume of paper, not all of uniform value. Graeme Hall and his colleagues regarded it as essential to arrange for an expert scrutiny of more that 20 years of files of *Der Spiegel*, comparing the contents, and especially the presentation of the news, with that of the Soviet propaganda organs, theme by theme.

In this, and other strictly German aspects of the case, I relied heavily upon the advice of a number of friends and associates, especially Hans-Josef ('Jupp') Horchem, Gerhard Löwenthal, Count Hans Huyn and Baron Hans Christoph ('Döld') von Stauffenberg.

Horchem, a small ebullient Rhinelander, had been head of the Security Service for the Land of Hamburg[1]; until, driven to distraction by the sniping and pressures of the left-wing government there, he left the Service and joined the famous Axel Springer newspaper group as a columnist.

Gerhard Löwenthal, an outstanding television personality with his own political show, had interviewed Sejna. Huyn, at that time a very active Member of the Bundestag for Strauss's CSU, ex-diplomat and son of a diplomat, born in Warsaw, multilingual, was a recognised authority on international affairs, with special reference to the Soviet threat.

Döld von Stauffenberg, a cousin of the Bomb Plot count who almost succeeded in ridding the Third Reich of Hitler, had been for years a shadowy presence in General Gehlen's BND. In common with a number of his colleagues, he had quit in disgust when Willy Brandt came to power in 1969 and decreed that he himself, as Federal Chancellor, and all members of his cabinet, were to be given the human sources of all West German intelligence: a perfect recipe for the destruction of the

BND. His reward came when his private secretary, Günther Guillaume, was exposed as an East German spy, and he was forced to step down as Chancellor.

Our choice for the onerous task of analysing the long-term coverage and presentation of the news in *Der Spiegel* fell upon Professor Dr. Hans Mathias Kepplinger who had founded, and headed, a public opinion polling organisation called Institut für Publizistik. He tackled his monumental task with typically Teutonic thoroughness. The findings, which he sent us at the end of February 1983, filled two large volumes of statistical notes and graphs.

It could not be claimed that the Kepplinger Report made exciting reading. Yet it had its importance, which is best conveyed by quoting Ron Baxter's covering letter to Graeme Hall, dated 4 March 1983:

> Dear Graeme,
>
> I enclose both volumes of the Kepplinger Report.
>
> With enormous analytic science it plots the twists and turns of *Spiegel* news coverage through the years. In all my experience, I have never known one journal to change its tune so incessantly. Without direct experience, of course, it is impossible to prove why. But as everyone knows, the USSR has changed its tactics frequently during the past 20 years during which it has launched a number of frenzied campaigns (such as the current unilateralist one) to further its objectives. Overall, the survey demonstrates a marked tilt towards the Soviet side over the years, with the same scare stories cropping up in varied forms time and time again. However, there have been occasional cracks, too, at the Soviet Union — but there would be, wouldn't there?

Baxter went on to quote a crucial paragraph (5), p.67:

> In spite of all contradictions and variations in the news coverage, it is possible to recognise a constant military objective and a constant political objective in the *Spiegel*'s news coverage since 1962/63. The political objective, a detailed analysis of which is not given here, was as follows: The FRG should disengage itself from the USA regarding foreign policy and should seek an alternative to NATO. The military objective was: NATO should renounce nuclear weapons completely,

or to a great extent. The *Spiegel* pursued both objectives with varying reasons and changing intensity. In spite of all military and political changes, however, the *Spiegel* maintained these objectives to the end of the period of investigations. The *Spiegel* never or seldom mentioned these objectives. It did, however — at least during the campaigns mentioned — present the military and political situation in such a way, that the reader would have to draw this conclusion.

The military and political objectives referred to above are identical with those pursued by the Soviet Union.

R.W.Baxter

In itself, of course, the Kepplinger Report could not be of decisive importance, but as a contribution to the education of lawyers, a prospective jury and the reading public, it would have had its value, had the case come to trial.

A complementary report, equally impressive and Teutonic in scale and conception, was prepared by another German contact who wished not to be named. This one covered only the period of the *Spiegel* affair, and yielded the following statistics, culled from many pages of heavy-going prose:

In 1961 there were 249 mentions of Strauss of which 183 appear to be negative, 51 neutral and 15 positive. In 1962, the fateful year, there were no fewer than 385 pages — an average of more than seven an issue — in which Strauss featured, and the overwhelming majority were hostile.

There were also many pages of quotations from *Pravda* and *Izvestiya* on the left and *Der Spiegel* on the right, showing striking similarities.

For my part, I was after more exciting stuff. When Augstein issued his writ, early in 1981, the Social Democrats (SPD) and their Liberal (FDP) partners were still in office in Bonn. Although Chancellor Helmut Schmidt was a strong NATO supporter, there was a marked and growing undercurrent of appeasement in his party. Under the long-serving Foreign Minister and Liberal leader, Hans-Dietrich Genscher, no possible co-operation could be expected from official quarters in the Federal Republic. The BND remained under the same management even after the collapse of the Schmidt-Genscher coalition in October 1982, with a protégé of Genscher's, Klaus Kinkel, in charge. It was not until March 1983, when fresh general elections brought the CDU (Christian Democrat) leader, Helmut Kohl, to power that our opportunity came to take our problem to the BND.

Not that West Germany's foreign policy had changed. Lacking an absolute majority in the Bundestag and any personal interest in foreign affairs, Kohl needed the support of the liberals, and invited Genscher to stay on as Foreign Minister. It was at this point that Strauss made what his friends regarded as a fundamental error of judgement. He had asked for the Foreign Ministry, but the new Chancellor turned him down and offered him Defence instead, reportedly well aware that Strauss would spurn the offer (perhaps because of the painful memories of 1962, or more likely because he regarded the Foreign Ministry as his by natural right). Already, Strauss had resigned his seat in the Bundestag, opting instead for unquestioned authority in his Bavarian fief and for whatever influence he could exert from afar. It was almost an act of abdication.

From our standpoint, however, there was an important silver lining to these dark clouds: Kinkel had gone, and the new head of the BND, Eberhard Blum, was a natural ally. Although I had never met him, he was a personal friend of several of my associates. For several years, unfortunately, *after* the *Spiegel* affair, Blum had been the closest associate of Reinhard Gehlen, the one-time Hitler General who had made a deal with the Americans after the war, in return for access to the secret Nazi documents, which he had hidden away. This was the deal that enabled him to create the BND, with himself as its head. Allowing Blum time to settle in, I telephoned his office, after the ground had been prepared by a mutual friend. An invitation to lunch awaited me. The date was 8 September 1983.

Although I had had occasional dealings with the BND in the pre- and post-Brandt days, I had never been to its headquarters at Pullach in Bavaria. I was met at Munich airport by a smartly dressed young BND official, who drove me to our destination. Pullach had a pre-fab air about it: a huge complex of low-lying huts and buildings behind high walls and barbed wire. The Director's office was in an older building, apparently once a private residence, with a charming courtyard, complete with fountain and statuary. Tall and slim, with iron grey hair and intelligent black eyes, Blum greeted me with friendly courtesy. The lunch, *à deux*, was excellent. I am no lover of German wines, but the bottle he had chosen was from the vineyards of Franconia, dry and delectable. The rapport between us was instant, helped by the fact that he seemed to have little affection for *Der Spiegel*.

I had taken with me photocopies of relevant passages from three separate editions of Gehlen's memoirs, *The Service* (in German, *Der Dienst*). Our team had picked out interesting discrepancies between them. The English language versions provided two or three pages of significant detail obviously edited out of the German original. One particularly interesting point, which appeared in the American, but not the British, edition was that an East German had been recruited by the BND as a double agent, one of whose jobs (on behalf of the East Germans) was to feed documents to *Der Spiegel*.

Blum didn't hesitate. He told me that the best informed man on the affair was a former BND official named Kurt Weiss. Now 69 and retired, but in excellent health, Weiss had handled all aspects of the affair for the BND, during and after the event, but his name had never appeared in public. 'I'll brief him,' said Blum, 'and put him in touch with you.'

Not long after, with communications duly established, I brought Kurt Weiss to London, for a lunch-time meeting in a private room at the Stafford Hotel, an ideal place for such gatherings, which I had learned to know and appreciate during my years at *The Economist* on the other side of St. James's Street.

The two Ronnies (Baxter and Scrivener) were present. Weiss had a clear recollection of distant events, but the important thing was that Eberhard Blum was going to give him access to the BND's secret archives, so that he could refresh his memory.

I have to record, anticlimactically, that although Weiss produced much interesting detail, nothing of decisive importance emerged from his lengthy communion with the archives. One big disappointment, which none of us could have foreseen, was that the 'East German double agent' turned out to be fictional — a fabrication by Gehlen's office to make his curiously dry narrative more attractive to the American public.... This was one occasion when I wished that the infinite ingenuity of secret services in obscuring the truth had not been in play. This was the closest we had got in attempting to prove that the affair had been 'orchestrated' by the KGB. And the story on which we had built our hopes was false!

The expanded American team, meanwhile, was yielding more and more material, obviously of variable interest. Ron Baxter made several trips to the US, mainly to meet Soviet Bloc defectors. Jimmy Goldsmith himself, increasingly interested in the battle, gave more of his time to it. Soon he was meeting both the defectors we had lined up, and high officials in the Reagan Administration, especially Bill Casey, with whom he developed a cordial and fruitful relationship.

Ron was surprised, as I too had been, at his first meeting with our key witness, Sejna. He wrote:

> The General turned out to be a very small general, with a marked absence of those patrician qualities, naturally assumed, which I had encountered in such very seniors as I had met (and quailed before) during my wartime service. Sejna looks like the peasant he was before he was adopted and advanced by the Czech Communist elite.
>
> But, like most sons of the soil, Jan Sejna was obviously a pretty shrewd fellow when fighting for personal survival, though much less so in handling his finances. The heady air of freedom, so beloved by those who desert their restrictive Communist homelands, can also bring agonising problems. You are not allowed to carve your own way in the world in Czechoslovakia; the Party does all the planning and takes all the decisions. To find yourself in a country where you can do what you like with the money you earn is greeted, first with a sense of elation, and later, quite often, with rueful regrets. One's new human rights include that of falling flat on one's face.
>
> This, figuratively, was what happened to Sejna. After years of emptying his memory of all he knew for the CIA, he was sent on his way, drained, but with a changed identity and final cash bonus of $100,000. He went to Chicago, where many compatriots of his had settled, and decided that since he was now in a capitalist society he would use his bonus to invest in a restaurant that would serve East European dishes to his fellow exiles.
>
> Alas, smart Chicagoans saw him coming all the way from Washington. It took them only a month to relieve him of his money. The real estators charged him an extortionate sum for the premises, sharp lawyers feasted on the remains, our defector failed to make sure that his restaurant would be granted a licence to sell alcoholic beverages

(it wasn't) and the poor chap was back in Washington, where he told his astonished minders that the $100,000 had gone with the wind in the Windy City.

As the investigation gathered breadth and impetus, I grew increasingly concerned about the way Graeme Hall was handling the legal side. Ron Baxter shared my concern. The burden of our concern had nothing to do with the man's professional competence. The problem lay in his personality. Time and again, he made a deplorable impression.

I was particularly incensed with his behaviour at a crucial meeting I had set up for him in the Pentagon with the top people in the CIA, and in the presence of Sejna. On 20 May 1983, I wrote to Sir James Gold-smith on this and similar incidents. After praising his thoroughness and legal professionalism, I wrote:

> You will remember that after considerable effort, I managed at last to gain access to our main witness, and official approval of what we were trying to do. On that occasion, Hall created what could have been a disastrous impression, when meeting the high Pentagon offi-cials, and saying that 'it didn't matter a damn' to you whether you won the case or lost it! At that time, I did suggest that you might consider taking him off the case.

> I just mention two or three recent developments:

> 1.   Ron returned this week from Washington, where he had apparently highly successful meetings with John Barron, and our two main witnesses S [Sejna] and F [Josef Frolik]. Ron and Graeme were staying at the Capital Hilton, but Graeme had sent a telegram to F to meet the two of them in the lobby of the Washington Hilton. Bear in mind that F had travelled 2,000 miles for this meeting. When he didn't turn up, Ron had the initiative to go to the other Hilton, where he did finally find our man, by then somewhat inebriated, in the bar after a very long wait.

> 2.   Ron is concerned at the hectoring manner which Graeme adopts when trying to elicit further facts from both these witnesses. It is as though he were cross-examining them in court. There is some danger in this, particularly in the case of S, in that when pressed for further information and further recollections, defectors have been known to start embroidering or imagining things in order to please

the questioner. Ron has apparently drawn Graeme's attention to this on a number of occasions, but without success.

(..............)

4.   I had a call a few days ago from our German friend, Herbert Schmidt. Ron had arranged for Graeme Hall to go to Munich to talk to several of Strauss's senior assistants at the time of the *Spiegel* affair 20 years ago. Schmidt happened to be in Munich, and was brought in as interpreter, as one of the Germans had hardly any English. Schmidt told me that Hall made 'a deplorable impression' on the Germans, both by his manner and by his general ignorance of the political background, I myself have now arranged to go over to Germany on 9 June to meet Schmidt and find out what damage, if any, has been done.

It may well be that at this stage it is too late to take Hall off this case. But I thought I ought to put these things on the record for your consideration.

In the event, Jimmy took no action, and Hall stayed on the case. Sad to record, when it was all over, he was killed, with others, in a car crash in the south of France when returning from a ski-ing holiday in the Alps.

It is only fair to add that, starting from an initial attitude of scepticism amounting to indifference, Hall progressively became convinced and committed. It is also fair to say that it is possible for a relative stranger to Washington to be unaware that the Federal capital boasts two Hiltons; and that, however unfortunate his manner may have been, there was method and purpose in his cross-examining of our witnesses. Thus, on 3 December 1982, he had written to Sir James to say:

Ron Baxter and I ... had a successful series of meetings with Sejna ... and Frolik. The last was most informative. He will make an excellent witness and ... I believe that every effort should be made so that ... he is able to give oral evidence in court. (.......)

Sejna explained one or two apparent inconsistencies in his statement satisfactorily. I do not believe he has the fabulous memory he claims to have. He is human like the rest of us and if he were just a little more careful over recalling these events which occurred a long time ago these mistakes would not occur, but I believe we are getting towards the truth and a very useful statement.

That letter was, of course, Graeme Hall's account of his first meetings with Sejna. Of the later occasion mentioned in my letter to Sir James Goldsmith of 20 May 1983, Ron Baxter had this to say in an office memorandum to me:

> Sejna polished up his memory and recalled several occasions in Prague when *Der Spiegel* was mentioned at the highest levels as the organ which was most potent in helping to further Soviet Bloc designs on the West. He also elaborated still further on the functions of the department in which he was involved; these discourses helped further to verify his original story.

In a later account of Graeme Hall's cross-examination of Sejna, Ron Baxter wrote:

> Graeme Hall and I spent two full days with Sejna, locked in a hotel room, while the general went into the most minute details about the organisation and methods of the Czech Politburo and Defence Ministry. Hall was an aggressive, no-nonsense interrogator and was determined to find out whether Sejna was inventing 'convenient' facts to prove his allegations against the Prague conspirators who had been responsible for the *Spiegel* coup.
>
> But he could not break Sejna down. Time and again, Sejna reiterated, and expanded on, the facts as he had first revealed them to Walter Hahn. At the end of two gruelling days, the tough rowing coach was satisfied that Sejna's story was true; every trick in the Law Courts' trade had been tried; no lie detector could have been so rigorous. Even after a substantial number of Scotches, Sejna made complete sense. (It is remarkable, by the way, how Eastern defectors develop a taste for Scotch and spurn the vodka.)

Josef Frolik was another of Ron's Czechoslovak targets, and very different in personality and character from Sejna. A senior officer in the StB, he had defected from Bulgaria in 1969 in perilous circumstances, which he recalled in his book, *The Frolik Defection* (1975). After various threats and attempts on his life — one from a driverless car aimed at him — he took refuge in a remote spot in Louisiana. His CIA minders were unhelpful: he didn't want to see anyone, I was assured. Reluctant to bother Bill Casey a second time, I chose another channel: my old (and now lamented) friend, Frolik's compatriot, Josef Josten. Later, faced with the accomplished fact of my being in touch with him, the CIA relented and helped to set up our team's meetings with Frolik.

Unlike Sejna and Frolik, Josten was a dissident, not a defector from inside the system, but one who disowned the system from the start. Twice, he had sought refuge from tyranny in Britain: in 1938, when Hitler's troops marched in; and ten years later, when the Czech Communists, under the shadow of the occupying Red Army, took over 'without a shot being fired'. In Britain after the first escape, he had served in the British Army during the war. Returning to Prague, he had been press officer to Foreign Minister Jan Masaryk. Not long after the Prague coup, Masaryk was defenestrated by his Communist interrogators.

Settling down in England, Josten had become a tireless fighter against Communist violations of human rights, and not merely in his own country. As such, he had become a prime target for assassination. Responding to an invitation, he had gone to Geneva to meet a compatriot who had written to say he was planning to defect. The two had met in a hotel lounge and the man from Prague had ordered tea, then absented himself, ostensibly to attend to his natural needs. Within minutes, Josten was taken ill, and was near death and reduced to a skeleton for several months.

Nor was that the only attempt. In his memoirs, Frolik gave chilling details of a plot to kill Josten, authorised by the then Party boss in Czechoslovakia, Novotny[2].

Despite this unpromising background, Josten made contact with Frolik some time after his defection, and arranged a meeting between him and Ron Baxter. There were a number of subsequent meetings, at one of which, in the Army and Navy Club in Washington, I had a long talk with him. A tense, vigorous man, he gave a strong impression of straightforward frankness and honesty, not usually associated with his former calling. Perhaps, however, that was one of the reasons why he defected.

A letter from Frolik to Josten, hand-written in capital letters and dated 28 September 1983, throws a revealing light on the life of a defector. These are selected passages (unedited):

WHEN I ARRIVE 5.30 P.M. TODAY I HAD A MESSAGE AT THE RECEPTION DESK TO CALL HOME RIGHT AWAY. I DID AND LEARNT THAT TODAY SEPT.28 AT ABOUT 11 A.M. A MAILGRAM WAS DELIVERED BY MAIL SAYING NOT TO GO TO D.C..

I AM SORRY WHAT HAD HAPPEN BUT IT IS NOT MY FAULT.
YOU IN ENGLAND SIMPLY DO NOT REALISE THAT CABLE
SERVICE IN THE UNITED STATES HAS THE SAME EFFICIENCY
AS IN THE TIME OF A CZARS.

(...............)

AFTER MR. GRAEME WOULD COME TO D.C. I WILL GIVE
HIM ADDRESS FOR CABLE SERVICE (...........) IT IS A BICYCLE
REPAIR SHOP OPEN FOR BUSINESS FROM 10 A.M. TO 6 P.M.

(...............)

I WAS CALLED TO D.C. IN A MIDDLE OF AUGUST BY
FRIENDS TO BE TOLD THAT SOMETHING FISHY IS GOING
ON IN CONNECTION WITH OUR BUSINESS AND THAT THERE
IS A INVOLVEMENT OF CZECH SERVICE IN IT TO DAMAGE
MY CREDIBILITY, TO SHOW ME AS AN UNPRINCIPLED CRIMI-
NAL, LIAR, SWINDLER, ETC. BUT NOT EVERYTHING COULD
BE PUT ON PAPER.

WHEN I RETURNED HOME I WROTE A MEMO ABOUT MY
EXPERIENCES I GOT IN THIS CONNECTION. A RUMOUR THAT
I STOLE A TRUCK WITH APPROX. 3 MILLION CROWNS AND
NEGOTIATE SECURITIES.

I ONLY MENTION IN ONE SENTENCE BUSINESS OF THE
MEETING IN D.C. AUGUST 9 AND AUGUST 10, BECAUSE
FRIEND OF MINE WAS WELL AWARE ABOUT THE BUSINESS
AND HAS WANTED A WRITTEN MEMO ABOUT
THIS...BUSINESS.

BUT THE BUSINESS CAN BE DISCUSS ONLY IN PERSON
AND WHAT U ALREADY WROTE IS *VERY STRICTLY CONFI-
DENTIAL.*

THE COPY OF THE MEMO I AM SENDING WITH THIS LET-
TER I PREPARED FOR GRAEME AND I HAD TO MAKE THE
NAMES OF OFFICERS BLANK.

IT IS QUITE CLEAR THAT THE SMEAR AND DEFAMATION
CAMPAIGN BY CIS [Czech Intelligence Service — BC] IS NOT A
CHARITABLE HELP AND INDICATE SOMETHING. AND IT IS
NOT A FUNNY BUSINESS.

I WAS TOLD 'JOE THE LAWYERS FOR THE OPPOSITE SIDE
WILL TEAR YOU IN PIECES, IF THERE IS NOT SOMETHING
MORE SERIOUS WE STILL DO NOT KNOW ABOUT.'

(...........)

PS. HOW THE CZECH GOT THE NEWS THAT I WILL BE A

WITNESS? OR THIS LAWYER KNOW THAT I WILL TESTIFY?

The jittery impression so clearly conveyed in this note was confirmed and emphasised by the CIA minders who arranged Ron Baxter's meetings with him. Yet on the first occasion, it was shown to be somewhat misleading. Ron had been told Frolik was indeed afraid of Communist revenge and had hidden away in a town a thousand miles from Washington. He would only come to the capital in his own car, as he was unwilling to risk public transport. For the first meeting, the Army and Navy Club, Ron was instructed to stand at a certain spot. Frolik would enter unobtrusively and stand in the shadows waiting to be approached and be greeted quietly.

In the event, at the agreed time, the front door of the Club was pushed open vigorously, a burly figure strode in, looked across at the waiting Ron Baxter and said in a loud and jovial voice: 'I am Josef Frolik.' As with Sejna, a great deal of Scotch was consumed before, during and after the ensuing meal.

Whatever the degree of fear in which Frolik lived, he went on to produce 200 pages or more of comparative analysis of the Czechoslovak-controlled press and contemporary issues of *Der Spiegel*, which confirmed the entirely independent analyses of the Germans, Kepplinger and Schmidt, in demonstrating the striking similarities in the treatment and interpretation of current affairs.

Such analyses can never be conclusive, unless accompanied by the statements of secret intelligence officers testifying that the similarities were intentional and 'orchestrated' by their respective services. But they did support the overall conclusion that what Sir James Goldsmith had said in January 1981 was the simple truth.

Notes

1.   The *Landesamt für Verfassungsschutz*, or Land Office for the Defence of the Constitution, a branch of the Federal Office or BfV, created for the defeated Germans by the occupying British after World War II.

2.   Josef Frolik, *The Memoirs of an Intelligence Agent* (Leo Cooper, London, 1975), pp 65-69.

4. Conclusive Evidence

Our second and decisive breakthrough came in May and June 1984, but we were not to know that in late 1983 and early 1984 — a period marked by increasingly frenetic activity on the part of the team and of Sir James Goldsmith.

Baxter and I made several more trips to the United States, Scrivener multiplied his German contacts, commissioning research by ex-*Spiegel* employees and others. As for Sir James, his will and enthusiasm stirred by the looming prospect of a trial, he was everywhere. He sent his private jet to Washington, to bring Sejna and his dazzling wife to New York for dinner. He sought out and cultivated the company of other defectors. He discussed the case with that legendary, complex and sometimes misguided genius of the CIA, the former head of counter-intelligence, James Jesus Angleton. He went to Munich with Ronald Scrivener for a meeting with Strauss on 18 September 1984 — very late, as by then (in the absence of an out-of-court settlement) the trial was scheduled to begin on 8 October.

Not all the defectors were of equal value. Some were ready to confirm what the Western experts had been saying about the KGB and its work; which was useful but in a limited way. And one went back to Moscow in mysterious circumstances. Of that one, more later.

The useful defectors — already mentioned — included two ex-KGB men, Yuri Bezmenov (Tomas D. Schuman) and Stanislav Levchenko; and the former senior officer from the Czech StB, Ladislaw Bittman. There were pros and cons about each.

Ron Baxter met Bezmenov. I did not, but I corresponded with him. He produced a lengthy biographical note almost constituting, in its own

right, a short story worthy of a literary prize; and a good essay on Soviet Active Measures (see Appendices). He had a sardonic sense of
humour, not always to the taste of his employers. Co-opted by the
KGB, he chose the code-name 'Musafirov', which in Urdu means 'passenger': he had learnt Urdu at the Oriental Languages Institute of Moscow State University. He regarded the choice of name as a dangerous
joke about his secret intention to 'take the KGB for a ride'. He realised
later that it was he who was being taken for a ride.

Bezmenov served in India, where his assignment was to spread
disinformation, to corrupt the locals and, on occasion, to contribute to
the character assassination of the incorruptible. Everything Bezmenov
said contributed to the overall picture of KGB methods we needed for
the case; but none of it was directly relevant to our needs.

Levchenko is one of the most important of KGB defectors — not
because of his rank (he was a Major) but because of the amazing wealth
of material he brought with him, which formed the core of John Barron's
second major work: *KGB Today: the Hidden Hand* (1983). With
names and all the incidental details, Levchenko revealed a previously
unsuspected story: the KGB's massive recruitment of journalists and
officials in Japan, where he was stationed. The KGB treated such assignments with commendable thoroughness. Bezmenov had mastered
Urdu; Levchenko read and spoke Japanese.

A highly strung man with a black moustache, Levchenko suffered in
full measure from the difficulties of adjustment to life in a free society,
compounded in his case by the breakdown of his American marriage.
None of this affected the obvious authenticity of his extensive revelations.

Two men, both friends of mine, had non-official access to Levchenko:
John Barron of the *Reader's Digest*, and Donald 'Jamie' Jameson, whom
we have already met. At that time, John was too busy writing his book
to be much help, though he later contributed a splendid Statement on
Active Measures. 'Jamie' did the necessary.

Severely crippled by the after-effects of polio, which he had con-
tracted in Germany in the 1950s, Jamie coped with his affliction with
great courage and cheerfulness. A fluent Russian speaker, he was the
best informed American specialist on the Soviet system I ever met.

One early morning in September 1982, Jamie brought Levchenko to my room at the Madison for breakfast. We had a long and (for me) illuminating talk on Soviet disinformation techniques.

Some months later, Jimmy Goldsmith met Levchenko, having brought him to Southampton for lunch, as he recorded in a letter to Graeme Hall dated 7 September 1983:

> He is an intense man of about 40. He is tough and looks like a man who could have been a Colonel in the Secret Services. However, he is also clearly under pressure and is at present number one on the KGB hit list. So he was probably under some form of sedation. On a normal day he would make an excellent witness. He thinks for quite a long time before answering questions and is still not sufficiently relaxed to answer difficult questions freely. He has not yet definitely decided to trust us but I think he is on the way.
>
> He wants to think about whether or not to come and his considerations are:
>
> 1. Personal security
> 2. Whether or not he wants to participate in what he calls 'the potential destruction of *Der Spiegel*'.

This last point must have seemed strange to Sir James. However, not long after his meeting with Sir James, Levchenko gave a major interview to *Der Spiegel* obviously with the approval of his CIA minders, who must have thought (not without reason) that this was a good and easy way to counter the pro-Soviet line usually taken by the news magazine.

Another controversial witness, for quite different reasons, was Ladislaw Bittman, whom Ron met several times on his North American travels and found 'by far the most impressive person' he encountered on the *Spiegel* assignment. After a successful career in Czech disinformation (always, it should be remembered, for the ultimate benefit, and under the guidance, of the KGB), he escaped to the West and, under another name, was running an academic course in disinformation at a major US university. His books certainly rank as some of the best ever written by a defector. With a commanding and charismatic presence, he spoke impressively and would have made a first-class witness.

However, Bittman knew nothing about the *Spiegel* affair. This was not surprising, even though he had been Deputy Chief of the StB's

Disinformation Department. Any such 'top secret' would be made known only to those who 'needed to know'; and he had reached his high post long after the 1962 affair.

There were some more material considerations in Bittman's mind. Against relentless hostility from the American 'liberal' establishment, he had persuaded his university to set up his Disinformation Studies Department and he now had 30 students from many countries. If he came to London as a witness, the fact would be widely reported in his local newspaper. Then, if the jury decided not to credit Sejna's evidence, Bittman would be seen as associated with the losing side. This in turn would destroy his credibility and with it his university course. He made it quite clear, understandably, that he wasn't about to risk all.

The strangest of our potential witnesses was the defector who possibly wasn't: Oleg Bitov. Unlike the others, Bitov was not in secret intelligence. He claimed to be a dissident, not a defector. Nevertheless, as a staff translator on the prestigious *Literaturnaya Gazeta*, he had been a member of the Soviet Union's privileged elite, the Nomenklatura. He had, to all appearances, defected to the West while on an official trip to Italy. By the time he came into our case, he seemed to have settled in London and was making good money from articles and advances on books.

Sir James, by now, was collecting defectors — a relevant pastime, with the trial looming ahead. On 28 May 1984, he wrote to Graeme Hall to brief him on what appeared to have been a very fruitful talk over lunch with Oleg Bitov. The *Literary Gazette*, said Bitov, had briefed a special correspondent to prepare a series of five articles refuting allegations by the American (ex-Communist) writer Claire Sterling, in her book *The Time of the Assassins* (1984) that the KGB was behind the plot to assassinate the Pope.

Nothing special about that. The special point was that now the articles had duly appeared, *Der Spiegel* had just published a condensed version of them, promoting the same conclusions: that is, that the KGB had nothing to do with the plot, which was the work of the CIA. More interesting still: according to Bitov, the author of the *Gazette* articles, Iona Andronov, was a Colonel in the KGB.[1]

In the last paragraph of his letter to Hall, Sir James Goldsmith expressed his glee at this revelation:

I believe the information concerning the current issue of *Spiegel* is game, set and match if we can prove that in reality it was written by a KGB Colonel. No doubt Brian will want to study this more carefully and discuss it with John Barron.

I shared Jimmy's enthusiasm and when, some weeks later, Bitov had returned to London from his US tour, I contacted him and he came to my office. The date was Tuesday 26 June, the time 4 p.m..

I found myself talking to a Russian intellectual, with all the soulful self-doubt and torture of a Dostoievsky character. He told me that the author of the *Gazette* articles blaming the CIA for the papal murder plot was indeed the KGB Colonel Andronov. He explained that Andronov, although theoretically No. 2 on the editorial staff, was the man whose veto was absolute.

The next move was to invite Bitov to translate at least key passages of the *Literaturnaya Gazeta* articles for us (his English was excellent), so that we could compare what he said with what had now come out in *Der Spiegel*. I called in Ronald Scrivener, and introduced him to Bitov. Over the next few weeks, they had several meetings. The first problem was where to find copies of the *Gazette*. Scrivener solved that one fast: the London School of Slavonic Studies kept a full file. He obtained the necessary permission, went to the School and came out armed with photocopies of the articles. Bitov started work.

Over the next few weeks, I played little and in the end no part in the proceedings, as I entered the Middlesex Hospital to have my gall bladder removed.

One day the telephone rang next to my bed. It was Ron Baxter to tell me that all his efforts to contact Oleg Bitov were failing. The telephone went unanswered; his letters likewise.

The mystery was solved when, with a suitable fanfare, Bitov turned up at a press conference in Moscow on 18 September. On television, the wretched man looked even more tortured than in my office. He declared that he had been kidnapped in Venice by British agents, smuggled to the UK, and there subjected to drugs, blackmail and bribery to make him co-operate. In London, the Foreign Office issued a not-unexpected denial, suggesting, semi-officially, that Bitov had made his allegations as part of an agreement with the Soviet authorities in order to rejoin his wife and daughter in Moscow. This may well have been true, but it was certainly only part of the truth, leaving unanswered the question whether Bitov was a true or a false defector/dissident?

A conversation I had with another ex-member of the Soviet establishment not long after provided a possible answer. On returning to Moscow, I learned, Bitov had been promoted from translator to 'columnist'. He now rated an office and chauffeur-driven car and a country dacha. This seemed conclusive enough. A true defector who repents and goes home was generally not heard of again, either because a bullet was lodged in the back of his neck or because he was whiling away his time in prison or the gulag. A true defector who repents is not promoted. *Ergo*, Oleg Bitov was neither a defector nor a dissident, but a KGB plant, whose 'redefection' provides a massive propaganda stick with which to beat the countries that had offered him hospitality.

My own theory was simple. Bitov was probably due to stay on a little longer in the West. However, he had evidently gone too far when he revealed to us that the papal plot articles had been written by a KGB agent. Establishing credibility is one thing; helping the enemy, a different matter. Had Bitov gone on to translate the articles for us, and provided us with a Statement on Andronov, he might well, as Jimmy had put it, have given us game, set and match. It was time to bring him home.

The fact that his departure was so precipitate supports this theory. It suggests that Bitov had reported the matter to the KGB and that a decision was taken to whisk him away there and then in the clothes he stood in, sans car, sans money, sans toothbrush.

Convincing though these explanations sounded, they may not have been the whole truth. According to another ex-Soviet friend of mine, who had known Bitov during his stay in London, the man was actually overpowered and bundled into the Soviet embassy before being whisked away. He had talked to one of Bitov's *Literaturnaya Gazeta* colleagues who told him that far from being promoted, Bitov was barely tolerated, shunned or ostracised by his work-mates. The only reason he had escaped a worse fate still was that he had agreed to co-operate with the KGB in spreading the story that he had been kidnapped by British agents, etc..

Perhaps the whole truth will never be known. In a long article in

Literaturnaya Gazeta, on 3 October 1984, Bitov told his own story, or at any rate the approved version of it, under the title 'Failure of a Provocation'. He also told the story of his meetings with Sir James Goldsmith and myself, in terms which Jimmy found so 'fanciful and entertaining' that he reproduced a translation of the whole article in a collection of his own writings and speeches, published privately in 1985 under the title *Counter Culture.*

'He sat with his legs crossed picturesquely,' wrote Bitov of Sir James, 'chewing a cigar of prestige, numbered, made as fat as a factory chimney. He looked down on his visitor from the height of his millions as though they were a throne.'

About his visit to my office, he had this to say:

> A respectable building in a respectable street — Regent Street. A sign in prominent letters at the entrance: 'Linen Hall'. If only Londoners knew what dirty linen they deal in beneath this sign!
>
> Third floor. A deserted air-conditioned passage, doors without signs on them. This is the location of a major ideological subversion centre run by Brian Crozier, British intelligence officer, extreme right-wing journalist and biographer of Franco and Chiang Kai-shek. Crozier also holds the office of protecting Mr Goldsmith's interests in the British Isles. Maybe not all of his interests, but his political interests for sure. It was he who gave details of the programme which was only sketched out by the 'boss'.

Bitov went on to describe the task Ron Baxter and I had set him: to translate the Andronov articles from the Russian original in the *Gazette,* and added: 'I won't conceal the fact that I was tempted to concoct such a phoney "analysis" that even the most biased court would reject it.' He had found a 'different solution no less risky yet more sensible'. He 'worked up a storm', asking for more and more material. His 'immediate "guardians" from the "Intelligence Service"...were delighted that I had "finally come to my senses". So pleased were they that they that they even stopped watching me. And so I was able to break through the circle of my captivity and leave without giving Goldsmith and company a single line.'

As Euclid put it: *Quod erat demonstrandum.*

Fortunately, by the time Bitov had gone back to Moscow, his relative importance for us had diminished considerably. For by then I had enlisted the help of a true and major defector.

His name was Ilya Dzhirkvelov, a senior KGB man who had defected to Britain from a United Nations post in Geneva. I had heard through my grapevine that Ilya had knowledge of the *Spiegel* affair as a KGB operation. At a Guildhall function in the City of London, I had run into an old friend — a genuine dissident — who told me that if I needed to meet Ilya, he could arrange it for me.

I stored this offer away, in case it should be needed. Meanwhile, I thought I would try official channels first. I had what I thought were good reasons for this. The rule of the game was that once a defector has come over and been debriefed by MI-6 (Secret Intelligence), he is 'minded' by the Security Service (MI-5). I thought it could prove useful to me and to the team to have a co-operative contact with MI-5, with which, at that time, I had no contact whatever.

I mentioned the matter to an old Foreign Office friend whom I had known for many years going back to the now defunct Information Research Department with which I had developed a close professional relationship when I was on *The Economist*. The friend — let us call him Paul — promised to do his best but warned me that 'Five' were 'awfully sticky' about this kind of thing.

'Awfully sticky' turned out to be an understatement. For a whole week, it seems, Paul had battled it out with his colleagues of the Security Service, pleading, cajoling, appealing to a wider sense of duty; all to no avail. The rock of the Security Service was immovable. He was sorry, he reported back to me: he had done his best but failed. It looked as though there was no way I could meet Dzhirkvelov.

'Well, thanks for going into battle for me, Paul,' I said. 'It looks as if I'll have to use my own channels.'

Within half an hour, I had contacted my friendly dissident by telephone and invited him and Ilya to lunch. The date, my diary tells me, was Monday 11 June 1984, and the venue was a pleasant restaurant in Beak Street, fully a minute from my office.

The man who joined us for lunch was about 5ft.7in. tall but powerfully built, with grey hair and a pencil-line grey moustache.

Dzhirkvelov confirmed that he did indeed have personal knowledge of the *Spiegel* affair. His wife was also ex-KGB; his former wife likewise. Indeed, he thought that was the reason why there had been no reprisals against his family when he defected.

Ilya Dzhirkvelov had joined the KGB in 1944. His Statement (see Appendices) gave important details about the merging of the political and military intelligence into one supraministerial organisation in September 1947, under the then Foreign Minister, Vyacheslav Molotov ('Mr. Nyet' as he was popularly known in the West).

Through his entire career, until his defection in 1980, Ilya was involved in disinformation work. From 1957 to 1965, he was Deputy Secretary-General of the Soviet Union of Journalists. From 1965 to 1977, he was a Tass correspondent in Tanzania and the Sudan; then, until his defection, he was stationed in Geneva in the Information Department of the World Health Organisation, with the diplomatic rank of Counsellor.

Early in 1960, Dzhirkvelov was summoned to a top level secret meeting of the International Department of the Soviet ruling party's Central Committee. The ID was the direct descendant of Lenin's Comintern, which Stalin 'dissolved' in 1943 to reassure his wartime allies, Churchill and Roosevelt, that the Soviets had given up world revolution. In this, he succeeded beyond any reasonable expectations. In the chair was the Comintern veteran and head of the ID, Boris Ponomarev. Also present was the Politburo's top ideologist, Mikhail Suslov.

Not enough attention was being paid to West Germany, said Ponomarev. In more general terms, he spoke of Turkey, Iceland, the Netherlands and Japan. Much could be done in all these countries, he declared, to prevent politicians undesirable in Soviet eyes from coming to power. *The only name he specifically mentioned, however, was F.J.Strauss.* Those present, including Dzhirkvelov, were instructed to work out, urgently, practical proposals to 'improve the situation'.

Not long afterwards, he discussed the German situation with Khrushchev's son-in-law, Alexei Adzhubei, who at that time was Editor of the government daily, *Izvestiya*, and one of the most powerful people in Russia. Forget the rest, was Adzhubei's command, and concentrate on West Germany. 'With West Germany in our hands,' he said, 'we would control the whole of Western Europe and could liquidate NATO, because West Germany is NATO's striking force.' Heady words.

Dhirkvelov was instructed by KGB General Agayants, who was in charge of all disinformation operations, to take every opportunity to tell West German journalists that the Soviets had proof that Strauss was linked with US intelligence. This was the message drummed into the heads of a party of West German journalists, all Social Democrats, invited to the USSR and given VIP treatment. Privately, Dhirkvelov was required to tell them that the Americans were paying large sums to Strauss, whose interest in self-enrichment meant far more to him than the future of Germany.

The line was that the Soviets would give the journalists all the material they could wish for, for publication in the Federal Republic — but on condition that the Soviet origin of it was not revealed.

Much later, Dhirkvelov learned of a successful secret operation against Strauss. It was Ponomarev himself who first told him and colleagues, at another top secret meeting in 1963, that 'we successfully used *Der Spiegel* to undermine Strauss'. Corroboration of Ponomarev's claim came to Dzhirkvelov from several sources.

One of these was a close friend of his, Colonel Arkady Boiko, who had been posted to Dresden, in East Germany, to take charge of an important Residency set up by the KGB in the 1950s. The purpose of the Dresden Residency was to conduct Active Measures against West Germany and Austria. The choice of location was deliberate. It was felt that any such activities, if based in East Berlin, would attract unwelcome attention.

The biggest coup of the Dresden Residency, Boiko told Dzhirkvelov, was when it succeeded in using *Der Spiegel* to compromise Franz Josef Strauss. Others, too, mentioned the *Spiegel* affair as a great success. Among these were Adzhubei, Pavel Gevorkyan and Leonid Zavgorodniy, another close friend of Dhirkvelov's.

Yet another man who mentioned the affair was the Soviet Deputy Secretary-General of the International Organisation of Journalists (IOJ: one of the main Soviet international front organisations), Alexander Yefremov. 'One of the best jobs ever,' was Yefremov's verdict.

There could be no doubt at all, Dzhirkvelov averred, that the anti-Strauss campaign in *Der Spiegel* was launched on the basis of material planted by the KGB. The last few lines of Dzhirkvelov's formal statement deserve to be quoted, however, as they make an important point which is relevant to the whole theme of this book:

> This, of course, does not imply any collaboration between the KGB and *Der Spiegel*: many respectable and politically impeccable publications fell victim to the KGB's 'Active Measures' without knowing by whom they had been used.

And that, indeed, is the true state of the art. To use people and organisations in such a way that they do not know they are being used. This was the standing rule for journalists, politicians and academics. And it seems likely that it was also standard practice in 'the KGB lawsuits'.

Notes

1.   In fact, according to the senior KGB defector Oleg Gordievsky, Andronov was not a staff member of the KGB, but a very active KGB agent.

5. The End of the Affair

With the statement from Dzhirkvelov safely in our files, I felt confident of victory — should the *Spiegel* case come to court. But I was a novice in these matters. With his enormous experience of litigation and especially of the vagaries of the English legal system, Sir James Goldsmith knew that we couldn't afford to relax.

The case had been scheduled for hearing in May 1984, but was postponed until 8 October, which was now the definitive deadline. Material, mostly from expert witnesses, had been pouring in. Our various German sources were also delivering, but we were all disappointed in the quality of the material they provided, most of which was too vague, general and unspecific to carry weight with judge and jury. Weiss, the man designated by the head of the BND, Eberhard Blum, was particularly disappointing in this respect.

Suddenly, in early September, the other side gave in. What amounted to an admission of defeat came in the form of a telephone call to Sir James's Counsel, Lord Rawlinson, QC, from the Plaintiffs' Counsel, John Wilmers, QC. Rudolf Augstein, Mr. Wilmers said, was ready to drop the action. There was only one condition, to which Rawlinson, after consulting Sir James, readily agreed. The Defendants were required to make it clear in an agreed statement that they did not maintain that Mr Wilmers's clients were 'controlled by the KGB'. Indeed, Sir James had never said that they were.

Even at this late hour and in the face of victory Sir James took nothing for granted. He felt he might yet need further and more convincing evidence from the German side. Only one man, he felt, could produce, or cause to be produced, the missing bits which he (and I) had felt all along must be there, somewhere. So, on 18 September 1984, Sir James, accompanied by Ronald Scrivener, flew to Munich for a long talk with Franz Josef Strauss himself.

Next day, Scrivener wrote a detailed account of the conversation. 'There was need for speedy action,' as he put it, adding:

> One such need was to overcome the problem that whereas the BND President had been helpful we had only been able to secure from the man he had asked to help us general indications of what material existed but no details and no material as such. Thus we knew that the double agent referred to by Gehlen had existed; that there had been the highly placed courier between East Berlin and *Spiegel*; that there had been four or five *Spiegel* staff who had been in receipt of material from Eastern Secret Services; and that documents found in Augstein's safe during the 1962 search of the *Spiegel* offices were held in the *Bundeskriminalamt* in Würzburg. But because of the obligation which ex-BND officers had not to reveal classified information this was in each case as far as we had got. We needed definite and not circumstantial evidence, with names and dates and, if possible, actual documents, to ensure our success if — as we must still anticipate — the case went to court.

It was only at this late stage, under pressure from Strauss and his lawyers that Weiss, with obvious embarrassment, revealed the awful truth that there never had been an East German double agent.[1]

As it happened, the revelation, and Sir James's personal intervention, made no difference, for shortly after his return to London agreement was reached on an out-of-court settlement. Graeme Hall telephoned me with the good news. So did Sir James. It was a busy morning. Sir James sent me by hand the draft of his side of a proposed statement to be read out in court. In a protracted telephone conversation, I made numerous drafting changes, which Sir James took down by hand at his end.

The time came for a final meeting with the lawyers. With Lord Rawlinson urbanely presiding in his own cramped Chambers in the Middle Temple, Sir James went through the text of his portion of the statement and also of a personal statement he intended to deliver to the press. This, too, had been sent to me for comments and drafting changes. The two Ronnies were there, and there was a lively discussion about exactly what to say and how. I felt for an hour or so like a junior sub-editor (or, as Americans call the species, copy-reader) in a pre-hightech Fleet Street office. Every now and then, I would leave the group to go to the ancient, heavy, steam-age typewriter which was all the distinguished Counsel's Chambers could find for my use. The ribbon, moreover, was so old and faint that the results of my labours were scarcely legible.

After a couple of hours or so, final versions were ready and approved: ready for the court and ready for the press. Already, Sir James Goldsmith had instructed his office to arrange for full-page advertisements to appear in Britain, the US and Germany. The newspapers carrying it were: in the UK, *The Times, Daily Telegraph* and *Financial Times*; in the US, the *New York Times*, the *Wall Street Journal* and the *Washington Post*; and in the German-speaking world, the *Frankfurter Allgemeine Zeitung* and *Die Welt*. (It was turned down by *The Guardian, Neue Zuercher* and *Die Zeit*.) Apart from minor changes, the advertisements were identical.

In the British press, the headlines were:

SOVIET METHODS ADMITTED
SPIEGEL V. NOW! MAGAZINE
AUGSTEIN v. GOLDSMITH

The final agreed statement read in the High Court of Justice, Queen's Bench Division, on 8 October 1984, incorporated three separate statements: by John Wilmers, QC, Counsel for the Plaintiffs; by Lord Rawlinson, QC, Counsel for the Defendants; and a second one from Mr Wilmers.

In his first statement, Mr. Wilmers explained that the Plaintiffs had taken exception to Sir James Goldsmith's claim that the campaign in *Der Spiegel* to discredit Strauss had been orchestrated by the KGB. His clients felt that this claim implied that the magazine was under the control of the KGB, that it knowingly employed journalists who were Communist agents and that in fact it was a KGB front organisation.

Lord Rawlinson's statement recalled the main facts of the *Spiegel* affair of 1962, and went on:

In support of his case, Sir James had arranged to call witnesses

from this country, the USA and West Germany who would have testified as to Soviet policy in general and to the special role and organisational structure of Soviet covert propaganda. In addition, Sir James
would have called high level Soviet and Soviet bloc defectors, who in
their former capacity as officers of the KGB or satellite intelligence
services, had themselves been involved in disinformation and penetration of the Western media including the recruitment of Western
agents of influence, among them journalists. They would have given
evidence of a number of instances of Soviet 'active measures'. More
specifically, certain of these high level officials (who have since defected to the West) would have given evidence of meetings at which
plans were approved to seek to discredit Dr. Strauss and to use *Der
Spiegel* in the manner I have indicated.

Such witnesses would have testified to the fact that the vast majority of the Western media which are used do not know that they are
being so used and further that an important part of the planning of
such operations is to ensure that the publications remain unaware of
the source of the material which is supplied to them and that most of
the individuals concerned do not know that they are ultimately serving Soviet purposes.

(................)

I am happy to state publicly on behalf of all the Defendants, as was
indicated before these proceedings began, that it was never intended
by Sir James to imply that the Plaintiffs or their paper were controlled
by or co-operated with Soviet Intelligence or knowingly employed any
journalist who was a KGB agent.

To this, Mr John Wilmers replied that his clients now took the view that
it was unnecessary to proceed any further with the action. They fully
accepted that Soviet Intelligence did operate as described by Lord
Rawlinson, but wanted to make it clear that they were not conscious of
having been so used.

At the foot of the advertisements came Sir James Goldsmith's personal Declaration, headed: '**A Victory for the West**'. In it, he placed
the *Spiegel* affair in the wider context of a vast number of similar examples the world over. It was to prove the existence of this world-wide
activity of the KGB, as well as the truth of his charge about the manipulation of *Der Spiegel*, that he had 'sponsored a massive international
research effort'. He added, however, an important rider:

It was never my intention to imply that *Der Spiegel* was at any time aware that it was being used by the KGB. Indeed the whole point of Soviet manipulation of Western media is that the publications so used should be unaware of the source of the material fed to them. I was therefore happy to make this matter clear in the agreed Statement.

He ended by describing the agreed Statement of 8 October 1984 as 'a famous victory for the defence of the West against its main enemy, Soviet imperialism'.

It was indeed just that: a famous victory. Sad to record, however, Rudolf Augstein was a bad loser. On our 'D-Day', *Der Spiegel* carried an article distorting the facts, notably by alleging that 'Goldsmith instigated a settlement' of the dispute — a straight falsehood. Goldsmith immediately issued a corrective statement. In its issue of 15 October, the newsmagazine came back to the charge, with two further articles. One was an editorial on the first inside page, unsigned, but not difficult to attribute to Augstein himself. Here is a sample paragraph:

What Sir James failed to do after three and a half years he now tries to achieve by expensive advertising — to which *Neue Zuercher*, *Zeit* and *Bild* have not lent themselves. He maintains there was a 'decision in Moscow' to stop Strauss succeeding Adenauer. What an honour for *Spiegel* to carry this out.

On the last inside page, *Der Spiegel* carried an article from the newspaper *Die Zeit* (which had indeed turned down Sir James Goldsmith's advertisement), criticising Sir James's statement on the ground that:

Of course the KGB spreads false statements, but there are responsible editorial staffs between the KGB and the readership. Sir James should not try to manipulate us.

A fair comment on the above might be that some editorial staffs are more 'responsible' than others. Understandably, Sir James was incensed by Augstein's defiance of the settlement and of the form of words approved by his lawyers as well as our own. Goldsmith sued *Der Spiegel* in Germany, and won. He obtained an injunction to stop any repetition of the lies that were being published.

I leave the last word to Walter Hahn, the man who first drew attention to Sejna's revelations. In a powerful editorial in *Strategic Review* (Fall issue, November 1984), under the headline 'A Case of Media Manipulation', he recalled the background, ending with these words:

> There are, in the final analysis, no viable bulwarks against the [KGB's] offensive other than the alertness of the media themselves. Let us hope that Sir James Goldsmith's courageous effort to expose the problem can set the standards for a searching self-examination by the media in all Western nations — even at the occasional cost, as in *Der Spiegel*'s case, of self-effacement.

A few sour remarks were only to be expected. In any event, although an important battle had been won, it was not, nor could it be, the end of the war which, by definition, would not end so long as a Leninist regime was in power in Moscow, or indeed anywhere else in the world to a lesser degree. In pursuance of his wider concept of the KGB's permanent campaign to penetrate and influence Western media, Sir James had already announced a typically generous plan which, however, turned out to be unrealistic. Early on in the *Spiegel* case, in a letter to the London *Times* of 16 September 1981, he had offered an annual prize of £50,000 for 'the best investigative journalism into subversion in the media'.

This was indeed a vast sum in the scale of literary or journalistic awards. The problem was: who was going to claim it? As a former working journalist myself, in what used to be called 'Fleet Street', I knew that nobody, certainly no member of the National Union of Journalists (NUJ), would come forward, thus branding himself or herself as an informer against fellow-journalists. The outcome could be expulsion from the NUJ and loss of livelihood.

Not every journalist would be perturbed on becoming aware that one of his or her colleagues was an agent of influence of the KGB or of some other Soviet Bloc intelligence agency. Or, at any rate, perturbed enough to do something about it, unless protected by secrecy, with a guarantee that the source would never be revealed to third parties: the exact antithesis of coming forward in broad daylight as a candidate for a public award.

Not surprisingly, to me, the original announcement had aroused little visible interest, apart from one or two irreverent gossip paragraphs. Visibly puzzled by this lack of response, Sir James at one stage offered to present the prize to me, but I declined unhesitatingly, though with gratitude. I felt the purpose of the award would be served only if the person receiving it were a 'working journalist' — that is, employed by a newspaper or magazine, or a radio or television concern. Although still a journalist, I had for years been a free-lance.

Another reason for declining the £50,000 was that I was handling the *Spiegel* research effort on contract and my acceptance of such a prize might throw doubt on the genuineness of my search for the truth. In the end, but not before some sarcastic comments in the London media about an award nobody was claiming, Sir James made his decision. He consulted me before making an announcement, and I approved his choice, wholeheartedly.

Sir James's choice was a dual one. The prize would be shared equally between John Barron and Paul Anastasi. He had asked me to sound out the two candidates discreetly, and I did: directly with Barron, and through Ron Baxter with Anastasi. Both were delighted, in Anastasi's case not only because he considered it an honour (as Barron did) but because it came as a very welcome contribution to the mounting expenses of the litigation that followed his courageous investigative exposure of the *Ethnos* affair (covered later in this book).

Jimmy asked me to draft a letter to *The Times*, for publication on 8 October 1985, one year after the first announcement of the award through the same channel. The letter defined Sir James Goldsmith's motive as encouraging the press 'to cleanse itself' by revealing the sources of any funds accepted by publications or individual journalists. It admitted, sadly, that 'there has been a dearth of applicants for the prize', but went on to announce that he had decided to award the prize jointly to two outstanding investigative journalists:

> PAUL ANASTASI, Athens correspondent of the *Daily Telegraph* and the *New York Times* and Managing Editor of the *Athens Star*, for his outstanding courage in exposing Soviet subversion in the Greek press;

and

> JOHN BARRON, Senior Editor of the *Reader's Digest*, for his
> admirable and pioneering exposure of Soviet subversion of the inter-
> national media in two major works: *KGB: The Secret Work of Soviet
> Secret Agents* (1974) and *KGB Today: The Hidden Hand* (1983); as
> well as for his continuing work of high quality and integrity in this
> important field.

Paul Anastasi had approved the wording of the reference to himself, which was deliberately unspecific, in view of the fact that he was defending a libel suit brought by the tabloid daily *Ethnos* in Athens.

The letter duly appeared and inspired only marginal comment. Sir James had written to me on 2 October to ask me, in addition, to draft a short statement to be issued to the big international agencies, AFP (France), AP (USA) and Reuters (UK). I agreed, but suggested that the statement should also be offered to the British Press Association (PA), which serves the entire British press with domestic news.

Although AFP and AP carried the statement, it was ignored by the two UK agencies, PA and Reuters. I was astonished. For it was one thing to ignore the announcement of a forthcoming prize likely to embarrass the press; surely quite another to ignore the news that the prize had actually been awarded. Clearly, I had underestimated the degree of hostile penetration of the British press, or alternatively of fear of action by the print unions as well as by the NUJ. Left-wing influences were indeed strong among both printers and working journalists. And yet, as Sir James wryly commented to me, the £50,000 prize was not exactly negligible. In comparison, the annual Booker Prize for the British novel held to be the best of the past year was (at that time) a mere £15,000, yet it always inspired an awesome number of column inches of newspaper space.

The Goldsmith Prize was of course regarded by Sir James as an integral part of his war to expose subversive influence in the Western media, as indeed was his speech of 21 January 1981. In Washington on 22 May 1984, while our *Spiegel* investigation was in full swing, Sir James made another speech, even more wide-ranging and hard-hitting. Jimmy had invited me to lunch at Wilton's so that he could show me his draft and ask for my comments.

I was sorry not to have been in the audience, which included the American Director of Central Intelligence, William Casey, and a galaxy of personalities from the conservative establishment then in power.

The title Sir James had chosen was: 'SOVIET ACTIVE MEASURES V. THE FREE PRESS — a European Perspective'.

The occasion was sponsored by Frank Barnett's National Strategy Information Centre, in co-operation with the National Security Studies Program of Georgetown University and the Institute for Sino-Soviet Studies of George Washington University.

By all accounts, the speech was a great success, not merely because Sir James was addressing an invited and committed audience but because of the directness and succinctness of his presentation. The 'European perspective' helped, too, by broadening the terms of reference.

Sir James referred to the revelations of Stanislav Levchenko (through John Barron) about his recruitment of Japanese agents of influence; mentioned Andrei Sakharov, the Soviet Nobel Prize winner (long in internal exile, then freed by Gorbachev) and his 'testament to the West' in which he described agents of influence including some political figures, businessmen and a great many writers, journalists, government advisers and heads of press and TV; gave details of Anastasi's exposure of the *Ethnos* affair; described the main Soviet international front organisations; gave numerous examples of Soviet 'active measures'; and recalled the campaign to discredit Franz Josef Strauss (no doubt feeling free to do so since he was speaking in the US, not Britain). He went on to suggest ways in which Soviet covert influences could be countered, while categorically ruling out any form of official censorship.

The financial cost of Sir James Goldsmith's 'famous victory for the defence of the West' was enormous. My own research contract, including special payments to researchers, ran to about £439,000. Payments to the UK law firm may be estimated at about £200,000 and to the German law firm at about £15,000.

Only big organisations or very rich individuals can afford justice at this kind of price. And legal aid is not on offer to defendants in libel suits in the United Kingdom.

So, it was a costly victory, as well as a 'famous' one. But how much costlier it would have been, had it come to trial!

Six years after Sir James Goldsmith's 'famous victory', two major revelations came to light which, in my view, vindicated Sir James Goldsmith's stand. Indeed, it is fair to speculate that had these facts been known at the time, Rudolf Augstein would not have sued Jimmy.

The first was the admission by *Spiegel* magazine, in its issue of 17 December 1990, that its East Berlin bureau chief, one Diethelm Schröder, was an agent for the East German security service, known as the STASI (short for Staatssicherheitsdienst). Reporting on it from Berlin in *The Times* the following day, Anne McElvoy used the words 'sheepishly admitted', and added that Schröder's mission was to disseminate disinformation through the columns of the magazine.

He had been called in for questioning and accused of passing military and political information to the East Germans. Before being sent to East Berlin, Schröder had been *Der Spiegel*'s military specialist. As such, he was reported to have been on good terms with NATO's secretary-general, Manfred Wörner (who, of course, was in no way to blame for whatever use Diethelm Schröder might make of this relationship).

In that same issue of the magazine, *Der Spiegel* had this to say:

> Only now, three months after unification, it is becoming clear that the long arm of the STASI reached not only into the offices of ministries but into almost all social circles of the Federal Republic of Germany.

Some of us had been saying just that for years, and been widely dismissed as 'paranoid'. It has to be added, however, that Schröder had not been working for *Der Spiegel* at the time of the Strauss affair, so that the news of his STASI connection merely confirmed that the magazine was a target for STASI penetration.

Fourteen months passed. Then, in the March 1992 of the long established Paris review of Communist affairs, *Est & Ouest,* I read these words:

> I can say that for many years, *Der Spiegel* had put its columns at the disposal of the KGB.

Now, if Jimmy Goldsmith or I had said these words, they would have been no more than an unsubstantiated allegation. But they were attributed to a man who was bound to know what he was talking about, who indeed would qualify for the 'smoking gun' label so eagerly sought by libel lawyers: the ex-KGB General Oleg Kalugin. I rang Jimmy in New York, and he invited me to check the attribution and to write an article for publication in the next volume of his occasional collection of speeches and articles under the generic title of COUNTER CULTURE.[2]

As it happened, I had met Kalugin in November 1991 at a conference in Potsdam organised by the Washington-based International Freedom Foundation. We had indeed dined together, itself a reunion that would have been unthinkable during the Cold War, and made still less believable by the fact that another dinner companion on that occasion was Bill Colby, whom I had known when he was Director of the CIA. On parting company, Kalugin had given me his card as a People's Deputy, which had made him immune from prosecution when he had been fired as head of Soviet Counter-Intelligence after speaking his mind about his employers.

I tried to reach him but the number he had given me appeared to have been cut off. So more 'detective' work was needed. The article quoting Kalugin was signed by one Jürg Steinacher. My friends at *Est & Ouest* told me that Steinacher's article had originally appeared in the Swiss publication *ZeitBild*. When I got through to Steinacher, he referred me to his own source: an article in the Hamburg daily *Die Zeit*, which he kindly faxed to me. I failed to reach the author, Christian Schmidt-Häuer.

There was a problem, which only Kalugin could resolve. The three publications involved had carried incompatible versions of the circumstances. It was impossible to tell whether he had said what he was reported to have said in a television interview, and if so whether it had been seen on Soviet or German TV; or whether he had been addressing the Soviet parliament.

I was rescued from my dilemma by the intelligent and amiable Chairman of the International Freedom Foundation, Duncan Sellars, who had invited Kalugin to the Potsdam conference where I had met him. Armed with Kalugin's direct line, I reached him at first attempt and was glad that I had gone through my convoluted journey, for it turned out that he had indeed said the words attributed to him, but neither on television nor in the Soviet parliament. He had in fact had his say at a press conference immediately after the failed hardline coup of August 1991, which had provoked the fall of Mikhail Gorbachev and brought Boris Yeltsin to power.

Der Spiegel itself had then approached him to check the words attributed to him, and he had confirmed them. At my request, a well placed German friend made an exhaustive search through the files of the magazine and failed to find any reference to his statement which their own staff had confirmed.

Unsurprisingly for a man of his seniority, Kalugin had long known of the KGB's use of the *Spiegel* connection to ruin Strauss's career, although he had not been personally involved in that particular Active Measure. And of course he did know that the magazine was open to the KGB. The question remained: could Rudolf Augstein not have known? Perhaps the Diethelm Schröder story was as much as *Der Spiegel* could take. Embarrassment doubtless has its limits.

Notes

1.   See Chapter 3.
2.   *Counter Culture*, Vol.5, 1992.

6. IPS: The Battle Starts

I have to admit that I brought this battle upon myself, albeit unwittingly. I had long been familiar with the works of the American writer Richard Barnet, and with the activities of the Institute for Policy Studies (IPS) which he had co-founded two decades earlier. I therefore read with special interest a review of Barnet's latest book — *Allies: America, Europe and Japan since the War*, published in England by Jonathan Cape in 1983.

Not the least interesting point about the review, which appeared in the (London) *Spectator* on 7 April 1984, was that it was by Enoch Powell, at that time the most celebrated of Britain's backbench MPs. Every politically conscious reader in the country had views about Mr Powell and I was no exception. I admired him, but not uncritically. Like General de Gaulle, whom he resembled in certain respects, Enoch Powell came as a package deal. It was impossible to take only the bits you liked and reject the others.

One bit I did not like was Powell's anti-American bias. Should he ever read this passage, he would doubtless argue with his usual logic that he has no such bias: that he approves of some things American and disapproves of others. Indeed, that is his right, and in that respect, we have something in common. I found very little to approve of in the conduct of public affairs during the four years of Jimmy Carter's Presidency and it is quite possible that some readers of my regular column in William Buckley's conservative *National Review* during that period may have wrongly concluded that I, too, was anti-American.

Back to Mr. Richard Barnet. When Barnet wrote about East-West relations, which he did frequently, more often than not he reached the conclusion that America was wrong and Russia right. That, certainly, was the message of *Allies*. It was therefore hardly surprising to find that Enoch Powell had given Barnet (an anti-American American, by my definition) what might fairly be called a 'rave review'.

Had I kept my views to myself, I might have saved myself several years of hard work and anxiety. That is why I say that I brought this on myself. I couldn't resist the temptation to unburden myself in a short letter to the Editor of *The Spectator,* which was duly published in the issue dated 21 April 1984. The letter read:

> Sir: Mr Enoch Powell never ceases to puzzle. How can such erudition cohabit with such innocence? The most important point about *Allies: America, Europe and Japan since the War,* upon which he heaps such praise, is that the author, Richard J.Barnet, is a co-founder and is still a mainstay of the Institute for Policy Studies, a major front for Cuban intelligence, itself controlled by the Soviet KGB. Are readers not entitled to be forewarned?

Although Richard Barnet did not issue his writ against me until 16 August 1984, he had fired his first shot in the long battle two months earlier: on 15 June, to be specific. That day, a courier had delivered to my Regent Street office a bellicose letter from Bindman and Partners, describing my allegations as 'utterly false' and 'highly defamatory'. According to Bindman and Partners, my letter to *The Spectator* 'states wholly inaccurately that the Institute for Policy Studies is a "major front for Cuban Intelligence" and is "controlled by the Soviet KGB"'. Their client required me forthwith to take the following steps:

> 1. To make a statement in Open Court withdrawing the allegations you have made and apologising for them in terms to be agreed with us.
> 2. To pay our client an appropriate sum in respect of damages to compensate him for the injury you have done him.
> 3. To undertake in a form to be agreed not to repeat such allegations about our client.
> 4. To indemnify him in respect of his legal costs.

The 15th was a Friday and the lawyers had given me a week-end to think things over. By noon on Monday 18th, I was to let them know that I would comply with these requirements. 'If we do not hear from you,' the letter had gone on, 'proceedings will be instituted and pursued until adequate redress is secured.'

Menacing words. By good fortune, Sir James was spending that week-end at his London home. He would not take kindly to any threatening letter from his old enemies, (Geoffrey) Bindman and Partners, well-known to him for their defence of *Private Eye* against writs he had issued.

At that time, my *Spiegel* investigation was still in full flood. I saw this new battle as the opening of another front in the same war, and felt sure Sir James would see it in the same light.

He received me at home the next day, a Saturday, not as before in his small, book-lined study, but in the huge and comfortable drawing room.

Sir James read through the writ carefully. 'Are you sure of your facts?' he asked.

'I can't claim to have "smoking gun" evidence, Jimmy, but the circumstantial evidence is very strong. Besides, what I said about the IPS has been said repeatedly in America, and as far as I know, no writs have ever been issued before.'

It didn't take Sir James long to make up his mind. His gambler's instincts were aroused, and his fighting instinct as well. 'I'll see you through,' he said. 'To the end.'

To be honest, I don't really know what I would have done if Sir James had decided not to back me. I would have headed straight for a quick bankruptcy without his help, for which I shall always be deeply grateful. And yet, I firmly believed that what I had written was the truth.

Had I written what I did in any American (or French) publication, there would have been no problems. To say it in England was to expose myself to the rigours of libel laws. For nearly 50 years (since 1935), I had been a journalist, and this had never happened to me before, although I had had some close shaves. The risks of libel are drummed into the skulls of cub reporters and once absorbed are never forgotten. Care in the formulation of allegations becomes second nature. I thought I had conformed to my own rules, and, greatly strengthened by Jimmy's promise, the first thing I did on arriving at my office on 18 June was to dictate a letter which said:

> Dear Sirs,
> I have your letter of 15 June. You do not seem to have read my letter in the issue of The Spectator dated 28 April 1984 with due care, even though you have quoted portions of it which your client Mr. Richard Barnet alleges to be 'utterly false'.
>
> I therefore draw your attention to the following points:
>
> 1. I described the Institute for Policy Studies as 'a major front for Cuban intelligence, itself controlled by the Soviet KGB'. The use of the preposition 'for' is significant. I did not use the word 'of'. The clear implication is that the IPS has been used by Cuban intelligence for its own purposes, not necessarily with the knowledge of the IPS itself.
> 2. You allege in your second paragraph that I said that the Institute for Policy Studies is 'controlled by the Soviet KGB'. Syntactically, in context, I said nothing of the kind. What the phrase you quote means, in plain English, is that Cuban intelligence is itself controlled by the KGB. This is well-documented. I did not say, as you allege that I did, that the IPS is itself controlled by the KGB.

I added that I had no intention of apologising and was prepared to justify my allegations in open court.

Two unexpected conversations made me realise, for the first time, the dimensions of the problem I faced.

The first was with Dzhirkvelov, not long after we had learned that Augstein was dropping his lawsuit against Sir James. Looking me in the eye, Dzhirkvelov said: 'In the KGB before I left, we were always told: "Public Enemy number one is Brian Crozier."'

This was a startling piece of information, even though attacks on me in the Soviet press and radio were by no means rare. It was also, of course, flattering, to learn that I ranked so high in the KGB hate list.

There was a natural rejoinder. 'Who was Public Enemy number two?' I asked.

The answer was appropriate, and could hardly have been rehearsed. 'Robert Moss,' said Dzhirkvelov, referring to the gifted young Australian journalist and author, one of my successors as Editor of the confidential bulletin, *Foreign Report*, who had dedicated his first book, *Urban Guerrillas*, to me in 1972 in the following words: 'For Brian, who helped to make this work possible and who understands the problem better than any of us.'

These remarks left me pensive.

The second conversation was still heavier with implied menace. It took place over a coffee house lunch at the Madison Hotel in Washington. A friendly contact of mine, formerly of the District of Columbia police force, had brought an ex-colleague of his to meet me. The few plain clothes detectives I have met have always startled me by their unkempt appearance, designed no doubt to enable them to merge unsuspected into a hostile human environment. This one was no exception. Tall and gangling, he wore his hair long and had an untidy beard to match.

'I'd gotten myself accepted in the IPS,' he volunteered between mouthfuls. 'They'd invite me round for social evenings, poker evenings, really. I remember one evening very clearly.' He interrupted his eating to look me in the eye, over the rim of his glass of beer. 'You were the sole topic of conversation.'

'Me?'

'Yeah. Brian Crozier. One of them kept on asking: "How can we finish that guy off?" A number of suggestions came up. One guy wanted to do a research project on everything you'd written, so as to prove you were an agent of influence of the CIA. They kept mentioning a book on Chile.'

That reference, at least, rang a bell. More than a decade earlier, as Editor of the 'World Realities' series, I had commissioned Robert Moss to write a book on the short-lived regime of President Salvador Allende, which had duly appeared under the title: '*Chile's Marxist Experiment*' (London, 1973). Deposed in a military coup in September that year, the disastrous Allende regime had been adopted by the Soviet propaganda apparatus, and therefore by the international Left, as a 'cause' for agitation, as in their respective times, the Spanish Republic and Vietnam had been and as South Africa would be when its time came.

Moss's book became the focus of intensive and at times virulent agitation, which caused the author many problems in his profession and much time consumed in writs but at least brought him the compensation of published apologies. The conversation during the IPS 'poker evening' thus appeared to confirm and complement the remarks of Dzhirkvelov.

'Oh, and something else,' said my hippie-looking detective. 'Two names kept coming up.' He paused, scratching his head. 'Newbirt. No, Newbury. And Bolton. Yeah, Newbury and Bolton. Mean anything to you?'[1]

'Indeed they do. Both were former employees of mine. In what context were these names mentioned?'

'They were the main sources the IPS had, about you, I mean.'

'Can you remember when this took place, this poker evening?'

He searched his memory. 'Oh, I guess about two years ago.'

The lunch we were having took place on Wednesday 2 April 1986, and my offending letter to *The Spectator* had appeared on 28 April 1984. If the plain-clothesman's memory was accurate, the plan to 'finish that guy off' would have been discussed only three or four weeks earlier. Unwittingly, it seemed, I really had played into the hands of my declared enemies.

During the two months after the first threatening letter from Bindman, I occasionally allowed myself to hope that Richard Barnet and his Institute might have second thoughts about proceeding with the case, in view of my uncompromising response to the threats. In any case, I was still deeply involved in the *Spiegel* case. I had lost no time, however, in letting selected friends in the US know what had happened. I say 'friends in the US deliberately, rather than 'American friends', for two of them at least were not US citizens. They were Robert Moss, who was Australian-born, and John Rees, who was British born but had spent many years in the United States.

Each had a strong interest in anything concerning the IPS, an interest that was professional and ideological as well as personal. In 1968, Robert Moss, then aged 22, had called to see me in my office at 200 Piccadilly, London, with a written introduction from Geoffrey Fairbairn, an Australian academic specialist on guerrilla war in South-East Asia, who was a member of the Founding Committee of my Institute for the Study of Conflict, and who happened to be Robert's father-in-law.

Tall and energetic, Robert Moss was brimful of self-confidence. He had brought with him a book of cuttings that impressed me: already, at his young age, he had had about 100 articles published in various Australian newspapers and journals. He had been lecturing on Latin American history at the Australian National University. I introduced him to *The Economist*, where he started a meteoric career. He had excellent contacts in Washington, and had been the first British journalist to gain access to 'the Letelier documents' — the incriminating contents of a briefcase belonging to the late Orlando Letelier, who had been the ambassador in Washington of the extreme leftist Chilean President Salvador Allende. The briefcase turned up, intact, in Letelier's car after a bomb deposited there had killed its owner. The assassination had been carried out on the orders of General Pinochet's secret service. The documents proved that Letelier had worked for Richard Barnet's Institute and that he had also been on Fidel Castro's payroll.

Robert Moss had run a well-informed, authentic account of the Letelier documents in *Foreign Report*. (A parallel role had been played in the US by Reed Irvine, a combative ex-Communist, in his own widely read bulletin, *Accuracy in Media*.)

In 1980, in collaboration with the distinguished Belgian-born American journalist, Arnaud de Borchgrave, Robert Moss co-authored a best-selling roman-à-clef, *The Spike*, which was widely interpreted as an exposure of the IPS.

John Rees, an ample man with a dark-red beard, had been a journalist on the London *Daily Mirror*, before settling in Baltimore. There, from his home, and with his wife Louise, he ran an impressively well-informed bulletin, *Information Digest*, which documented the activities of the extreme Left in the United States. His bulletin and his massive files included excellent material on the IPS.

The three of them — Moss, Rees and de Borchgrave — had formed a partnership to launch a monthly confidential bulletin (yet another!) entitled *Early Warning*.

As it happened, the writ from Barnet was issued on the day — 16 August 1984 — of my gall-bladder operation at the Middlesex Hospital, when I was in no condition to read it, let alone fight back.

One day the telephone rang next to my hospital bed. It was Robert Moss, who was in London. 'I've brought you a special packet,' he announced. He left it with me that afternoon. It was a weighty package indeed: a full set of photocopies of the contents of Orlando Letelier's briefcase — essential evidence for my defence.

After leaving hospital, much emaciated, I found I was too weak to type and indeed to do anything much. I went through the documents, and wrote a brief note by hand to the Hon. Fiona Black, a smiling and pleasant junior partner in Peter Carter-Ruck's team, who had been assigned to my case.

On 10 September, still at home in my dressing gown, I mustered enough intellectual energy to tape a letter and memorandum to Carter-Ruck, which I sent to Regent Street for typing.

As I said in a covering letter, most of the Letelier documents were in Spanish. At the present stage of my convalescence, I didn't feel up to translating them, but summarised the political background. I had divided the documents into three groups: Group A, consisting mainly of diaries; Group B, the vital papers about Letelier's activities and links with Havana; and Group C, consisting largely of a long list of friends and contacts, both individuals and organisations. The former included the eccentric American multimillionaire Cyrus Eaton, a great supporter of Communist or pro-Communist causes. I had numbered the documents in each group.

It was clear, very early on, that *The Spectator* would be trying, if at all possible, to extricate itself from the problems arising out of my letter — and of that journal's decision to publish it. One more of the unfair aspects of the English Laws of libel is that the blame falls not only on the writer of the offending words, and on the Editor of the journal or book where they appeared, but equally on the publisher and printer.

The complicating factor in this case was that the ownership of the old and distinguished journal in which my letter appeared had frequently changed hands. The owner, at the time, was Mr Algy Cluff, a (relatively) minor oil tycoon. Some time after my letter appeared, however, Mr. Cluff sold *The Spectator*, and pursued his other business interests. This did not abrogate his personal responsibility in the matter; but it considerably diminished his interest in defending the action. This was bound to create problems that did not arise in the *Spiegel* case, where Sir James, the owner of the publication in which the alleged libel had appeared, was also the main Defendant.

On 17 September, Fiona Black wrote to say that *The Spectator*'s solicitors had proposed that I should indemnify it against damages and costs, as they had 'no particular interest in fighting the action'. Carter-

Ruck's advice was negative, on the ground that '*The Spectator* accepted your letter for publication and there is no reason why they should not adopt the normal practice of standing by their correspondent'. These were, indeed, my own sentiments.

I was not able to see Fiona Black until Thursday 27 September, when I briefed her in some detail on what I knew about the IPS. It was clear, as it had been with Graeme Hall in the earlier case, that her excellent mind was blank in respect of the complicated political background of the IPS, of the Washington scene and of the machinations of the Castro regime.

Long hours of work, stretching to weeks, months, years, lay ahead. Mountains of documents, shoals of letters. The Laws of libel, on both sides of the Atlantic, were tailor-made for the highly profitable consumption of legal man-hours. Profitable, that is, to the lawyers, regardless of the outcome. The citizen at the receiving end is caught in a vice, once he decides to fight an action. There will be a 'Defence of Justification', 'Particulars' and 'Further and Better Particulars', on either side; and 'discovery', a device enabling the Defendant to oblige the Plaintiff to produce specific documents the existence of which, of course, must first have come to his attention. There will be this manoeuvre and that counter-manoeuvre, each with its own price-tag.

What it amounts to is a protracted war of nerves, in which the dominant element is staying power. The consumption of time as well as of nervous energy is monumental. At all times until the eve of the date set aside for the trial, the initiative is in the hands of the Plaintiff. What he has started, only he can stop. On the Defendant's side, the only recourse lies in causing the Plaintiff to consume as many man-hours as possible in the hope that he, too, will feel the strain, and reach the point where it is no longer worth his while to pursue the matter to its possibly bitter end.

To stay the course requires not merely stamina, but also a deep pocket. I had the former; Jimmy Goldsmith provided the latter.

Notes

1. The names, though not the persons, are fictitious.

7. Frustrations in Washington

I was acutely aware that in one particular, the IPS case was going to prove tougher than the *Spiegel* affair. There was indeed a significant difference between the two. In the Spiegel case, the main scene of the action was in the German Federal Republic, even though one of the principal witnesses, and several minor ones, resided in the United States. I had encountered obstacles in America and had overcome them, but they were bureaucratic and human obstacles, amenable to personal contacts and persuasion.

In the IPS case, as I knew in advance the obstacles were constitutional, political and legal, as well as bureaucratic. In retrospect, I had overestimated my ability to overcome them. But then, they turned out to be even more formidable than I could have imagined.

The political background has to be understood, for without it the constitutional and legal obstacles would make no sense. The Vietnam War had traumatised and divided American public opinion. In common with many other commentators on world affairs, I had written and spoken a great deal on the subject. In so doing, I had added greatly to the number of my political enemies who, even when they had not bothered to read what I had actually said, listed me among the champions of the American intervention.

To put the record straight, I was indeed whole-heartedly in favour of the American intervention; but was also highly critical of the form that intervention took, and of what, to my mind, was a profound failure of diagnosis and method on the American side.[1] This reservation, as might be expected, was normally omitted in the many attacks on me in the left-wing press.

The opponents of American intervention fell into two categories. One, symbolised by the film star Jane Fonda, was explicitly committed to the Vietnamese Communist side in the protracted war. The other, while by no means pro-Communist, felt (by no means without reason) that the American involvement, whether or not it was initially justifiable, was doing, or had done, immensely more harm than good, not least by dividing American society and public opinion on deeply antagonistic lines. This was, in my view, a perfectly honourable and defensible view to take, although I never shared it. My own efforts were directed to the end of trying to improve official America's understanding of the problems it faced in Vietnam, some of which were of its own making, and to modify its military, political and psychological approach accordingly. Long before the end, I had grasped the fact that it was a forlorn task.

The Watergate affair was hardly less traumatic and divisive. President Richard Nixon had been a hate-symbol for the Left, ever since as a thrusting young lawyer, he had exposed the esteemed State Department officer, Alger Hiss, as a Soviet spy and perjurer in the Congressional inquiries initiated by Senator Joseph McCarthy in the 1950s. The break-in at the Watergate Hotel in Washington during the Democratic Party's Convention in 1972, was a sordid incident. And Nixon, much involved at the time in Strategic Arms Limitation Talks (SALT) with the Soviets, handled the growing crisis ineptly. His political enemies exploited the situation for all it was worth until he was forced to step down as President.

The consequences were far-reaching. Without doubt, the great Soviet subversion machine was not initially involved by the affair. Indeed, Leonid Brezhnev and his Politburo colleagues in Moscow were at first dismayed that the man who had been negotiating with them was in trouble at home.

What followed has been described as an orgy of self-flagellation. The journalists and their Congressional allies seemed intent on destroying anything that might have helped Nixon to stay in the White House. In particular, both the Federal Bureau of Investigation (FBI) and the Central Intelligence Agency (CIA) became targets of interminable media exposés and Congressional hearings. Month after month, year after year, the failings or abuses, imaginary as well as real, were relentlessly exposed. The Watergate affair did lasting damage to the security of America's free society and resulted in a deep-seated malaise.

Briefly, the legislators approved steps to curb the activities of the FBI and the CIA, by bringing them both under public as well as Congressional scrutiny. While they were about it, they made it very difficult for the main law-enforcement agencies, such as the police and customs departments, to go about their legitimate business.

The two particular pieces of legislation that did the most lasting harm were the Freedom of Information Act and the Privacy Act. The first of these played into the hands of hostile agencies, including the KGB, by making available to Soviet agents, as well as journalists and the public, many matters best kept secret.

It should be added that as both the CIA and the FBI had residual censorship powers, many of the documents released contained heavy deletions that made some of them unintelligible. The amount of official time thereupon consumed, both in revealing and in concealing, was a monstrous misuse of the bureaucracies concerned. An illuminating example was provided by the CIA defector, Philip Agee, who exercised his new 'rights' by requesting all documents relating to his own case. Responding, the Agency searched its files and located 8,699 such documents, but refused to release 8,175 of them, and released most of the rest only in part, as was their right under the FOIA. The CIA's decision was upheld in court and the presiding judge noted that in responding to Agee's request, the Agency had had to spend some 25,000 man-hours at a cost of over $400,000 in the retrieval and review of the documents their former employee had requested.

As for the Privacy Act, the main effect of it was to make it impossible for any government agencies to keep files on either individuals or groups, regardless of their purposes or intentions. A charter for criminals and subversives, especially terrorists.

Disgraced, though not impeached, Nixon was succeeded as President by Gerald Ford who, not having been elected, was never more than a stop-gap Chief of State. The next elected President was Jimmy Carter. The very fact that he won the Presidential election of November 1976, albeit narrowly, was indicative of the national mood. By a small majority — less than 2 per cent — American voters wanted the man in the White House to leave things as the Congress had left them.

In that sense, Carter was the perfect post-Watergate incumbent. He encouraged his chosen Director of Central Intelligence (DCI), Admiral

Stansfield Turner, to dismantle the Agency's covert action capabilities so that, before Jimmy Carter stepped down, the CIA had been reduced to a shell of its former self, with some 800 resignations or early retirements. Of these some 400 officers were eased out because they had been involved in anti-Soviet work. Carter's Executive Order 12036 of January 1978, which became known as his Charter for the intelligence Community, made things worse. Congressional Oversight turned into a device for leaking top secrets to the media — and therefore to the KGB.

The fact that Ronald Reagan was elected President in November 1980 with a sweeping majority over Jimmy Carter, the Democratic candidate, reflected a marked swing in the national mood. Reagan and his campaign team had made it clear that they deplored the emasculation of the FBI and CIA and intended to do all they could to restore both to full efficiency and effectiveness.

As I have related (Chapter 2), the post-Watergate mood had not been fully dispersed when I went to Washington in 1981 in search of witnesses in the *Spiegel* case. I had hoped that things would be better in 1985 but they were not. If anything, the mood was less co-operative. To be fair to the bureaucracy, however, this time I was treading on ground that was even more sensitive. One of the issues on which the CIA had been hounded in the aftermath of Vietnam and Watergate was the charge that it had spied, unconstitutionally, on US citizens. And now, here was an alien intruder, a British investigator, poking his nose into US domestic issues.

In retrospect, 1985 was perhaps the most frustrating year of all. A busy one in other respects, it had yielded little more than an admittedly vast, and constantly growing, pile of press cuttings — useful in building up a picture of how the IPS had started, the kind of activities it went in for and what various writers thought about it but little of it acceptable as evidence in an English court of law.

Whatever the renown of the writers, and however many of them confirm each other's findings, their printed words amount in sum merely to 'hearsay'. This was the professional advice constantly reiterated for my benefit by a bright young solicitor when he took over my case from the Hon. Fiona Black, who had pulled out to have a baby. His name was Alasdair Pepper, his age 28 and he towered above us all at 6 feet 8 inches. I found him sharp, thorough, precociously mature and professionally pessimistic. Without live witnesses who could stand up to hostile cross-examination, he never tired of telling me, I stood little chance of winning.

Some of the most interesting material came from a young American researcher, Steven Scot Powell, who was writing a book on the IPS and had attended meetings there in the guise of a sympathiser.[2] From the draft chapters he sent me, it was clear that Soviet and Soviet Bloc officials frequently attended IPS functions: useful, but hardly conclusive in proving my allegations in *The Spectator.*

Knowing the restrictions on the official side, I tried through many private channels to reach the key Cuban defectors who had testified in public about the Soviet control over Fidel Castro's intelligence service, the DGI, to which they had belonged. I badly needed access to two of them in particular: Orlando Castro Hidalgo, and Gerardo Jesús Peraza Amechazurra.

I had been familiar with their revelations for many years. Indeed I had incorporated them in my *Conflict Study No. 35, Soviet Pressures in the Caribbean: The Satellisation of Cuba*, published in May 1973. Perhaps, indeed, it was that study, as much as anything else, that had gone down in whatever 'black book' had been compiled by those who wanted to find ways of 'finishing that guy off'? Aged 31 at the time and serving at the Cuban embassy in Paris, Orlando Castro had crossed into Luxembourg and sought asylum in the American embassy in the Grand Duchy. His colleague Gerardo Peraza had been serving at the Cuban embassy in London when he defected to the American embassy in Grosvenor Square in November 1971, aged 40.

Castro Hidalgo had written a book, entitled *Spy for Fidel* (1971). Two years earlier, he had testified before Congress, explaining that he had defected because his service had been taken over by the Soviets. Interestingly, his colleague had named the same reason for his own defection, but had not been able to testify until 1982 — a reflection of the change of political atmosphere in the US.

Although my own study had drawn upon the evidence of these defectors, it had been largely based on a Top Secret intelligence paper, which gave specific details of the KGB personnel sent from Moscow to Havana to supervise the creation of the DGI. Again, even if I had been able to obtain permission to produce the secret document in court, it would not have been admissible, unless its original author had also been permitted — and persuaded — to appear as a witness.

It was thus a major objective of mine to find the two Cubans and to persuade them to come to London at the critical time and take the stand and the oath as witnesses. There was one snag: nobody seemed to know what had happened to them. Everywhere, I drew a blank. My own friends and associates had tried and failed.

Essentially, my strategy was to draw what seemed to be the logical lesson from my success in the *Spiegel* case, when I had bypassed the blocked official channels, to reach the key potential witness, the KGB defector Ilya Dzhirkvelov. True, there was a different lesson to be drawn from my other success in gaining access to the Czech defector Jan Sejna through the personal intervention of Bill Casey: start at the top!

The 'top' was indeed open to me, in the sense that by then, I had had an 'audience' with President Reagan, but I decided that, tempting though it was, my personal problem was not one I should inflict on the President of the United States.

On that visit, therefore, and at intervals through 1985, I tried the first method; and got nowhere. One of my long-standing contracts in Washington was Dr. Ernest Lefever, an austere and erudite man who ran a small but distinguished think-tank called the Ethics and Public Policy Center. Lefever had been President Reagan's choice to fill the 'Human Rights' slot at the State department but his nomination had attracted a smear campaign of such venom from the liberal Left that he had been forced to withdraw. Thus we shared the unsolicited distinction of being targets of hostile propaganda, and he wanted to help. Not greatly to my surprise, he told me that his Center was engaged in writing a definitive study about the IPS.

My visit had begun as his offices were closing for the day. After listening to me, Lefever went to a filing cabinet, produced a card, and said: 'This guy is a member of our study group on the IPS, and may be able to help you. He's ex-FBI, and probably knows a lot about the Cuban connections of the IPS.' He photocopied the card for me.

Let us call the man Richard Wicken. I wrote to him on 12 June, after returning to London, and he replied at length and with great courtesy on 17 July. He had retired nine years ago, he explained, and such information as he had was not very significant, and out of date. However, he enclosed a cutting from the *Washington Times* of 15 July 1985, asked me if I knew the Editor-in-Chief of that newspaper, Arnaud de Borchgrave, and suggested that the latter might be helpful. (In fact, I had recently had an interesting but hurried talk with Arnaud in the impressive headquarters of his newspaper.)

As Mr Wicken said, the cutting he enclosed included a comment on the IPS which 'seems to be precisely the same as the one giving basis for action against you by Richard Barnet'. This observation was true, but did not take my investigation much further.

It was, as the bureaucrats put it, not without interest to note that yet again, one could say in America with impunity what I had said in Britain with dire consequences. One more document to add to the deepening pile.

One day in late June, John Rees had rung me from Baltimore in a state of some excitement. He had been reading a book entitled *Labyrinth* published two years earlier, and had found a passage which, he was convinced, would win the case for me. He airmailed the book to me and I had to agree that the passage he had in mind was potentially of explosive interest and relevance.

A co-author of *Labyrinth* was Eugene Propper[3], the prosecuting attorney in the Letelier assassination case, and his working relationship with the FBI man assigned to the case formed the core of the book. His name was Carter Cornick. Even now, the actual passage is worth quoting in full. It occurs on pp.125-126:

> Cornick walked into Propper's office on the morning of November 24 with his daily update and a new item. Saul Landau [a Senior Fellow of IPS] was complaining that a prominent Chilean exile who worked for IPS had been followed the day before in New York. According to Landau, someone had followed the exile through Grand Central Station so clumsily and aggressively that the exile had asked a policeman to speak to the man. This having no effect, the exile had left Grand Central, whereupon the man following him had hopped into a car. The exile had taken down the license number, and he had a description of the man. Landau thought the exile's life was in danger and wanted FBI protection for him.
> The next day Cornick was back with a grin.
> 'You won't believe this,' he said after closing Propper's door.

'Guess who was following the guy up in Grand Central?'

'Who?'

'It was our people, Gene,' said Cornick. 'That license plate comes off a Bureau car.'

'What do you mean it was our people?'

'It was the Bureau, Gene,' said Cornick. 'They were following the guy the Chilean was meeting in Grand Central.'

'The son-of-a-bitch was meeting with a Cuban who is an officer of Castro's intelligence. The upshot of it is that our Palm Tree Peekers were following Castro's spooks and this Chilean got mixed up in it.'

'Jesus Christ, Carter,' sighed Propper. 'They did a damn good job of being discreet about it! They were so bad they got chewed out for spying by a cop. Can you believe that?'

'They weren't supposed to be discreet, Gene,' Cornick said, a bit defensively. 'They wanted the Cuban to know they were on him. That's what they tell me, anyway.'

'Yeah, right,' said Propper. 'What are you going to tell Landau?'

'Well, that's a problem,' said Cornick. 'I can't tell him the truth because I can't tell him we were following the Cuban agent. Besides that, he would go apeshit if I told him it was the Bureau. My God! Those people at IPS would have a paranoid fit over that. I'll just tell him I've checked it out and it's under control. I'll tell him the FBI is on top of it.'

This was indeed sensational information: a Chilean protégé of the IPS meeting a DGI man under FBI surveillance; and an FBI man acknowledging the facts and concerned to placate the IPS man best known for his close relationship with Fidel Castro and his regime.

As soon as my copy of the book arrived, I photocopied the relevant pages, sent the book to Alasdair Pepper, and telephoned him. He was suitably impressed, but came back with the usual proviso. *Per se*, the book was inadmissible as evidence. The information could be very useful, but only on condition that either Eugene Propper or, better still, the FBI man Carter Cornick, would agree to appear as our witnesses at the trial, or at least, give us a signed statement.

There, indeed, was the rub. Propper was not going to be worth our time and attention. In circumstances I come back to later, he had conducted his investigation into the Letelier assassination purely as a case of homicide, and entirely without regard to the all-important political background. That left Cornick. Replying to the friendly Mr. Wicken's letter, in one of my own dated 5 August 1985, I summarised the passage in *Labyrinth* and asked: 'Did you know Cornick? Is he a friend of yours? Would you be able to put me in touch with him? I think he could be a key witness for us.'

Alas, the trail petered out. Contacted by one of my Washington friends, Cornick professed to have no recollection whatever of the incident. From this amazing lapse of memory, and from other indications, it became clear that Carter Cornick, whatever his powers of recall, would not be any use to us.

I pulled out all the other Cuban 'stops' I could think of. One of them was a distinguished exile, Professor Alberto Piedra, with whom I had a number of pleasant bilingual conversations. Now an American citizen, he had held high office in the State Department and had just been appointed US ambassador in Guatemala. On 19 August, I wrote to him, offering my congratulations and asking him if he could put me in touch with Orlando Castro Hidalgo and Gerardo Peraza. That same day, I wrote to Mr D. Craig Russel of the Cuban American National Foundation which, I had been told, was likely to know the whereabouts of my two Cubans. Both my letters brought friendly replies, and suggested names of ex-Cubans who might help. I followed up the suggestions, to no avail.

In March, another possibility occurred to me. I had met the Editor of the Spanish language daily, *Diario Las Americas*, published in Miami, Ariel Remos, and he had interviewed me at length in London. Early in March 1986, I telephoned him from London and explained my problem. On the 11th, he wrote, telling me of his own (abortive) efforts on my behalf. He had tried good contacts of his, with negative results.

My frustration was growing, but had not yet reached its peak. Nor was it altogether surprising. By now, I realised that I was up against the familiar problem of the defector as an endangered species but in a more extreme form than any I had yet encountered. After months, and even years, of debriefing, they are all, to some degree or other, subject to the law of diminishing returns; which means, diminishing utility to the host intelligence or security services.

At this point, they become potentially embarrassing and even dangerous. The host organisation begins to find them, accordingly, somewhat tiresome. Some have expertise of such quality that they will be offered employment on secret work. Others want no part of the world they have left. They are afraid of assassination. They want to change their names, move far away from the centres of power, get a job, merge into their new background. We have seen Sejna's problems in this respect; and Frolik's fear for his life.

Some at least of these 'difficult' cases had been shamefully neglected by the CIA (though perhaps understandably when, as has happened, they begin to invent in an attempt to prolong their usefulness). To deal with this very real problem and to ensure that continuing use is made of the expertise of defectors from the Soviet Bloc, the Jamestown Foundation had been set up some years earlier. From hints dropped in official quarters, it looked as though both my Cuban quarries fell into the 'difficult' category. Both had changed their names. Castro Hidalgo, in the end (I was told), had set up a successful garage business. Peraza had lived through difficult times but had now been rehabilitated by the CIA, which had paid for him to take a technical college course.

By March 1986, it was clear that I was getting nowhere and I decided the time had come to appeal to my old friend Bill Casey, whom I had hoped to preserve from possible embarrassment. In a letter dated 3 March, I told him about the IPS lawsuit and spelt out the theory which forms the basis of this book and which I had already mentioned to Sir James Goldsmith. My letter to the DCI, which was marked 'CONFIDENTIAL', was hand-delivered by a friend. It went on:

> This case is similar in kind, and possibly no less important in its implications, to the *Spiegel*/Augstein case against our friend Sir James Goldsmith, the international research for which I handled. Moreover, it appears to be part of a new pattern presumably decided in Moscow, of using 'capitalist' courts to damage 'capitalist' writers. There are similar cases, recent or current, launched on behalf of the KGB-funded *Ethnos* daily in Athens.
>
> As you will remember, it looked at a certain stage of the *Spiegel* case as though we might be stymied for lack of material witnesses, as the DIA was refusing us access to General Jan Sejna. When I explained the situation to you, you responded immediately and decisively: Sejna was made available. In the end, the other side asked for an out-of-court settlement and Sir James (and I) were vindicated.

Bill, I am now up against the same kind of frustration that almost caused us to lose the *Spiegel* case. Intensive efforts by myself and my American associates have yielded a vast pile of documents, all tending to confirm my allegations about the IPS. In particular, the evidence of KGB control over the Cuban DGI is very strong, as you know.

However, Counsel's advice to me, as of a few days ago, is that in the absence of material witnesses, I am bound to lose the case if it comes to trial. Despite all my efforts and the use of about eight different channels, I have been unable to contact such vital witnesses as the Cuban defectors Orlando Castro Hidalgo and G.J.Peraza Amechazurra, who between them revealed the Soviet pressures which, between 1968 and 1970, brought the DGI under Moscow's control. Nor have we been able to contact any more recent Cuban defectors, or even any Soviet defectors with knowledge of Cuban operations involving the IPS.

(...........)

Now, I am of course aware that the IPS is an American institution and that therefore you and the Agency are forbidden by law from playing any official part in this case. I am nevertheless hoping that in view of the importance of this case, you will be able, at least, to talk to your opposite number, the Director of the Bureau, and possibly to receive me personally when I am next in Washington.

I just add that I believe it would be very bad news for the Bureau (and even for the Agency) if I lost this case. Conversely, it would be very good news if I am enabled to win it. A victory in this country could indeed avoid all the hassle you might expect from Congress and the media if the battle were fought on American soil.

It ended with the hand-written words: 'Grateful for anything you can do. Warm regards.' Then came a PS:

It occurs to me that to get over the main difficulty of your involvement, there are two angles to be considered: the role of the IPS offshoot, the Transnational Institute in Amsterdam, and the involvement of the IPS in Central America, both of which take the case into the foreign realm.

Before writing that letter, I had telephoned the DCI's office at Langley to set up a meeting, which in fact was scheduled for Thursday 3 March at 4 p.m. in Casey's office in the Old Executive Building adjoining the White House.

A busy day. Before turning up for my appointment I had lunched Alfonso Tarabochia, whom I had met 11 years earlier when I testified before the Senate subcommittee of which he was Chief Investigator. Tarabochia, a tall, placid man, was difficult to place in ethnic terms; and no wonder, for he was born a Greek on the isle of Chios, but brought up in Italy. Some held it against him that he had joined the Italian police force while Mussolini was still in power, but I was not among them. A careful man with an excellent policeman's memory, he was a remarkable linguist. In retirement, he supplemented his income by translating from Greek originals. He also spoke accentless Latin American Spanish, and indeed the main reason I wanted to see him again was that he had interpreted for Peraza when the latter testified before what was now the Senate Subcommittee on Security and Terrorism, on four days between 26 February and 12 March 1982.

I shall return to Tarabochia's evidence, which I regarded as my first real breakthrough in this intractable case. Apart from the very important things he said, which he later repeated in a formal Statement, he gave me something potentially very precious: Peraza's telephone number in Boston, where the Cuban had settled. He did not, however, have Peraza's address. This I hoped to obtain from William J. Casey.

To my intense disappointment, I left Casey's office empty-handed. He had greeted me as cordially as always, in his friendly mumble. I explained that although I had Peraza's telephone number from one of my own sources, I lacked his address, and thought it only fair that I should write to the man and explain why I wanted to see him before ringing to set up a meeting.

The other Casey — the tough Irish New York lawyer — came to the surface. 'No, damn it, Brian, I won't give you his number! Look, I have a duty to protect these people. First we'll ask him whether he wants to see you. If he does, we can set up a meeting for you.'

Nothing I could say would shake the DCI when his mind was made up. I had no way of knowing for certain whether his concern for the defector's privacy was genuine, or expeditious, and perhaps it didn't matter which it was: the result was the same. Certainly it was a case in which the CIA's duty to defectors happened to coincide with the self-interest of the Agency in keeping out of a possibly damaging domestic affair.

Bill lectured me on the statutory limitations on the Agency's freedom of manoeuvre in this kind of situation (which I already knew), and gave me the name of a senior member of his staff who headed a department which had grown, inexorably, since the post-Watergate follies: the Legal Department. The man was out of town that day, but would expect my call.

On the Saturday, before my departure to New York and Pittsburgh, two conservatively dressed men came to my room at the Madison: the Chief Legal Counsellor, and his deputy. With bland and (I thought) well rehearsed efficiency, they gave me a further lecture on the restrictions that prevented the Agency from inquiring into the affairs of an American institution and on the duty the Agency had to protect men like Gerardo Peraza.

I pointed out that I was already well briefed on both these aspects of the CIA's limited freedom of action. I now mentioned that I already had Peraza's telephone number but thought it would be fairer to the man himself to explain in writing just why I wanted to see him rather than disturb his privacy with the voice of a stranger. I didn't add, as perhaps I should have done, that I didn't want to run the risk of having the telephone hung up on me, perhaps with final intent.

The two men could see I was not going to be easily deflected. One of them appeared to soften and gave me a name and a telephone number in Boston. 'Look, Mr Crozier,' he said, as blandly as ever, 'this is our man in Boston, on what we call "domestic collection". We'll tell him about this conversation by the time you call him and he'll be prepared to see Peraza in your behalf.'

This was the most I could have hoped for. I thanked the two lawyers for their time and shook hands with them.

From my hotel room at the St. Regis in New York, I duly telephoned the 'Domestic Collection' man, as suggested, connecting with him on the third attempt. He explained that Gerardo Peraza had gone through difficult times and was 'very touchy'. I had begun to guess as much.

'Look,' I said, 'will you do me a small favour? I want to write a friendly letter to our Cuban, in his own language. May I send it to you, and will you see that it is delivered?'

He could hardly say No to a man who enjoyed access to the DCI, so he grudgingly said Yes.

That evening, I wrote my letter to Peraza, by hand, keeping a photo-copy for my files and posted it to the accommodation address I had been given. I thought to myself how much fairer to Peraza it would have been simply to have received my letter through the post, when he could have taken his own decision, unencumbered by any intimidatory third party. This way, who knew what the Agency people would tell him, what subtle discouragements might be fed to him?

I had drafted the letter with great care, both linguistically and in tactful presentation. I had tried to address him as one fighter to another in a wider conflict. Moreover, I had made it clear that at this stage all I wanted from him was a signed Statement, not even an Affidavit. He would not have to obtain a lawyer's endorsement, or even have his State-ment witnessed. In all probability, he would not be called upon as a witness. Indeed, the purpose of the Statement, together with other State-ments I had obtained, was to dissuade the Plaintiffs from proceeding with the case.

On 17 April, back in London, I wrote to Casey to thank him for his help and to give him my own account of what had happened since I had seen him. I again stressed the importance of my meeting Peraza and asked him to set up contacts for me with more recent defectors from Cuba.

The weeks passed, turning into months. In mid-September, I was back in Washington, and still no word from Peraza. On Tuesday the 16th, Bill Casey again received me in the Old Executive Building. Hav-ing waved me to a seat, he produced a document and read out certain passages to me. I wish he had shown it to me, but could see that he wanted to keep bits of it to himself.

It was bad news. Peraza had refused to take delivery of my letter.

Next morning, I met two of Casey's top officials for breakfast, at their invitation. The news, in detail, was even worse than the appar-ently bland report in the DCI's hands had indicated. A female colleague of theirs had called to see Peraza. On hearing what she wanted to see him about, he had made a scene, raising his voice and shouting exple-tives at her. Seizing my letter from her hand, he had torn it up, unread, and scattered the contents in the air. He then flung the door open and ordered her out.

A day or two later, a male officer, suitably burly, had gone to see the Cuban. By that time, the Cuban had calmed down. He merely said that he wanted nothing to do with the case.

'Did he have something against me in particular?' I wanted to know.

'No, not you. It's just that he's had enough of hearings and wants out.'

I had wasted my time. It was a dismal end to what had seemed a promising initiative. There was no point in telephoning Peraza. Had he read my letter in solitude, it is conceivable that he would have consented to see me. I shall never know.

Notes

1.   See, for example, my book, *South-East Asia in Turmoil* (Penguin, 3rd edition, 1968, pp. 189 et seq.); and David Rees, 'Student of Subversion' in *National Review* (New York, 31 Dec. 1985), and 'Global Realities: A Survey of the Work of Brian Crozier' in *The Salisbury Review* (London, Oct. 1986).

2.   His book, *COVERT CADRE: Inside the Institute for Policy Studies* (Greenhill, Ottawa, Illinois, 1987) reached me in 1988 after I had completed my own work. It is a remarkable piece of research. Henceforth, CADRE.

3.   With Taylor Branch (Penguin, 1983).

8. The Team in Action

To assist me in the Herculean task that lay ahead, I could count on the help of friends and allies, such as Robert Moss, John Rees, and many other whose names people these pages. More directly involved, however, were the American associates in my international consultancy[1], the existence of which was presumably not known to Richard Barnet when he embarked on his challenge. Those principally involved were Lee Edwards, David Martin and Donald Jameson. They made an interesting trio.

Edwards, a journalist and a teacher of journalists, was a Republican activist who had written a handbook for aspirant activists, appropriately entitled *You Can Make the Difference* (1980). A slight, dapper man of about 50 when the case began, with thinning black hair and intelligent dark eyes, he had also written a revealing political biography of Ronald Reagan, timed to coincide with his subject's assumption of the Presidency but revised to include a chapter on the failed attempt to assassinate him in March 1981. Not the least of his qualifications was a wide-ranging knowledge of Congress and its elected occupants.

David Martin, when I first met him, had been a member of that submerged but influential community known as Congressional staffers, in his case as Senior Analyst on the staff of Senator Strom Thurmond, Chairman of the Subcommittee on Internal Security of the Senate Committee on the Judiciary, to give it its abridged but cumbersome title. He had rung me in London to invite me to Washington to testify in hearings on international terrorism that were about to begin, in July 1975.

In common with many (but never enough) committed leftists, David had made the intellectual and ideological journey from Marx to anti-Marx. A Canadian by birth, he had been a Trotskyist in New York (as indeed had my mentor, James Burnham) and had that special insider's knowledge which no amount of study from the outside can ever fully replace.

He had served in London both in the Royal Canadian Air Force and the RAF. He had developed an almost obsessive interest in the strange and tragic case of the Yugoslav Chetnik leader, Drazha Mihailovich, initially supported by the Allies, then dropped in favour of the Communist partisan leader, Tito, who in 1946 had him hanged. Having studied the wartime manoeuvres of a group of British Communists in Cairo, especially one James Klugmann, undoubtedly a Comintern agent, Martin had established that telegrams, intended for Churchill's eyes, had been diverted by this group, so that the decision to switch support to Tito had been taken in the absence of vital evidence. He had published his findings in a major study, *Patriot or Traitor* (Hoover, 1978)[2].

David Martin, a few years older than I, later developed Parkinson's Disease, a severe physical handicap which, however, left his mental faculties absolutely intact. His knowledge of communism was profound, as was his understanding of the complex workings of government in the American capital.

No less remarkable was Donald Jameson ('Jamie'), whom we have already met several times. Apart from his Russian and Soviet expertise, he spoke fluent Spanish and had a special interest in Central America that would prove most useful in my investigation of the Cuban connection.

Of the other American members of the team, two do not wish to be named. One I shall call Harold. He belonged to the growing but by definition select company of former 'card carrying' members of a Communist Party. Harold provided some vitally important material, especially on the early connections of the man whose fortune made the IPS possible, Samuel Rubin.

The other anonymous member of the team I shall call Harriet. A tall, thin 'blue stocking' lady, she came up with an imposing, and at times breathtaking, collection of revealing documents of the kind historians call 'primary source material' (as distinct from, say a published book or article which, however carefully researched and written, only counts as 'hearsay' evidence in the eyes of an English judge and jury). An American tax return, for instance, is 'primary source material'; an 'op-ed' piece in the *Washington Post* is not.

Many others were helpful, if only as conduits to people with special knowledge of Richard Barnet and his associates. My friend John Barron, for example, the *Reader's Digest* specialist on the KGB, put me in touch with the able young researcher, Scott Powell[3], who produced several interesting papers for my file.

In my necessarily incomplete 'Story of the IPS', in the ensuing chapters, I draw heavily upon the statements, signed or not, from all the above, and also from Alfonso Tarabochia; Michael Waller, a brilliant young analyst specialising in Central American affairs; Joshua Muravchik, another gifted young academic and journalist, who conducted a sensationally revealing interview with Saul Landau of IPS; David Horowitz, another member of the select band of ex-Communists; and two key Hispanic witnesses: Huber Matos, a survivor of Fidel Castro's prisons and torture chambers, and Arturo Cruz, Jr., son of a leader of the Nicaraguan contras, who was briefly in the news during the so-called 'Irangate' hearings in Washington in 1987, in part because the media described him (accurately, it seems) as the former boyfriend of the glamorous Ms Fawn Hall, secretary to Lt-Col 'Ollie' North, formerly of the National Security Council, a celebrity through his trial — and later acquittal — for his part in the 'Iran-Contra' affair.

It was 'Jamie' Jameson who first produced a detailed account of the Communist origins of the IPS, in a paper that reached me in May 1985. He described the use of groups by intelligence services, such as the Soviet KGB and the Cuban DGI, to obtain 'operational intelligence', which he defined as: '...information on target individuals and organisations, and on local security practices, that enables an intelligence service to do its business effectively and with greater security.'

He distinguished such groups from front organisations, such as the Institute for the Study of the USA and Canada in Moscow, and the US Peace Council in America, whose purpose was the broader one of influencing US policies.

In his paper, Jamie went on to record that the IPS staged frequent conferences with Soviet organisations; was regularly involved with Communist front organisations, such as the World Peace Council; and maintained contacts with Cuban intelligence vehicles, such as the 'Venceremos' Brigades.

'Venceremos' means 'We will vanquish' in Spanish. In his testimony, Al Tarabochia (see preceding chapter) had an illuminating passage about these Brigades of young Americans recruited by the Cubans:

> One passenger manifest of the government-owned Cuban airline, Cubana de Aviación, on a flight from Mexico City to Havana showed that Saul Landau [a Senior Fellow of IPS] travelled in July or August 1969 to Havana at the same time as the leadership of the Students for a Democratic Society or SDS [the key organisation of the American New Left in the 1960s], to meet with the North Vietnamese and Vietcong delegation and plan the 'Days of Rage' to bring the war home and also lay the foundation for the creation of the Venceremos Brigade, which was one of the most successful operations of the DGI/KGB.

An interpretative passage in Tarabochia's testimony also calls for quotation:

> As regards connections of IPS Fellows and Cuba, let me make one aspect clear. In my opinion, and in the opinion of those who worked for the DGI, the distinction between the agency itself [the DGI] and other [Cuban] agencies in contact with foreigners, be it in Cuba or outside, was minimal or non-existent. In other words, everyone worked towards the common goal. The information collected by an operative of a different agency ultimately ended in the hands of the DGI. So far as I am concerned, and so far as the DGI officers who defected are concerned, there was no distinction whatsoever.
>
> This was true of the embassies. It was true of the commercial missions. It was true of any mission that came to the United States or went to the West, and it involved every Westerner or foreigner who visited Cuba. Suffice it to say that all these people were lodged at a special hotel which was equipped for the monitoring of conversations. In colloquial terms, the hotel was bugged, for one purpose: to monitor the conversations of the guests who had been put there for that one purpose.

As Scott Powell's study of the IPS progressed, in 1985, he sent me chapters relevant to my case, of which the most useful were those dealing with connections between the Institute and the Soviet Union; the

Soviet bloc; Cuba and Nicaragua; and North Vietnam. There was also an interesting chapter on the IPS and the CIA defector, Philip Agee, and on its relations with the Communist Party USA. Finally, in January 1986, he signed a Statement, specifically for me, naming the various Soviet personalities who frequented the IPS. He knew, because he, too, had been 'frequenting' the IPS, and had seen them there.[4]

Despite the continuing inflow of reports and statements, and the already vast pile of press cuttings, two gaps in my defence were beginning to loom. I needed files from the FBI under the Freedom of Information Act (FOIA), and I needed an American law firm to do some of the chasing that could not be done from London.

Initially, request had indeed been made to the FBI on my behalf, under the FOIA, by two members of the team, but without result. Sir James Goldsmith had demurred at my request for his permission to retain a New York firm of lawyers, on the ground that the American specimens of the legal genus were even more exorbitantly expensive than the British. I argued the point with him once, in a little office he sometimes used when in London, in Aspinall's Club in Curzon Street, in which he had a share. 'Do you know how much they charge for just one letter?' he asked me. I confessed ignorance.

'Two thousand dollars!'

'Jimmy,' I insisted, 'there are some areas of this case that can only be handled by American lawyers.

'Who did you have in mind?'

I mentioned a man strongly recommended by John Rees, who had handled a number of similar cases, was committed on our side, and already knew a lot about the IPS. His name was Allan Altman, and his senior partner was Henry Dressel. They had a reputation for winning the lawsuits they handled.

'Right,' was Jimmy's response. 'Go ahead. But fix an initial limit of, say, $10,000, and make them stick to it.'

It was on this somewhat discouraging basis that, on my next visit to New York, I went to see Altman and Dressel at their office at 150 Broadway, close to Wall Street. They made a contrasting pair. Altman, compact, dark, friendly, had a soft voice and great personal warmth and charm. Dressel was a tough, no nonsense, 'we'll skin the pants off their asses' New Yorker. Not, on reflection, a bad combination. They did indeed know a lot about the IPS, which was a help. Over the next 16 months or so, I had several meetings with them, each time in a different place, as they moved uptown, settling (finally?) on an entire floor at 600 Madison Avenue in the firm of Berger and Steingut.

I explained my problem and stated Sir James's cash limit, which they accepted, expressing determination and professional optimism.

One of my requirements had been whatever papers they could extract from the FBI. Here again, they expressed optimism. And yet, the months still passed without so much as a single document under the FOIA. Once again, it seemed, a bit of independent initiative was going to be needed. An intermediary was called for, and the obvious choice was a man I had known for more than 20 years: Bill Mott.

Rear-Adm. William C. Mott, USN (Ret.), was one of the Founders of Frank Barnett's National Strategy Information Center. Himself a lawyer by training, he had a varied and distinguished career, becoming Judge Advocate-General to the US Navy and serving as an aide under Presidents Roosevelt and Truman. In civilian life, he had a highly successful career, becoming President of the US Independent Telephone Association. For many years, he had run the American Bar Association's Committee on Education about Communism (restyled in the post-Watergate period, as the ABA Standing Committee on Law and National Security). We had attended many conferences together and met privately in various countries.

Quintessentially American, he was outstandingly generous and was once described in my hearing as 'invincibly friendly'. He was also an avid reader and an erudite student of history. When my large biography of General de Gaulle had come out in one volume in the US in 1973, he had staged a launching dinner for me and presented each of the 14 guests with a copy.

More to the point, he was now the Editor of *Intelligence Report* (with my other friend David Martin as Associate Editor), and a personal friend of Judge William Webster, at that time Director of the FBI (later succeeding the late Bill Casey as Director of Central Intelligence). If anybody could speed the process of unlocking the official files, Mott was the man.

Having reached him by telephone as one message after another finally caught up with my ever-moving target, I wrote to him on 13 March

1986, giving him the full background to the case and asking him to use his influence to arrange an appointment for me with Judge Webster and his Legal Counsellor, John Mintz.

A fortnight later, a photocopy of his letter to Mintz reached me in London. The date was Saturday 22 March. He had sent Mintz a copy of my own letter, and the key passage read:

> I do hope we can help Brian — he has one of the sharpest intelligence minds in the Western world and we should protect it from the likes of Richard Barnet and the IPS... . I have not yet contacted Judge Webster deeming it preferable to come to you first.

As unsolicited testimonials go, I could hardly have asked for more. I arrived in Washington on Easter Monday, 31 March, and telephoned Judge Webster's office the following morning. His secretary was ready for me and gave me an appointment at FBI headquarters on Wednesday 2 April at 4 p.m..

Bill Mott had offered to accompany me, but had been called away on business. I decided to ask David Martin to come along, not least because his deep knowledge of security issues could prompt questions that might not have occurred to me.

It was my first visit to the headquarters of the Federal Bureau of Investigation, with its imposing courtyard and the massive statue of the late and legendary J. Edgar Hoover, who had dominated the Bureau as its Director for more than 37 years. David and I had arrived together and on time and we were not kept waiting. Alas, Judge Webster was not there to greet us. Instead, we were shown into the office of his Deputy, Joseph Davies, who explained that the Judge had been called away unexpectedly to the White House. I had no reason to doubt the reason given.

Joseph Davies was quiet, civilised and helpful. Bill Mott's friend John Mintz was there too, tall, smiling and attentive, but leaving the conversation mainly to Davies. Somewhere along the line, I had heard it said that the IPS, taking advantage of the drastic change in the political climate that followed the Watergate affair and the resignation of President Nixon, had felt able to challenge the FBI through the courts. But I was unaware until that moment of the enormity of the Institute's success.

The IPS writ against the FBI alleged that over many years the Bureau had conducted 'illegal surveillance' of the Institute and its officers. The FBI had contested the lawsuit and defended itself in a protracted action that had lasted five years. The 'end of the day' came on 3 October 1979 when a decision of the United States District Court for the District of Columbia (Washington) upheld the Plaintiffs' allegation and ordered the Defendants to discontinue all investigation of the IPS. Game, set and match to Richard Barnet and his colleagues.

There was, however, nothing to stop the Bureau from acceding to my request for material on file about the IPS: material, that is, earlier than October 1979. I thanked Messrs. Davies and Mintz. Exchanging courtesies, David Martin and I took our leave.

It was not until this visit that the full significance of the FBI investigation into the assassination of Orlando Letelier hit me. The booby-trap bomb that killed Letelier exploded on 21 September 1976. The IPS lawsuit against the FBI had already lasted two years and was therefore still *sub judice*. The murdered ex-Ambassador was running the European offshoot of the IPS, the Transnational Institute. Even if the prevailing political climate had been more favourable than it obviously was, there were strong legal considerations to inhibit anything other than a *criminal* investigation.

My visit to the FBI was nevertheless successful in that it undoubtedly speeded up the FOIA process. On 9 June 1986, the Bureau wrote to advise me that no fewer than 1,681 pages of 'processed documents' were on their way to me, pending payment of $168.10 cents — at the standard fee of 10 cents a page for duplication. Before the end of the month, the enormous package reached me: 15 volumes of Memoranda on the Richard Barnet Institute, its personalities, its activities.

I grasped at one glance the significance of the word 'processed'. Not only were many pages missing, but the black deletions were numerous. On many of the pages, only a few words survived. There was another discovery to be made: the almost invariable rule was that the deletions occurred at the precise stage where the material was becoming interesting!

Having said that, the 1,681 pages rewarded my necessarily long and patient study. In sum, they built up a fascinating picture of protracted involvement with Marxist groups, not only in the United States but in other countries as well, principally in Cuba and North Vietnam. More hours, more days of study and analysis lay ahead. In London, at any rate, this was not a job I could delegate. With his sharp mind and trained eye, Alasdair Pepper would doubtless home in on points of legal interest; only I could fill in the political background and the significance of every item.

My detailed analysis of the documents ran to 16 pages of A-4, single-spaced, say about 9,000 words. This may seem paltry in comparison with the mass of material that had reached me, but it should be remembered that much of the stuff was repetitive (for instance, almost every major Memorandum began with lengthy quotes from an evidently fundamental article by Edith Kermit Roosevelt that had appeared in the Washington journal *The Examiner* of 24 September 1967, under the title 'Think Factory Trains Extremists'. Moreover, the deletions and omissions often reduced pages by up to 90 per cent.

My first discovery was that the IPS had been under surveillance from 3 April 1965, when Marcus Raskin (Barnet's co-founder) had addressed an anti-Vietnam War rally at the University of Wisconsin. As for Richard Barnet himself, he had been under FBI investigation from 30 October 1968 until 3 April 1974, when the IPS writ took effect.

As always, the political background is all-important. In their earlier years, a number of IPS personalities had been members of the SDS: the Students for a Democratic Society, rallying point for the New Left, best defined as born-again Communists who wished to disown the dreadful inheritance of Soviet communism and, in effect start all over again.

On 1 November 1968, an FBI report reported that personnel of the IPS had 'featured prominently in ... anti-draft [conscription], anti-war and mobilisation activities...'. The report (File 100-447935), which had heavy deletions, singled out Arthur Waskow, a senior staff member of IPS, as 'an advocate of what he calls "creative disorder"'. For example, he was said to favour a kind of guerrilla warfare technique of training nurses, teachers' assistants and others to sit in on employers' premises, forcing either employment or arrest.

On 4 November 1968, at an SDS rally at American University in Washington, DC, Waskow had condoned looting and burning by Negroes and said that they should not stop until the black communities owned the businesses and property in the areas where they lived. Not surprisingly, perhaps, Waskow was among 98 persons arrested for demonstrating without a permit on Election Day, 6 November 1968, after repeated clashes with the police[5].

In a further report, marked 'SECRET' and dated 16 October 1970, Arthur Waskow was described as a New Left activist who supported the actions of the Black Panther Party (BPP), a Negro terrorist group advocating the killing of police as 'pigs'.

An early mention of Richard Barnet appears in the last entry of Volume 1 of the FBI files. Dated 17 December 1969, it quotes the *Washington Post* of 13 November 1969 on Barnet's visit to Hanoi as a participant in a meeting to register support of 'massive [American] demonstrations against the United States aggression in Vietnam'.

Despite the many and tantalising deletions, the FBI documents, in conjunction with the statements of my potential witnesses and much published material, did help to build up a picture of the IPS as an organisation, some of whose members were ready to fraternise with terrorists and to make disproportionate allowance for any failings of Communist regimes while implacably critical of American democracy.

A Memorandum dated 14 March 1974, in Volume 6 of the released material, provides a typical example of FBI reporting on the IPS, almost telling the reader the worst but deleting the juicier' bits. The following sentences survive: 'In late 1970, IPS reportedly circulated a document calling for brigades [presumably the Venceremos Brigades] to descend on Washington, DC, and close down government agencies. The chief organiser of the program was reported to be [deletion] assisted by [deletion]'. The remaining pages had been suppressed.

By then, it was evident that the FBI was becoming nervous. A heavily deleted report, dated 7 September 1973, refers to a Civil Rights complaint by Marcus Raskin, the substance of which was the allegation that the Bureau had 'engaged in electronic surveillance, and breaking and entering upon the premises of IPS'. On investigating the complaint, the FBI decided that Raskin's allegations could not be substantiated.

The words 'breaking and entering', however, must have had a jolting effect at a time when the Watergate crisis was in full swing, even though it was not yet known whether President Nixon would be forced out of office.

The next passage suggested that the FBI was unlikely to obtain any evidence of the kind it was seeking (about an alleged violation of Federal Laws by the IPS) 'without a full physical surveillance program, technical surveillance, trash [rubbish or garbage], or live informant in place'. The FBI report added: *'None of these techniques is considered prudent or feasible at this time.'* (Emphasis added.)

To be cynical, in other words, the FBI now considered it unacceptably risky to break the law in order to expose an alleged breach of the law. This did not mean that surveillance was being dropped, merely that it would proceed without such methods although these were the only ones considered effective.

Even the relatively timid form of surveillance that continued after Raskin had launched his Civil Rights complaint was dropped early in 1974 (when the clamour arising out of the burglary at the Watergate Hotel had become deafening). On 28 February 1974, a Memorandum to the Director, FBI, brought him negative advice, couched in tortuously euphemistic terms which qualify for further quotation. The Memorandum recorded the view that 'a paucity of information exists that would support the likelihood of IPS or its leaders to be functioning in violation of Federal law'. The writer therefore advised the director 'that continued investigative efforts...would be unlikely to develop further substantial information detailing subversion on the part of the IPS', and could very likely again place the FBI into a position of attempting to prove a negative concept, i.e.. the Bureau's non-involvement in any illegal activity directed against the Institute.

In simpler and cruder terms, the writer was advising his chief to 'lay off, or we may have some explaining to do'. The Director (Clarence Kelley) accepted the advice and all investigation of the IPS was discontinued.

Against this background, I had to be grateful for the (heavily deleted) information that had come my way.

Notes

1.   My 'international consultancy', as I called it, was in fact a Pri-

vate Sector operational intelligence agency I launched in 1977 and ran for 10 years. See *FREE AGENT: the Unseen War, 1941-1991* (Harper Collins, 1993). Henceforth *AGENT*

2.   An enlarged version of his study appeared in 1990. (*The Web of Disinformation*: Churchill's Yugoslav Blunder; Harcourt, Brace, Jovanovich); a definitive version had not found a publisher when these lines were written.

3.   See Chapter 7. David Martin died in March 1995.

4.   Steven Powell gives specific details, including names, in the book mentioned in Chapter 7, *CADRE op.cit.* (1985), Ch19; pictures of those named also appear.

5.   For further details of Waskow's involvement in, and support of, violence, see Steven Powell, *op. cit.* pp 31 et seq.

9. Accusing Voices

By September 1986, I felt I had enough material to write a 'Draft Speech for the Defence', an exercise that served several purposes. It would provide political guidance for Alasdair Pepper and focus on the points I considered important. It would expose any remaining gaps and weaknesses in my case, and it would, I hoped, elicit constructive criticisms and suggestions from 'the Team'.

It served all these purposes. Pepper submitted it to Counsel, who pronounced it a 'substantial' document but repeated the pessimistic professional verdict: that I still lacked conclusive evidence admissible as such in an English court of law.

From Baltimore, John Rees described my draft as 'masterly, not to say magisterial' — an impressive alternative eulogy — and went on to pick relevant omissions and proffer cautionary words from his own lengthy experience of libel actions. Most of his points were valid, and I followed them through.

In any case, spurred on by news that the case was scheduled for hearing in the spring of 1987 (subject to any requests for postponement from my solicitors), new material of high quality was now pouring in. Harriet, my 'blue-stocking' friend, whom I had lost sight of for some years, surfaced by transatlantic telephone. The grapevine had done its work, and she was bubbling with enthusiasm, assuring me that some of the stuff she had on IPS would 'boggle your mind'. It did, when it came. She sent me some exciting material about the origins of Richard Barnet's Institute, useful Tax returns about grants to it, and, over a period of months, a vast amount of original IPS material, much of it confirming the closeness of the Cuban connection.

Just before I started work on the Draft Speech, I received an interesting signed paper from one of Lee Edwards's discoveries, J. Michael Waller, who specialised on Central American affairs (mentioned in Chapter 8). He had just brought out an impressively researched pamphlet, published by the Council for Inter-American Security, entitled *CONSOLIDATING THE REVOLUTION: How the Sandinistas' Support Apparatus Operates in the United States*, in which I had spotted a reference to 'the pro-Castro Institute for Policy Studies'.

In his conclusions in the Statement he made for me, Waller said: 'It is clear that judging by the evidence, the Institute for Policy Studies has a consistent record of support for the policies of the government of Cuba'.

Waller went on to say that evidence found in Orlando Letelier's briefcase 'showed his deep collaboration with the DGI's top agent in the United States, and revealed that he received regular payments from Cuba for his work'. The IPS, of course, has consistently refused to accept that the Cuban payments received by Letelier came from the DGI.

And Michael Waller added: 'Simple reasoning shows that the IPS is without doubt useful to the DGI and hence, the KGB.'

As on so many previous occasions, Alasdair Pepper read Waller's paper with an interest tinged with legal scepticism. All Waller was saying, he argued, was that he agreed with me about the IPS. But this coincidence of views did not constitute a defence. My counter-argument, as always, was that the more people came forward, each having reached the same conclusions, the more convincing their collective evidence would be to a prospective jury. Whereupon, as always, he would remind me of the need for a live witness with personal knowledge of the relations between the IPS and Cuban intelligence.

David Martin had been working hard, and to good effect. He had managed to trace a prominent New Leftist whom he had known in different circumstances, and who, like himself (and myself, much earlier), had repented and recanted. This one was a formidable potential recruit to our camp. His name was David Horowitz (see Chapter 8), and he had been travelling the campuses making anti-Left and anti-Communist speeches, and writing articles in the same vein. Of special relevance was the fact that he had been singling out his former close political friend, Saul Landau of IPS, as a special target for criticism.

There was, for me, a particular irony in the suggestion that David Horowitz should help me. Some 15 years earlier, he had been an Editor of the main organ of the New Left, *Ramparts*, which had launched and run a ferocious campaign against me. Indeed, this caused me to wonder whether he would join 'the Team', for who knows what might survive from ancient animosities, despite his conversion to the anti-revolutionary side?

I need not have worried. Early in September 1986, he sent me a signed Statement which was quite the most interesting, from a human as well as a political standpoint, in the entire collection. Indeed, it prompted a thought: it could easily have been inserted into one of the most important books of our time, as a chapter long missing but now brought to light. The author of the book I had in mind was long dead, and his name, better known by far in the US than in Britain, was Whittaker Chambers, the former member of the underground network of the Communist Party USA, who had come in from the cold and whose testimony had put Alger Hiss behind bars. The title of this huge and moving memoir was simply *Witness*, and its author had played an important role in the early years of William F.Buckley's *National Review*.

The 'missing chapter' is too long to quote in full here, but selected passages will give an idea of its importance:

> I was born in 1939. My parents were members of the Communist Party USA, as were all of their friends. Outwardly my parents were middle class high school teachers and as far as I know law abiding citizens... . But like all their friends and political associates, my parents inhabited another and secret world as members of the Third International founded by Lenin. (....)
>
> In their own minds, my parents were secret agents. They had been given secret names when they joined the Party for the time when their real political objectives would require them to 'go underground'.

What followed had a stunning effect on me as I read it: a chilling example of what a fundamental transfer of loyalties can mean in practice:

> Late in her life, the mother of my closest friend told me a story to relieve a guilt she had carried for more than thirty years. Her story illustrates the importance of intentions and the uses to which seeming innocence can be put. This woman was a high school teacher, no more than five feet tall, who lived a scrupulously middle class life.

Her only flirtation with excitement and risk was to have joined the Communist Party. But even her party life took place within humdrum channels, raising funds for the volunteers in Spain, doing her part in the Teachers' Union which the Party controlled. Except on one occasion. When my friend and I were a year old, she was asked to perform a special 'mission' for the Party, about which she could tell no one. It was a chance to perform one of the 'real' tasks, which gave all the others their meaning. She agreed and, as a good comrade, asked no questions at all. She left her son with her husband in New York, and took a sealed envelope to a contact in Mexico. The year was 1940. She had become a vital link in the chain by which Stalin was able to reach from to Moscow to Cayocoan and put an ice pick in Trotsky's head.

Thus, as David Horowitz put it, had his parents and their friends become 'secret agents of a foreign power'. Essentially, this is what had happened to his former friend, Saul Landau. In Horowitz's words:

> Because Saul Landau runs the Latin American section of IPS, the statement you [Brian Crozier] have made that IPS is 'a major front for Cuban intelligence, itself controlled by the KGB' seems uncontroversial and obvious to me. It's like saying the Communist Party is a front for the KGB, which it is. Does the DGI give Landau specific instructions and orders? I don't know. But in the sense that I understand your statement it makes no difference at all.

Was this, still, merely one man's opinion? I argued the point with Pepper. This was a statement from the inside, from a man who knew what being a 'revolutionary' really meant. This time, I think Pepper was impressed; but not yet to the extent of thinking that something decisive had come my way. There was still this problem of the witness with hard and specific evidence who would submit to penetrating cross-examination in the time-honoured adversarial tradition of English legal practice. On 25 September 1986, a telephone call from Allan Altman aroused a hope that the hypothetical 'smoking gun' witness could be drawing closer, perhaps even emerging into my line of vision. The day before, he told me, his senior partner, Henry Dressel, had an interesting lunch-time meeting in Miami, with a man who had long personal dealings with the right Cubans.

The typed sheets of paper that followed the call made interesting reading, indeed potential material for realistic fiction; but without taking us very far. They recorded Dressel's conversation with Frank A. Sturgis, whose main claim to notoriety was that he was one of the convicted Watergate burglars. Now aged 60, he was born Franco Angelo Firoini, but had been adopted by his mother's new husband, named Sturgis, when she had remarried.

Sturgis had a long connection with Cuba and the Cubans. He had been with Castro and his guerrillas in the mountains in 1957. That year, he had also been recruited by the CIA, and reported whenever he could to the Agency's Station Chief in Santiago, Chile. While Castro was in the mountains, he kept saying he wanted nothing to do with the Communists, but as soon as he had taken over from the departed dictator Fulgencio Batista, he sent out orders to eliminate all anti-Communists. The CIA ordered Sturgis to leave Cuba, and he did as he was told.

Later in the year, Harriet was sending me, in increasing numbers, documents of outstanding interest about the IPS, its origins, and its activities. Among them was a background note confirming the early communist involvement in the creation of the Institute.

Harold, too, was helpful, in the quality though not the quantity of his documentary information. One of the most useful items was an Official Report for the confidential use of the Special Committee on Un-American Activities, which listed the names and addresses of the voters for the Communist Party ticket in the 1936 general election of the five boroughs of New York City. This list included the following entries:

> Rubin, Samuel, 615 Pelham Parkway, Bronx, NY
> Rubin, Vera, 615 Pelham Parkway, Bronx, NY

The point was in the surname: Samuel Rubin was the main initial benefactor of the IPS, and Vera Rubin was his wife.

There were some fascinating confirmatory papers, unsigned and unusable as evidence, not least because, according to a hand-written note on one of them, "Persons who compiled these no longer alive". These obscure, unsung agents of the FBI, as I took them to be, knew what they were talking about, however, Here are some sample extracts:

According to Sylvia Langer, a Party member residing at 40 Feath-
erbed Lane, Bronx, Sam Rubin of Fabergé, and his wife, Vera, have
been members of the Communist Party for several years.... Rubin was
known to have been in the import-export business, which collapsed
when the Spanish Civil War broke out. He promptly entered perfume
manufacturing, which he continues today.

That note, typewritten, was dated 28 October 1946.

Here are extracts from another, dated 29 November of the same year:

Frank, the elevator operator, provided the following information
concerning Fabergé and SAM RUBIN.

When Sam Rubin first moved into 240 Madison Avenue, he was
conducting an oil and soap business, which consisted primarily of
importing and selling olive oil and castile soap from Spain. That was
in the early 1930s. At this time RUBIN and his father, whose first
name is believed to be JULIUS, operated the business, along with a
secretary and bookkeeper and a shipping clerk. RUBIN's father and
mother are presently living and Frank believes they reside in Seagate,
Coney Island.

The perfume business was started by them approximately eight
years ago when one BENNET, reputed to be a Russian Count, was
brought into the firm. This individual was supposed to have the original perfume formula which enabled them to get a start in this business. The perfume business prospered.....

From a later note, dated 17 June 1947, I cull the following obviously
authentic details:

It has been definitely established that the principal personnel operating the new Council of American Business, at least until recently,
were confirmed Communists who used every means to conceal their
convictions and the purpose to which the organisation was being put.
This was particularly true when the New York office was located on
the premises of Fabergé, Inc., owned by Sam Rubin.

(..........)

When Sam Rubin and his wife, Vera, joined the Communist movement some years ago, neither showed an inclination at the time to
conceal their political beliefs. Rubin became so absorbed in the move-

ment that he could express his feelings by naming his son Reed after John Reed, a foundation member of the American Communist Party, who is now buried in the Kremlin Wall. He has contributed heavily to numerous Communist fronts, including the Joint Anti-Fascist Refugee Committee, Birobidjan[1], the Council on African Affairs, etc..

In the last New York Congressional election, he contributed $250.00 to the campaign chest of George Rooney, a pro-Communist who ran on the ALP[2] ticket. Vera Rubin's Communist sympathies date from the time she attended New York University. They reside at Croton-on-the-Hudson, a community known as a well-heeled Communist colony. One of his closest friends is William Cropper, who achieved some fame as a cartoonist for the *New Masses* and the *Daily Worker*. As with the others, Sam and Vera Rubin have grown inordinately shy regarding their Communist beliefs. Rubin has resorted to the first lesson every Communist conspirator learns — that is to deny that he is one.

To remark, as I do, that these reports are obviously authentic implies merely that they are utterly in tune with everything else that is known about the late Samuel Rubin and with everything written (by Whittaker Chambers and others) about the Communist Party USA in that period. One further point: the unknown informants who wrote these reports were not doing it to please *me*, since they died long before Richard Barnet's writ was served on me!

David Martin, meanwhile, had been tenaciously pursuing a line of inquiry with highly emotive, and even dramatic, courtroom potential. His young friend Joshua Muravchik, the one who had interviewed Saul Landau for the *New York Times*, had trapped the IPS man into defending Fidel Castro's conduct of a notorious show trial. In the dock was one of his fighting comrades from the guerrilla days, Commandant Huber Matos, whose only crime on the available evidence was to have written to Fidel Castro shortly after the overthrow of the Cuban dictator Fulgencio Batista to resign as Military Chief in the Camagüey region on the ground that he was against the pro-Communist direction the Revolution was taking. For having thus implied that Castro had concealed his communist sympathies, but on a trumped up charge of sedition, he was gaoled for 20 years. No remission for good conduct in Cuban gaols: sentenced in December 1959, he was not set free until the last day of October 1979.

There was a callous irony in the Matos case, in that Fidel Castro, having denounced the prisoner in court (in a speech lasting seven hours!) for wrongly alleging that the Revolution was veering towards communism, was later to reveal that he had been a secret Communist for years. Matos was not freed on that account, however. Instead, he was kept in atrocious conditions and cruelly tortured.

Muravchik taped his interview with Saul Landau, in which the following exchange was recorded:

> Landau: Matos was tried and convicted
> Muravchik: Of what was he convicted?
> Landau: Of attempting to lead an armed insurrection against the State.
> Muravchik: Do you believe that?
> Landau: I certainly do. I've seen the trial transcripts and spoken to the witnesses. I don't think there's a question about it. The US press simply hasn't reported it. There was a trial: there was lots of testimony taken and Matos himself admitted that he was indeed planning to organise his officers to act against the government. Huber Matos was put in gaol, I think, for correct reasons.

This passage did not appear in the interview as published in *The New York Times*.[3] Joshua Muravchik had understandable professional and ethical scruples about allowing me to use this revealing exchange. Later, however, he solved the problem by reproducing a slightly modified version of it in a longer article by himself in *World Affairs* quarterly (Winter issue, 1984-85).

Martin's idea, with which I concurred, was to produce Huber Matos as a surprise witness for a courtroom confrontation with Saul Landau. In December 1986, however, David Martin persuaded Huber Matos, by then 68, to produce a signed Statement for me. With it came a transcript of his letter to Fidel Castro dated 19 October 1959, in which he expressed his concern over the increasingly Communist trend of the Revolution.

The Matos Statement is one of the most harrowing documents I have ever read. Matos, who had settled in Miami, where so many Cuban exiles had found refuge, spoke hardly any English and wrote in Spanish.

I translated his words literally, without either editing or embellishments. The following are extracts from the Matos Statement:

> The treatment which was meted out to me in those 20 years was far below anything deserved by a human being, a brutal treatment, coldly studied with the aim of destabilising me. During the first 10 years, the Castro brothers, through their gaolers, tried to send me mad; later, they changed their tactics and tried blows to try to intimidate me, moreover the idea of pushing me to suicide was present from the moment of my detention, for example, when they arrested me they took me to a room in the Colombia Encampment with a warder from the enclosure, the latter, believing I was asleep, came near me drawing a 45 pistol from its holster but I anticipated his intentions and asked him what he was doing.
>
> (.........)
>
> From 24 October 1959 until 15 December of that year, the date on which my trial ended, they kept me in a dungeon punishment cell in the ancient fortress of The Moor, which was no more than a window without any more space than the thickness of the wall in which it was embedded, with grills on either side and not even wide enough to stretch my arms. They constantly repeated that they were going to shoot me, they tried, what with the confinement and the threats to intimidate me before the trial, to which I was led without having seen a lawyer and without having been advised of the charges against me, all I knew was that they were going to condemn me to death.... Once the judiciary process was completed, they...moved us to the Isle of Pines. ..... I was immediately submitted to a discipline which made no sense except to humiliate me. I was always placed in the worst spots of the seven or eight prisons in which I was confined. Before each move, they prepared a special place in which they walled up the windows, if there were any, to accommodate me. On the Isle of Pines they installed me, under special vigilance, in a corner apart in which, apparently, was a hospital.
>
> From there, they put me in what was simply a concrete box with a hole for natural needs, in a minimum space for survival, without ventilation, where the light of the sun never penetrated. ...
>
> During a hunger strike in the year 1968, they transferred me to a cell of G-2 [military intelligence]. I found myself in appalling conditions. I looked like an inmate in a German Nazi concentration camp, I was a real skeleton, one could feel the roughness of my bones. The

strike lasted 165 days, they kept me alive by force-feeding me with a foul-smelling broth, introduced into my stomach by means of a catheter through the nose. ...

During another strike, they tortured me and believing me to be unconscious, my eyes being stuck together with pus, I heard one of the warders suggesting that they should cut off my testicles with a surgical knife, but the other one objected, arguing that castration with a surgical knife would leave a scar and they had not been given permission to mutilate me. He added that the problem was not to kill me but to provoke me into killing myself; they thought to leave me sexually incapable by destroying the cavernous bodies with substances which they injected into the genitals. They commented that they had received order 'from above' to create conditions so that I should take my own life.

(........)

I remember, specifically, the brutal beating up they subjected me to on 14 May 1973, half my ribs on either side were broken as though they were crumbling biscuits, my rib cage was deformed forever; the articulated muscles of my left arm were stretched in a special form of torture. I needed three years of exercise, perseverance and much pain before the arm, which half adhered to the thorax, could regain its power of movement.

Despite this appalling ill-treatment, and incarceration for just under 20 years, Huber Matos survived, broken in body but not in spirit. His Statement ends on a note of defiance:

During the 20 years I was a prisoner, and during the experiences I have briefly summarised in the foregoing paragraphs, I witnessed the fulfilment of what I had predicted in my letter of resignation to Castro, and which he had emphatically denied, that is, the betrayal of the revolution, the oppression of the people of Cuba and the total submission of our country to the Soviet Union.

Huber Matos Benítez[4]

There is a clear parallel between David Horowitz's Statement and the exchange between Joshua Muravchik and Saul Landau. Someone who brushes aside the circumstances of the trial and subsequent torture of a man guilty of no more than expressing a point of view is surely defending the Revolution. In one case, Stalin incarnated the Revolution to be served; in the other, Fidel Castro. The relevant point is that the man defending Castro's Revolution was a Fellow of the IPS. I return to the Matos case in a later chapter, in a wider context.

Before leaving the subject, I add only that the Matos case is unfortunately far from unique. A similar case is that of Armando Valladares, who spent 22 years in Castro's prisons, and wrote a book about his experiences, *Against All Hope* (New York, 1987). The enormous propaganda apparatus of the Soviet Union naturally focused attention on such selected targets as Pinochet's regime in Chile and on apartheid in South Africa. But the ultimate police State in Latin America was Cuba.

In the absence — still — of 'smoking gun' witnesses — Alasdair Pepper felt we needed comparative studies of Soviet and Cuban propaganda themes and of IPS statements or publications dealing with the same subjects. To this end, I compiled a list of such themes on the Soviet side, ranging from the Berlin Wall to Nicaragua, via arms control, Vietnam, Chile and Afghanistan.

During a long 'working holiday' in the US in the summer of 1986, Pepper had spent some time at the home and headquarters of John and Louise Rees in Baltimore. On 11 November, he wrote to them with a detailed list of themes and requested them to go ahead with the proposed analysis. This massive undertaking was never, to my knowledge, completed. Nor, as it happened, was it ever needed.

The search for material witnesses, especially Cubans, continued, however. John Rees had introduced me to a friend of his, whose name I do not feel at liberty to reveal, who had been heavily involved in Latin American affairs in the CIA. I could tell from his lack of enthusiasm that he had no very strong urge to expose himself to the possible adverse consequences of helping me in a specific sense. In this, he was of course entirely within his rights.

He did, however, give me the name of a former FBI man, now practising as a lawyer in Miami, whose name, too, I shall withhold. Let us call the ex-CIA man John and the ex-FBI man Peter. I followed up this potentially important lead and wrote to Peter, mentioning John. Peter replied promptly and helpfully, telling me that he did indeed know some Cubans who might be useful. One, in particular, he named as the link man to the others.

I passed the name to my friend in Washington, Lee Edwards, who lost no time flying to Miami. The helpful Cuban — let us call him Manuel — did indeed produce the names of no fewer than eight of his compatriots, all defectors from or dissidents against the Castro tyranny.

Armed with the names and bare details, I appealed to the contacts of mine in the intelligence community on either side of the Atlantic. This was a matter in which the provision of information entailed no legal risks, and I duly received fairly extensive biographies of all of them. Of the eight, however, only two were of possible interest. By then, we were well into 1987. More time consumed: John's, Peter's, Manuel's, Lee's; that of the intelligence agencies I approached; that of the lawyers, in London and New York; that of hard-working, anonymous secretaries everywhere; not to mention my own time. And that of course is largely what this kind of case is about: tying up valuable time, letting the costs mount: transatlantic travel and telephone calls, legal fees, Lee's trip to Miami, and this, and that....

For the record, not one of the Cubans turned out to have anything of relevance to contribute. And that, too, is part of the story.

In February 1987, Jamie sent me a further paper on the Institute for Policy Studies, supplementing the one he had prepared two years earlier. This, too, was an impressive piece of expertise and scholarship. Jamie listed no fewer than eight public references in the US to the IPS as a vehicle used by the KGB or the DGI, and commented: 'This had happened so often, it is puzzling that only one of them appears to have brought charges of libel.' To which, as the interested party in London, I breathed a private 'Hear, hear!'

Another comment from this lifelong specialist on Soviet methods should be quoted:

> [The] concentration on weakening US intelligence and counter-intelligence operations is unique in the history of American radical groups. Others have complained against the police, denounced informers, etc., but the systematic, broad gauged, sustained effort that the IPS and its subsidiaries have mounted is of a different order of magnitude. The effort includes not only the IPS but also the GAP [Government Accountability Project of IPS], the Center for National Security Studies and its subordinate organisations - the Project on In-

telligence and Covert Action, the Project on National Security and the Constitution, the Citizens' Projects on National Security, the Campaign to Stop Government Spying, the National Lawyers' Guild [a Soviet-founded front group, begun in 1936 and following a consistent line ever since: Note by Donald Jameson] and the publications *Counterspy* and *Covert Action Bulletin*.

In his paper, Jamie went on to provide notes on the activities of a number of persons involved with the IPS.

With this major interpretative document, and the mass of original source material reaching me from Harriet, I felt in April 1987 that the time had come to recast my first and tentative 'Draft Speech for the Defence'. Some of the gaps in the first draft could now be plugged; inaccuracies could be rectified; judgements modified, in the light of the many critical comments that had reached me. This second draft, fuller and much improved, would go to all concerned, for further criticism.

The expanded 'Story of the IPS' which follows is based on this second 'Draft Speech for the Defence'.

Notes

1.   Birobidjan: Stalin's 'answer' to Zionism - the Jewish autonomous region (oblast) in the Far Eastern Russian Soviet Federated Socialist Republic.

2.   ALP: American Labor Party, another name for the Communist Party's New York State political organisation.

3.   Russ Braley, in his massive study, *Bad News* (Regnery Gateway, Chicago, 1984) charges the *New York Times* with persistent political bias in its news coverage, with comprehensive documentation in support of his thesis.

4.   See Appendices II and IV.

10. In at the Birth

The authorised version of the creation of the Institute for Policy Studies is that it was sparked off, as though by spontaneous intellectual combustion, when the eyes of its co-founders, Marcus Raskin and Richard Barnet, met on 14 April 1961. There are several versions of this momentous event[1], but all agree that it occurred when the two men attended a meeting of a joint White House-State Department conference on disarmament.

At the time, Raskin was on the National Security Council as an aide to McGeorge Bundy, the well-known liberal academic, who was just starting a five-year stint as Special Assistant for National Security Affairs. Barnet was Deputy Director to John McCloy on the US Arms Control and Disarmament Agency. As one version put it, 'Raskin rolled his eyes. His gaze caught the look of another eye roller, Richard Barnet'[2].

As another version put it, Barnet later told an interviewer: ''Marc and I both grimaced at the same moment and knew we didn't belong there.'[3]

And so, out of a rolling of eyes and simultaneous grimaces, a moment of truth produced the 'think tank of the Left' known as the IPS. The 'truth' of which this was the moment was that these two apparently typical members of the liberal establishment had realised simultaneously that they no longer liked being what and where they were. They had turned against the whole thing and become revolutionaries.

Raskin had graduated from the law school of the University of Chicago. A child prodigy on the piano, he had given up an early ambition to be a Rubinstein or a Horowitz and turned instead to public policy. The first of the two versions of the moment of truth quoted above says this of him: 'His mind is a constant storm, raging simultaneously with clouds of abstraction and the most precise proposals. He was one of many bright young men who had been drawn into government in the wake of John F. Kennedy's Presidential.'

His soul-mate in more ways than one, Richard Barnet had graduated from Harvard *summa cum laude*, and had gone through the Harvard Law School, the Harvard Russian Research Center and the Princeton Center for International Studies. He wrote a book on disarmament, and indeed the diversion of public funds from Defence to social ends was to be a *Leitmotiv* of the IPS. If Raskin was a frustrated pianist, Barnet was a gifted amateur violinist who, it is said, liked to practise Bach partitas on his 18th century Carcassi violin.

In a sympathetic collective profile of the think tank, the writer described Barnet, in contrast to Raskin, as 'calm and rational'.

In launching a politically committed think tank, the two founders were pioneers. Like Karl Marx, who inspired much of their thinking, they wanted not merely to interpret the world, but to *change* it. And indeed, Marx would have approved the ways in which they proposed to change their world.

Ideas may be free but the practical application of ideas is costly. Having thought up the idea of an activist think tank, the founding pair needed money to set it up and run it. Various donors came forth, but all accounts agree that by far the most munificent was the Rubin Foundation.

I have already mentioned the late Sam Rubin, self-declared Communist and, by definition at that time, Comintern agent. A Communist who becomes a multimillionaire is a prime asset of the international apparatus created by Lenin in 1919 to extend Soviet-style communism to 'all countries of the world without exception'. Their wealth and success makes them acceptable in 'capitalist' society, but can usefully be diverted to the destruction of that same society. Rubin was by no means unique in that respect. A good recent example was the French Communist entrepreneur, Jean Baptiste Doumeng, now deceased, who used to buy cheap EEC butter and send it to the USSR on helpful terms.

It is important to understand just what it meant to be a Communist, and in particular a member of the Communist Party USA, in Rubin's time. The striking testimony of David Horowitz, quoted in the last chapter, throws a piercing light upon that issue, but a fuller picture is needed.

The terms 'McCarthyite' and 'McCarthyism' encapsulate the outraged feelings of American liberals before the 'witch hunt', as they saw it, conducted against them by the late Senator Joseph McCarthy. The hysteria engendered in part, be it said, by the Senator's crude and hectoring methods, and in part by the excessive outrage of perfectly innocent liberals who felt they were being victimised, has obscured the truth of this tense period in contemporary American history. The painful fact is that there really was a major Soviet spy ring operating at various levels in American officialdom. By 1947, most of the agents had been uncovered and removed. Senator McCarthy's 'witch hunt' did not begin until three years later, with a speech of his in February 1950.

By far the best contemporary account of these events, calm, lucid and concise, was James Burnham's *The Web of Subversion* (1954; 1976). In Burnham's view, 'McCarthyism' was a convenient invention of the international Communist propaganda apparatus, which had successfully sown confusion in the minds of the public in the liberal Establishment.

But the outraged liberals were not impressed by Burnham; for was he not that ex-Trotskyist renegade who had joined William Buckley's conservative *National Review*? A later effort of the historian's art left them almost literally speechless, however. An American scholar, Allen Weinstein, too young to have been emotionally involved in the great controversy, produced after long labour a monumental study of the whole business, simply entitled *Perjury: the Hiss-Chambers Case* (1978). The most interesting aspect of this painstaking work was that Weinstein had started off convinced that Hiss had not been guilty of perjury, and that Chambers's testimony was suspect. His exhaustive examination of the evidence had made him change his mind. There had indeed been a Soviet spy ring, and Hiss had been part of it.[4]

The key point to grasp is that the members of the spy ring were not merely sentimental leftists who supported their idea of the Russian Revolution, but actual Soviet agents, who received money from Moscow and got their orders from the NKVD, ancestor of the KGB. Some were spies in the true sense, obtaining and passing on official secrets; others were 'agents of influence', attempting often successfully to influence American policy in ways favourable to the Soviet Union.

I wrote earlier that Sam Rubin, by the fact of being a member of the

Communist Party, was by definition a Comintern agent. There is overwhelming evidence to confirm this view, in the testimony of American Communists, whether in their memoirs, in cross-examination by Congressional committees, or in the transcripts of various trials involving the Communist Party; and ample confirmation in the FBI archives now in the public domain.

An ex-leader of the American Communist Party (CPUSA), Earl Browder, in an account of the internecine clash which had removed him from the scene, made it clear that all his policies had been developed over 15 years with the 'knowledge, consent and support' of 'the whole international leadership of communism'.[5]

In an official report published in Washington in 1953, evidence was provided by Herbert Brownell, the then Attorney General, that between 1920 and 1934 , the Communist International (Comintern) had provided substantial funds for the CPUSA, including $50,000 for two Communist candidates in the Presidential elections, and $35,000 for the establishment of the *Daily Worker*. In 1940, the party had formally disaffiliated itself from the Comintern, but had received funds from that source in 1949.[6]

Moving forward to 1961 at the time of the momentous meeting of eyes and grimaces of the founders of the IPS we find the CPUSA appealing against the Subversive Activities Control Board before the US Supreme Court. The legal complexities of this action need not concern us here. Of interest, however, was the testimony of one Dr Philip Mosely, Director of the Russian Institute at Columbia University. Appearing as an expert witness for the Attorney General, Mosely listed some 45 major international issues during 30 years, during which there had been no substantial difference between the announced position of the Soviet Union and the CPUSA.[7]

In other words, at the material time, the CPUSA took its instructions from, and was at the disposal of, the ruling party in Moscow. Nor should it be thought that this subservience was a thing of the past. What happened was not that CPUSA ceased to receive funds and instructions from Moscow, merely that it became more careful in concealing the fact. As late as 1982, in Hearings on Soviet Active Measures, further evidence to this end was provided by Edward O'Malley, Assistant Director, Intelligence Division, Federal Bureau of Investigation. He said, for example:

> The CPUSA has been, as you know, one of the most loyal and pro-Soviet Communist Parties in the world and has unfalteringly accepted Soviet direction and funding over the years. *It continues to receive its policy direction from the Communist Party of the Soviet Union.* (Emphasis added)

O'Malley went on to give a number of examples.

The fact that Sam Rubin was a rich man may have deprived him of Soviet financial contributions, although not necessarily of money for specific operations; but had no bearing on his subservience to Moscow's directives . During the early post-war years of Rubin's political activities, Western intelligence and security services, including the FBI and the fledgling CIA, would have been unaware that Stalin had rebuilt and refined Lenin's Comintern. It is fair now (in the light of much later knowledge) to assume that Rubin would have been getting the Soviet Communist Party's orders through its Central Committee's International Department.

Although Rubin had registered as a Communist voter as early as 1936, he was not placed on the FBI'S Security Index until 18 May 1954. Questioned by the Bureau, Rubin gave evasive answers, refusing for instance to say definitely that he had enrolled with the CP, although he stated that he 'believed' he had done so on one occasion in the 1930s.[8]

In a further 'SECRET' document, described as a 'succinct' résumé and consisting, as released, mainly of deletions, it was stated (in the surviving sentence) that he should be placed on the 'Reserve Index' because of the above subversive information concerning him, and the fact that as a wealthy individual he could potentially furnish material financial aid to the CP'.[9]

In the event, he furnished more 'material financial aid' to the new IPS than anybody else. The hard-working Harriet, wading through Internal Revenue Service tax returns, compiled an analysis of funds reaching the IPS in the six-year period of 1971 to 1976. Some 86 per cent of the money ($5,292,500) came from Rubin. But there was more to the connection than money: indeed it was hard to determine where Rubin ended and the IPS began — for in organisational terms, there was a striking overlap.

Thus, the Chairman of the Board of the IPS was Rubin's son-in-law, Peter Weiss, who was also Director of the Rubin Foundation. Rubin's daughter Cora, wife of Peter Weiss, was Secretary of the Foundation. His son, John Reed Rubin, was Treasurer. As the unsigned FBI notes pointed out[10], that name has a powerful symbolism. The Rubin couple named him after John Reed, the American Communist journalist whose famous book *Ten Days that Shook the World* glorified the Bolshevik Revolution. In turn, the Revolution glorified him by burying him in the Kremlin. No more total emotional and sentimental commitment to Soviet communism could be conceived than the names chosen for Rubin's male offspring.

Rubin must have been proud, too, of his daughter Cora Weiss, who acted in effect as Hanoi's unofficial ambassadress. She made several trips to North Vietnam during the Vietnam War, and lobbied in favour of American 'reparations' to the Communist régime. When the Americans pulled out of Vietnam, it was Cora Weiss who organised a 'victory party' in New York and personally welcomed the Vietnamese Communist delegation. Over the years, she was equally devoted to Cuban causes. Allowance made for the rare schisms, such as Tito's in Yugoslavia and Mao Dzedong's in China, the Communist cause is indeed indivisible. It was natural that Rubin's daughter should support Communist Vietnam and Cuba, and that she should do so through the IPS, which Rubin had launched.

Let us now take a closer look at Rubin and the source of his wealth. According to one persistent report, the basis of that fortune was the cut-price ambergris shipped to him by the Spanish Republican government during the Civil War. I am indebted to the American philanthropist Mr Murray Baron for a corrected version of what happened, which supports, yet again, the adage that truth is stranger than fiction. Rubin did indeed receive shipments of cheap ambergris from Spain during the Civil War, but the shipments came from the *Nationalist* government, not from the Communists! His Muscovite masters must have been proud of him. There was a double merit in the deal, for the price concession came from General Franco's camp, which was desperately short of foreign currency. The NKVD's slush fund was spared; and attention was diverted away from Moscow. Mr Baron learned of the transaction from his brother, Sam Baron, who reported the Spanish Civil War (on the left side).

There is a further and no less ironical detail. One of Sam Rubin's friends was the richest and most influential of the exclusive club of Communist multimillionaires, who indeed helped Rubin to 'join the club': the legendary Armand Hammer himself. At this point, a short digression is necessary. There is an absurd notion still prevalent in the legal profession in Britain but not elsewhere, that it is defamatory to call anybody a Communist unless he or she is a member of a Communist Party. The notion is absurd because some of the most dedicated Communists (including the traitors Fuchs and Philby) never belonged to the party. In that sense, the late Armand Hammer was not a Communist (unlike the Frenchman Doumeng, mentioned earlier). On the other hand, his father Julius Hammer (like Rubin, a Russian immigrant to the US) was a founder-member of the CPUSA, and a friend of Lenin, whom Armand Hammer also met. Hammer's many favours to the Soviet regime are well known.

When Rubin was setting up his perfume company, it was Hammer who suggested to him that he should call it the 'Fabergé Perfume Company', after the famous Tsarist jeweller, Count Fabergé. Because of Hammer's Soviet connections, he acquired many Fabergé pieces, which are now in the Hammer Galleries in New York. The Fabergé family fought Rubin through the courts over his unauthorised use of the name, but lost because it had never been protected by trade mark registration. Rubin's purloining of the name was another instance of sound business sense allied to deception. For no name less likely to be identified with the Soviet regime could be imagined.

Another ironical detail: the Rubin Foundation owned stock in various multinational companies, such as Exxon, Chase Manhattan, Union Carbide and others, which were specifically denounced by Richard Barnet in a book of which he was co-author, *Global Reach*, and to which I shall return.

The Rubin connection with the IPS is obviously of major importance in confirming the Communist interest in the Institute. It leaves one question open, however: was it Rubin who proposed to Barnet and Raskin that they should set up an Institute? Or did the co-founders, having decided that they wanted to set up their politically motivated Institute, turn to Rubin as the most likely source of funds, in view precisely of the fact that their aims were, if not identical, at least compatible with his? Or, yet another possibility, did Rubin, on hearing about the IPS project, decide to offer funds from his Foundation? A further question is: Does it matter? Whichever explanation applies, or whether it was a combination of the three hypotheses, the end result is the same: an organisation which demonstrably engaged in activities helpful to Soviet policy aims over the years.

The Rubin connection, however, is not the only indication of Communist involvement in the genesis of the IPS. One of the fuller FBI documents gave me an interesting clue. Dated 19 March 1970, it consisted of a general assessment of IPS and quoted extensively from a two-part article in *Baron's Weekly* (6 and 13 October 1969). here are the relevant passages:

> IPS had its genesis in the Peace Research Institute, which began operations in Washington on April 5, 1961, with an announcement that it would serve as a private agency to undertake and stimulate research in all fields relevant to peace, security, disarmament and international order. Shortly afterwards, it obtained a $20,000 contract for a study for the Arms Control and Disarmament Agency.
>
> Signed by ARTHUR I. WASKOW, now the Senior Fellow of IPS, the document called for an international police force to keep world peace. (....)
>
> Late in 1963 the Peace Research Institute merged with the Institute for Policy Studies, which has been founded by MARCUS RASKIN and RICHARD BARNET.... Mr Waskow then went to work for IPS as a Senior Fellow.

It turned out that the 'merger' of the Peace Research Institute (PRI) with the IPS had a special significance. In real terms, the PRI was absorbed into the IPS, then vanished. While it still had its separate existence, Waskow, who was its President, invited a prominent member of the Soviet establishment, Igor Sergeyevich Glagolev, to the US. At that time, Glagolev was a member of another body known as the Peace Research Society (International). An informative 1965 pamphlet in my hands shows Glagolev as a contributor to the Society's publications.

From a confidential source, I learned that Glagolev and Waskow developed a close relationship. At the time of their meeting, Glagolev, a member of the Soviet Academy of Sciences, was much involved in the disarmament strategy of the World Peace Council. It may be inferred, therefore, that, at the very least, a Soviet propagandist was in a position to influence the course of events (or alternatively, to report back on the progress of negotiations between Waskow's Institute and the newly formed IPS, at the crucial time).

Some years later, Glagolev defected to the United States. As it happens, he came to see me when I was Director of the Institute for the Study of Conflict in London, and we met several times in the late 1970s, but I was not, at that time, inquiring into the origins of the IPS. His testimony would have been interesting, and probably very valuable, but I learned on trying to contact him that he had recently died.

The 'peace' connection does not exhaust the Soviet or Soviet Bloc's generic involvement in the IPS. Harriet, collected some revealing documents, including official tax returns, pointing strongly to a Cuban connection. The returns concerned the Louis M. Rabinowitz Foundation, which recorded grants to IPS personnel and affiliated organisations.

With the Internal Revenue documents came a full list of recipients of Rabinowitz grants and an illuminating article about this 'Private Foundation exempt from income tax', to use the official jargon. What was, and is, the Rabinowitz Foundation? The founder, a self-made millionaire, had made his fortune in the New York garment industry (specifically by making and selling hooks and eyes). He set up his Foundation in 1944 to help utterly respectable Jewish contributions to American life in the best tradition of true philanthropy: libraries and museums, chairs at major universities, archaeological expeditions — all strictly within the Foundation's charter.

And then, in 1957, the founder died, and his creation came under the direction of his son, his daughter and his daughter-in-law. Almost immediately, the funds started reaching radically different beneficiaries. In 1967, ten years after the death of Louis M. Rabinowitz, only 3 per cent of the grantees were connected with philanthropic Jewish causes. Instead, the money was going to 'Marxist' writers and scholars for 're-search' useful to Communist causes.

Many of the books thus fostered were being published by International Publishers, the publishing house of the Communist Party USA. Other beneficiaries were associated with the 'independent' Marxist publishing house, Monthly Review Press, and its magazine *Monthly Review*.

In 1967, the Rabinowitz Foundation had made a grant to Richard Barnet. Admittedly, the grant was not a very large one, a mere $1,500. The previous year, it had made a somewhat more generous grant of $5,000 to another man with close IPS connections., John Gerassi, a former *Newsweek* correspondent turned extremist who had made illegal trips to North Vietnam and to Cuba in 1966 and 1967.

Increasingly, from 1963 on, Rabinowitz money had been going to pro-Cuban recipients and causes. Nor was this, on further inquiry, surprising. For many years, according to the article from which I have extracted these facts, the founder's son, Victor Rabinowitz, a New York lawyer, was Fidel Castro's chief legal representative in the United States[11]. As such, and in accordance with US law, he was indeed registered as a foreign agent[12] The discovery that a man registered as a Cuban agent was actually sanctioning grants to IPS people and causes startled me, and I immediately requested my anchor-man, Lee Edwards, to check the facts. On 6 May 1987, Edwards wrote to me in these words:

> At last, after three weeks, I have been able to verify Victor Rabinowitz's foreign agent's status with Cuba. The government office took that long to move and make its records available The records show that Rabinowitz...registered with the Department of Justice as a foreign agent for Cuba from May 4, 1964 through September 10, 1968.

So it was true! It may be objected that a grant of $1,500 to the co-founder of IPS and of $5,000 to a writer with IPS links doesn't amount to very much. But that is hardly the point. The point is that a New York lawyer, representing Fidel Castro, thought it natural to help IPS writers. In that sense, if in no other, the IPS was a front for the Cuban regime; and therefore for Cuban intelligence.

Whether the considerable body of evidence assembled here would have been admitted as such in an English court of law remains untested. What is certain is that to any specialist in such questions, the evidence does show the Soviet and Cuban services were interested, *ab initio*, in using the IPS for their own purposes; in other words, as a front for those services,.

This is surely the moment to produce the confirmatory evidence for the second proposition disputed by Richard Barnet in his lawsuit against me, namely that Cuban intelligence is itself controlled by the KGB. As far as I know, I was the first writer to tell the full story of the creation of the DGI and its take-over by the Soviets, in an ISC report mentioned earlier (Chapter 7),

Later accounts were published by John Barron in his two books on the KGB; and by Melvin R, Laird, a former US Defence Secretary (under President Nixon)[13]. All these versions, however, my own included, were secondhand. The primary sources were the two elusive Cuban defectors, Orlando Castro Hidalgo and Gerardo Jesús Peraza Amechazurra. Castro, who had defected to the American embassy in Luxembourg in March 1969, testified before a Senate Committee later that year, and told his own story in book form two years later. Peraza, who defected in London in November 1971, did not testify until early in 1982. My own witness, Alfonso Tarabochia, played a leading role on both occasions.

Before quoting the key passages from each man's testimony, I recall the political background, without which the full significance of their revelations would be obscure.

Although Fidel Castro later stopped trying to hide his secret allegiance to Communism in his early years in power, he went so far as to gaol critics, such as Huber Matos, who had dared to criticise him for steering the Cuban revolution in that direction (see chapter 9). I was one of many commentators deceived by Castro's cover up. In fact, Castro had met secretly in the Sierra Maestra with Carlos Rafael Rodríguez, the leader of the old Popular Socialist Party (as Cuba's Communists called themselves). The two men agreed that Castro's Rebel Army would henceforth work closely together with the PSP. These facts were revealed by the American correspondent Daniel James in his book *CUBA: The First Soviet Satellite in the Americas*[14]. Once in power, Castro tried to keep his distance from Moscow, both for the sake of his international image and probably for his own ego. Flushed with his own revolutionary success, he aspired to export his version of revolution all over Latin America, in the face of cold discouragement from the Soviets who regarded his efforts as amateurish and adventurist.

Through an able KGB officer posing as a Tass correspondent, Aleksander Alekseyev, the Soviets created Castro's secret intelligence service, the DGI. Having done so, they naturally wanted to harness it to their own needs, but ran into resistance from the *Líder máximo*. A turning point came with the pathetic fiasco of 'Che' Guevara's Bolivian adventure. The 'Che', as Castro's Argentine lieutenant was known, had been the darling of the turbulent 'New Left' in the 1960s, in part because of his romantic notion that all you had to do to have a revolution was to start one. In 1967, he tried to do just that in Bolivia, where he had gone with a small band of followers, not one of whom spoke the Quechua language of the local Andean peasants. Moreover, the local Communists, under Moscow's instructions, refused the slightest cooperation. In the end, Guevara was captured and killed by the Bolivian security forces, promptly becoming a martyr in the eyes of the New Left.

At this point, the Soviet comrades decided that enough was enough. It was time to bring Fidel Castro to heel. Their first thought was to work through the pro-Moscow old guard of the ruling party, now calling itself the Communist Party of Cuba. The leader of the pro-Moscow faction was Aníbal Escalante. Fidel could see what was happening and sent Escalante to Prague. Back in Havana, Moscow's man made a further attempt to assert the Soviet line, but Fidel again came out on top. In January 1968, he summoned his Central Committee, denounced Escalante's 'micro-faction' and gaoled him for 15 years. Eight of Escalante's followers got 12 years.

Having tried, and failed, to influence the charismatic leader through his more pliant younger brother Raúl, the Soviets lost all patience and decided to use heavier methods. Not long after the 'micro-faction' incident, they threatened to cut off all economic aid unless Castro stopped criticising the Soviet Union and launching guerrilla plans without consulting Moscow. Let Orlando Castro Hidalgo pick up the story:

> In the Soviet Union Nikita Khrushchev was thrown out of power, and the hard-nosed bureaucrats who took over were not of the kind to tolerate indiscipline on the part of Castro, whom they viewed as a mere puppet, and a highly dependent one, at that.

Because Cuba was not capable of supporting itself economically, nor of obtaining in foreign trade all the goods it needed, a supply line from the Soviet Union to the island had been established. Vital to Cuban existence was petroleum that Russia kept flowing aboard a steady stream of tankers. The Kremlin hardened its position toward Castro, and the flow of petroleum was slowed. The Cuban economy found itself in grievous trouble. There was not enough fuel to keep sugar mills, industries and vehicles functioning. In a desperate move, military chief Raúl Castro allocated about one-third of military fuel stockpiles to civilian use. Other supplies from Russia on which Cuba was dependent also failed to arrive, forcing closure of a number of factories. The workers were sent to toil in the cane fields. (*Spy for Fidel*, p.61)

Where persuasion and internecine plotting had failed, the Soviet blockade worked. During the crisis, the Soviet advisers had been summoned home; Now they were sent back to Cuba. A large-scale economic aid plan was launched, and advanced Soviet weapons started flowing in. Bowing to his masters, Castro fired his DGI chief, Manuel Piñeiro Losada (known as 'Red Beard'), not for any professional failings, but because he was anti-Soviet, and with him those of his staff who had similar views. As a consolation prize, he was put in charge of a newly created 'Department of the Americas', theoretically autonomous, but ultimately under Soviet control.

As for the original DGI, the top job was given to a Soviet nominee. José Méndez Cominches. For good measure, the Soviets sent their own man, General Vitaly Petrovich Semënov (sometimes known as Viktor Simenov), to supervise Méndez from an office next door. The takeover was complete.

Let the other elusive Cuban defector, Gerardo Peraza, pick up the thread. During his testimony before a subcommittee of the US Senate in 1982, he was asked why he had left the service of the Cuban government in 1971. He replied:

> The fundamental facts are these: First, there was a law which was promulgated in the intelligence service of Cuba making it mandatory to belong to the Communist Party. And second, the intelligence service of Cuba was transferred directly to the services of the Soviet intel-

ligence service[15].

Peraza went on to give a detailed account of the Soviet takeover. Today, no serious student of international communism and of Soviet/ Cuban relations doubts the fact that the Cuban DGI was totally under the KGB's control, to the extent that all DGI operations had to be cleared first with the KGB's man on the spot, who in turn had to approve any allocation of funds.

During my investigation, and in the light of my failure to meet Castro Hidalgo and Peraza, Alasdair Pepper was anxious to establish the legal status of their testimonies before the Congressional Hearings. In other words, would their evidence be acceptable to an English court of law in their physical absence, since it would not be possible to cross-examine them? As far as I am aware, this point was never satisfactorily resolved. In scholarly terms, however, their testimony was decisive. Future historians of the period will rely upon it when both men are dead, as I did while they were still alive.

The interesting point, of relevance to this book, was why the IPS, having access to the facts, continued to support Fidel Castro's régime in various ways.

Notes

1.   Among other sympathetic accounts, see: Gary Wills, 'The Thinking of Positive Power', *Esquire*, March 1971; and Sidney Blumenthal, 'The Left Stuff: IPS & The Long Road Back', *The Washington Post*, 30 July 1986.
2.   Blumenthal..
3.   Wills.
4.   Allen Weinstein, *PERJURY: the Hiss-Chambers Case* (Knopf, New York, 1978). For further details, see *op cit*, pp 18, 20 and *AGENT*, 27-28.
5.   Earl Browder, *Modern Insurrections and Miracles* (self-published, 1950), p.49.
6.   Subversive Activities Control Board, Petition Herbert Brownell, Jr., Attorney-General of the United States (US Government Printing Office, Washington, 1953).

7.   Supreme Court of the United States, 5 June 1961, Communist Party of the United States v. Subversive Activities Control Board, Opinion of the Court, delivered by Mr Justice Frankfurter.

8.   FBI Office Memorandum to J. Edgar Hoover, 18 May 1954.

9.   FBI Memorandum from J. Edgar Hoover to Director Bureau of Intelligence and Research, Department of State, 3 August 1964.

10.   See Chapter 9.

11.   See *CADRE*, pp 16-17, and p 39, note 15; also Lawrence V.Cott and Ruth I.Matthews, 'Left Bank — the Louis B. Rabinowitz Foundation' in the journal *Combat'* 15 June 1969.

12.   Under US law, any American citizen working for *any* foreign government is required to register as an agent of that government. No distinction is made between allies or friendly governments on the one hand, and hostile or enemy governments on the other; nor between tiny countries, such as the Principality of Monaco, and a superpower , such as the USSR at the relevant time.

13.   Melvin R. Laird, 'The Moscow-Havana Connection', in *The Reader's Digest* (US Edition, August 1976).

14.   Daniel James's book was published in 1961 (Avon, New York). He also wrote a biography of Che Guevara and edited Guevara's diaries. The essence of his work appeared in his penetrating review of Tad Szulc's far from critical book, *FIDEL: A Critical Portrait* (William Morrow, New York, 1987).

15.   *The Role of Cuba in International Terrorism and Subversion* Hearings before the Subcommittee on Security and Terrorism, Committee on the Judiciary, United States Senate, 26 February, 4,11 and 12 March 1982; p6.

11. IPS: Founding Portrait

A man with strong political convictions will always be at risk of a collision with the government of the day, if those convictions are totally at odds with the prevailing public philosophy. This is true of Western countries as well as of Communist ones, though to a lesser degree. In the latter, total and unquestioning conformity was required. In such countries as the Soviet Union, even long after the death of Stalin, to be a dissident was to court persecution, arrest, torture or 'psychiatric' abuse.

The United States is one of the freest countries in the world. But Americans who choose to indulge strong political convictions through terrorism will run foul of the law; whereas if they merely express their dissent verbally nothing much will normally befall them. The McCarthy period in the early 1950s in the US was not a normal one, in the sense that it did limit free speech through fear of the consequences.

When a democracy is at war, public emotions are naturally exacerbated, and freedom of speech is an early victim. In Britain in World War II, members of the British Union of Fascists, including its leader Sir Oswald Mosley, were detained without trial under the notorious Regulation 18B, with many innocent Jewish refugees from Nazi Germany who were later deported to Australia and other distant places.

At the time the IPS was created, the United States was at war. True, it was an undeclared war against a distant enemy who did not directly threaten the territory of the US. And it was an unpopular war, especially in the East Coast liberal Establishment, to which Marcus Raskin and Richard Barnet belonged. Ironically, it was President John F. Kennedy, so revered by the liberals, who had first sent American combat troops to Vietnam. Doubtless it was Kennedy's commitment to the anti-Communist cause, more than anything else, that precipitated the political revulsion of Raskin and Barnet.

Had the two men confined themselves to verbal criticism of America's involvement, they would presumably not have attracted the hostile attention of the FBI, but they went well beyond the limits of passive opposition. They were anti-war activists, and proud of it. Increasingly, as the war dragged on, Barnet in particular was seen to consort with the North Vietnamese and their Soviet protectors; that is, with the *de facto* enemies of the US in a war to which his country had committed a large army of fighting men who were suffering heavy casualties, and with representatives of the power that made the North Vietnamese war effort possible.

It was hardly surprising to learn from the heavily deleted FBI files released to me that Barnet was under FBI investigation for some years, from 30 October 1968 until 3 April 1974. The Bureau file on Barnet (No. 105-185148), in an entry covering the investigative period from 9 February to 8 April 1970 included a recommendation that he should be placed on the Security Index, Priority I.

There followed a personal report, running to 40 pages. Some of the many New Left organisations with which Barnet had been associated were listed. 'Barnet's speeches,' we read, 'are anti-US in content'. On several occasions, the report went on, Barnet had travelled to Europe, the Soviet Union and North Vietnam. The purpose of his trip to Paris in 1969, at the height of the Vietnam War, was to hold meetings with North Vietnamese representatives. On that occasion he had been accompanied by Cora Weiss (Rubin's daughter, mentioned earlier), and by two men, Bernard Davis and Dave Bellinger, described as leaders of national prominence in the New Left movement and convicted defendants in a trial that had attracted much attention, known as the Chicago 'Conspiracy'.

Many entries in the report concern the Vietnam War. In July 1967, Barnet had attended a meeting of the Vietnam Organising Committee in Stockholm. There was nothing criminal about that, of course, but he had gone a good deal further in November 1969, when he went to Hanoi, capital of Communist North Vietnam, to take part in mass demonstrations against 'the United States aggression in Vietnam'.

The Hanoi trip was sponsored by two Communist-controlled bodies, the Vietnam Peace Committee and the Vietnam Committee for Solidarity with the American People. I have tried, objectively, to point to some of the differences between American participation on the Allied side in World War II, and US involvement in the war in Vietnam.

Some entries in the FBI report on Barnet are, in themselves, trivial. They become significant in the wider picture of the activities of the joint founder of the IPS. For instance: 'He acted as a character witness for a self-admitted Communist Party member who was his friend at his college....' On p.23, the identity of his Communist friend was given as John M. Bailey, and in September 1958 Barnet had testified as a character witness for Bailey before an Industrial Loyalty Hearing in New York City. Barnet stated that he first knew Bailey was a CP member after he had left the Party in 1949.

'So what?' might be the comment, and I would not dissent from it.

Another entry, again trivial in itself. On 12 July 1962, it was learned that Barnet had been having contacts with members of the Polish embassy. On 17 and 28 September 1962, Barnet had told an FBI man that he had had a dinner meeting on 11 September with Stefan Szymczykiewicz, who introduced him to his replacement, Kazimierz Oraczewski.

Again, 'So what?' As a working journalist in London, I had many such meetings.

A further trivial entry. In 1964, the IPS had invited a Soviet representative, Yuri I. Bobrakov, to a seminar on crime. More serious? Or is it a case, as in mathematics, that nought multiplied by any number is still nought?

To meet Communists, native-born and foreign, on numerous occasions is possibly another indication of where IPS sympathy lies.

The report included a lengthy entry on the IPS-linked Mobilisation Committee to end the war in Vietnam (WMC)[1] and various affiliated or interchangeable organisations,[1] was the National Mobilisation Committee to end the war in Vietnam (NMC). There was a quotation from a report of the House Un-American Activities Committee, dated 8-15 April 1967 and entitled 'Communist Origin and Manipulation of Vietnam Week': 'Communists are playing dominant roles in both the Student Mobilisation Committee and the Spring Mobilisation Committee.' (p.53). The report went on to cite the names of known Communists.

In a further report on Barnet, dated 4 May 1970, the FBI had hardened its view, in the following passage:

...it is indicated that he [Barnet] had demonstrated his willingness to use his position of influence with the IPS to discredit and undermine US policy, both foreign and domestic.

The Barnet file moves on. An entry dated 13 May 1971 declares: 'Barnet has been identified as having had contact with United States Soviet personnel, given a public speech stating that Nixon will use nuclear weapons in Vietnam...' The following page must have been interesting, before the censors got to it. It is headed 'Contacts with Soviet Embassy Personnel', and consists mainly of deletions.

Another tantalising entry is headed 'Contacts with North Vietnamese'. The heading, however, presides over a deleted paragraph.

The anti-Vietnam War activities of the co-founder were tireless. On 6 August 1970, an East Coast Communist newspaper, the *Daily World*, carried the text of a speech by Barnet to a meeting of the Business Executives Move for Vietnam Peace and New National Priorities.

A CIA report is quoted for the news that Richard J. Barnet of the IPS was planning to address an international conference of lawyers on Vietnam in Paris in September 1968, The name of the sponsoring body caught my attention: the International Association of Democratic Lawyers (IADL), somewhat euphemistically described as 'Communist-dominated'.

More accurately, the IADL was one of the major international front organisations set up by the Soviet Union after World War II, specifically through an International Congress of Jurists held in Paris in October 1946. By 1949, most of the non-communist members had grasped who was behind the body they had joined in all innocence, and had resigned. The following year, the French government expelled the IADL from its original headquarters in their capital, and it set up shop in Brussels. Richard Barnet, Harvard graduate, *summa cum laude*, should not have had any problem in acquiring the easily-available background given above.

Richard Barnet played a curious, but still in some respects obscure, role in the protracted negotiations in Paris in late 1972, which led in January 1973 to the departure of the American forces from Vietnam and to the Nobel Peace Prize for Henry Kissinger and the North Vietnamese negotiator, Le Duc Tho (who refused it). The obscurity simply arises from the heavy deletions both in his personal FBI file and in the general files released to me.

On a previous visit to Paris, Barnet had travelled with Cora Weiss. On this further visit, Cora's husband Peter Weiss was his fellow traveller, in his capacity as Chairman of the Board of Trustees of IPS. In Volume 5 of the general files, we read: 'Mr Barnet and Mr Weiss stated their beliefs that a "change of policy in Saigon, specifically the freeing of political prisoners in Saigon, the lifting of censorship and the ban on political meetings offered the best hope of a breakthrough in negotiations".' This passage appears to be a quotation from an IPS report on the Paris peace talks. I say 'appears' because the first page is deleted.

What Barnet and Weiss were advocating, in other words, was a list of unilateral concessions by South Vietnam, with no corresponding measures in Communist North Vietnam (the Democratic Republic of Vietnam or DRV). At that time, as at all times since the legendary, Moscow-trained Ho Chi Minh had set up his Republic in 1954, there were thousands of political prisoners in the DRV, blanket censorship and a total ban on unauthorised political meetings. Bearing in mind that the Soviet Union was providing some 90 per cent of the arms and equipment for the North Vietnamese army and for the Vietcong guerrillas in the South, the course advocated by the IPS could be interpreted as helpful to the policy interests of the USSR.

Let us leave Richard Barnet the activist for a moment, and look more closely at Richard Barnet the author and political thinker. His books and articles are a subtle form of anti-American, pro-Soviet propaganda. That is, the line he takes never blatantly favours Soviet policies. Instead, after an apparently dispassionate analysis of the evidence, written in a cool academic style, he almost invariably reaches the conclusion that the United States is in the wrong, in any phase of the protracted East-West conflict.

An interesting example of Barnet's communicating skill is the book mentioned earlier, *Global Reach* (New York, 1974), of which he was co-author with Ronald E. Müller. In this massive, well researched tome, we have a sustained and highly effective, apparently well-reasoned attack on multinational companies, including of course those to which the Communist 'angel' Rubin had entrusted his fortune. Not the least arresting aspect of this attack was that it preceded, by two years, a massive campaign against the multinationals launched from Moscow in 1976.

The Soviet campaign began in February of that year when the press agency Novosti castigated the multinationals in a publication signed M. Volkov and entitled *The Strategy of Neocolonialism Today*. The next move was a Conference of European Communist Parties held in East Berlin on 29 and 30 June 1976, at which it was resolved to intensify 'the struggle against the policies of multinational monopolies'. The time had come to broaden the campaign, and in 1977 the Programme of the Soviet-controlled World Peace Council named the multinationals as a target. I had duly chronicled this sequence in the ISC *Annual of Power and Conflict* for 1976-77.

Which, then, was the cart, and which the horse? Did *Global Reach* inspire the Soviet propaganda campaign? Or did Richard Barnet have advance knowledge of the forthcoming meeting of European Communist Parties and decided to give them something to talk about?

A fellow-student of the Barnet/IPS phenomenon is the American academic writer Rael Jean Isaac. As Dr Isaac notes, Barnet held the view that the freedoms enjoyed by US citizens were more than matched by those available to Soviet citizens in their own country. A startling view, that Dr Andrei Sakharov and Solzhenitsyn, among countless other persecuted dissidents, might have disputed. But let us pay attention to Dr Barnet. The US, he argued in his book *The Giants* (1977), offered 'procedural' freedoms, whereas Soviet freedoms were described as 'substantive'. By procedural freedoms, we learn, Barnet understood freedom of the press, of speech and of assembly. The substantive freedoms he claimed to identify in the Soviet Union were listed as medical care, jobs and housing. Given the choice, he was sure Soviet citizens would choose their substantive freedoms.

What Barnet refrained from saying was that Soviet citizens were in fact not given this choice, and that their freedom to travel and see for themselves how American and other Western citizens live was severely restricted even under Mikhail Gorbachev and his much trumpeted policy of *glasnost* (which again means 'publicity' but was flatteringly rendered as 'openness',) And the restrictions were far tougher when Barnet wrote *The Giants*.

Barnet was too intelligent to avoid all criticism of the Soviet Union, a fact which enhances credibility and costs nothing. When he did criticise the Soviets, however, he usually did so to make a comparison detrimental to the United States. For example, in *The Giants*, he referred to 'the outrageous' behaviour of the Soviet officials towards their own citizens', chronicled the Soviet failure to live up to its human rights commitments under the Final Act of the Helsinki Conference in 1975, sharply criticised the treatment of minorities, dissent and religious beliefs and denounced the oppressive use of mental hospitals as an 'Orwellian nightmare'.

But read on. Those strictures appear on p.51. On p.96, Barnet argued that the treatment of dissent in the Soviet Union was lenient compared to many dictatorships around the world with which the US had close and friendly relations. As Rael Jean points out,[2] 'so even this becomes yet another stick with which to beat the United States'.

On one important issue, Richard Barnet never blamed the Soviet side: invariably, he argued that the Soviet Union posed no threat to the US. In his 'Our Strangelovian suspicion of Russian intent'[3] and other published texts, he argued that the US military build-up since World War II and military activities had been entirely the fruit of internal domestic processes. The underlying premise was that there was no genuine and significant external threat to the United States, Soviet behaviour being defensive in nature. In an article published some years later, he declared that 'the alternative of a conventional arms build-up in the name of nuclear pacifism must be resisted'[4]. In other words, the US must not only discard its nuclear weapons, but refrain from any compensating increase in conventional weapons: a logical conclusion, if one admits the premise, is that there was no Soviet threat to guard against.

Re-enter Richard Barnet the activist. One of the most significant events, in the context of arms, was the joint IPS-Soviet meeting held in San Francisco in September 1985. The Soviet delegation was led by the Kremlin's top expert on the United States, Central Committee member Georgi Arbatov, Director of the Institute for the Study of the USA and Canada. As already pointed out, this 'Institute' had been exposed by various specialists as a vehicle for Soviet 'active measures' and disinformation.

In the paper he presented at this conference, Barnet blamed both superpowers, the United States and the Soviet Union, for blocking progress in arms control negotiations. He asserted that the American policy of trying to block the spread of communism in the developing world was counter-productive. It should be 'abandoned', because it was based upon what he claimed was an unfounded fear that the Soviet Union would use Marxist States for strategic purposes.[5]

It is always pleasant for a speaker to know he is addressing a sympathetic audience, and what could have been more sympathetic, at that time, than a Soviet delegation led by Georgi Arbatov, whose professional mission was to know all there was to know about the American polity and society, the better to destroy them? So it was hardly surprising that Barnet should go on to defend the Soviet deployment of the new SS-20 missiles in Europe as 'defensive', while he described as 'disastrous' the consequences of the deployment, then just beginning, of the new US Cruise and Pershing II intermediate-range missiles in Western Europe.

Arbatov and his team must have heard such arguments with smiles on their lips, for was this not an American speaker in his own country, condemning his own country's behaviour?

But there was more. Turning to Afghanistan, Barnet blamed *both* superpowers for not resolving the issue through improved bilateral co-operation. Evidently judging that such impartiality was out of character, he did his usual tilting act, chiding the United States for not doing more to end the war.

The factual background to the defence situation in the European 'theatre' at the time Barnet presented his paper is important. The Soviets started deploying their formidable SS-20s in 1978; deployment of the Pershing IIs and Cruise missiles on the Western side came *six years* later and only after the Soviets had walked out of the bilateral arms control talks in Geneva.

In the face of this background, of which Barnet was well aware, he blamed the US for responding to a heightened threat from the Soviet side. But then, it is all a question of definitions: if any deployment of nuclear weapons on the Soviet side was seen as 'defensive', then any counter-measures on the American side could only be 'disastrous'.

The same tendency to meet pro-Soviet definitions can be seen in Barnet's approach to the war in Afghanistan. President Amin was assassinated by the Soviet Spetsnaz[6] in December 1979, after a failed

KGB poisoning attempt[7]. His predecessor, Nur Mohammed Tarakki, had been installed in April 1978 in a coup masterminded by the KGB; then removed when he proved insufficiently obedient. Finally, after the murder of Amin, the Soviets had an unconditional puppet in Babrak Karmal: he it was who invited the Soviet Union to occupy his country and help deal with local unrest. It was thus that the Afghanistan war began. It is hard to believe that Richard Barnet was unaware of this sequence of events.

After the advent of President Reagan, in January 1981, the US began, initially on a small scale, a programme of aid to the Afghan resistance, known as the Mujaheddin. It was this response, evidently, that Barnet had in mind when chiding his own government for not doing more to end a war which the Soviets, not the US, had started.

Such consistent support for Soviet interests is noteworthy, to say no more.

Judging by the written evidence, there seems to have been a division of labour, tacit or explicit, between the two founders of the IPS; or three, if one counts Arthur Waskow, who was in almost at the birth when his Peace Research Institute was absorbed by the IPS.

Richard Barnet concentrated on foreign affairs and defence: that is, on opposing the conduct of both by successive US governments. Marcus Raskin and Arthur Waskow seem to have devoted most of their energies to subversion: that is, to undermining American society from within. Waskow, in particular, was involved with left-wing terrorist groups.

In Leninist terms, there is no clear dividing line between external and internal 'active measures', or between subverting a target country from within and undermining its foreign and defence policies. To the extent that a target country was weakened within, it became an easier prey to the Soviet Union's external policies.

Within the Institute, Marcus Raskin seemed to be regarded as its chief philosopher and ideologist. In his book *Being and Doing* (1971), Raskin presented his view of what he called 'the American imperium', seen by the poor and the young as 'the world's primary enemy'. Americans themselves, it seemed, were 'colonised', and this internal colony was subdivided into four:

    1. *The Violence Colony* (Raskin's capitals). Most political phi-

losophers distinguish between the necessary force of the State, as in its 'law enforcement' agencies, and criminal (that is, unauthorised and illegal) violence. In the more widely acceptable view, criminal violence may be committed by individual citizens, but also by the State itself (as in the use of excessive force, or even torture, by the police). In Raskin's philosophy, there was no such distinction: the rulers of the Violence Colony used 'the rest of society as their hostage'. Startlingly, their primary tool was the university, which Raskin saw as 'the fundamental shield and terrorising instrument of the State'.

2. *The Plantation Colony*, whose people 'work at meaningless and unreal jobs to obtain things that they are led to want' but which do not satisfy 'human needs' (as understood by Marcus Raskin).

3. *The Channelling Colony*, the inmates of which were 'broken into 'accepting authority structures'. As Rael Jean Isaac (from whose analysis I have drawn in these passages) says,[8] the Channelling Colony was 'known by less profound minds as the educational system'. Once 'broken', the inmates became 'bored, user-used and hollowed out.'

4. *The Dream Colony*, the purpose of which, apparently, was to lull the oppressed people into passive acceptance of the other colonies. The Dream Colony 'provides a surrogate of action and passion for the colonised, replacing their own actions and passions'.

There is more in the same vein. Having listed his 'colonies', Raskin offers his remedy: dismantle, destroy and start all over again. The Violence Colony had to go first, because that was what kept the whole show on the road. American society has to be cleansed and demilitarised by a model law. Any civil servant convicted of militarism would be discharged, and might even have his property confiscated and be sentenced to seven years of 'socially useful work' in custody.

The Plantation Colony was to be replaced by worker-controlled and operated industries. Gone, too, would be the Channelling Colony, with the wholesale destruction of records, grades and tests, to be replaced by free inquiry. As for the Dream Colony, it would yield to a television channel that would bind people together 'in an associative, democratic way'.

In Raskin's Reconstructed Society, local meetings would take all decisions and workers would fix their own taxes.

At the end of Raskin's day, it has to be said that, apart from the terminology, there is nothing new in his political thinking. The remedy proposed is a form of anarcho-syndicalism, remarkably similar to the 19th century nostrums of Proudhon, Godwin, Kropotkin and the other 'Utopians' whom Marx so despised (although his own philosophy was no less Utopian than theirs). If that were all there was to it, there would not be much cause for concern. The trouble is that, like Marx and Bakunin, Raskin and IPS wanted to *change* the world, starting with America. Dismantling meant dismantling. Thus on 13 March 1969, the *Washington Post* quoted Raskin as advocating the dismantling of the CIA, the Defence Department and the National Security Agency within the next decade, as the only sure way of reversing the 'national security State'.

It is at this point that Marcus Raskin, whether he was aware of it or not, was serving the foreign policy interests of the Soviet Union. To be honest about Raskin's anarcho-syndicalism, this was scarcely the kind of message that appealed to the leaders of a maximum security State such as the Soviet Union. But dismantling the CIA, and the Pentagon, and the NSA? Well, that was something else.

Similarly, the KGB may be presumed to have had an interest in an initiative of Raskin's in October 1970, when he wrote to a large number of US companies for confidential information. His stated motive for so doing was that he was working on a study on industrial security. The FBI contacted all such companies and asked them to advise the Bureau, should they be contacted by Raskin. In the early weeks of 1971, Raskin's exercise was still in progress, but thereafter the trail runs cold.

Perhaps the ultimate IPS exercise in anarchism was a campaign, launched in 1971, to abolish all prisons within the next five years. An IPS report to this end is quoted in full in Volume 4 of the IPS files released to me. The second paragraph reads: 'Ending prisons would require the transformation of American society: the abolition of poverty and the creation of participatory democracy and real community, at the least.' A later passage runs: 'The jails are the domestic equivalent of Vietnam that is, the *worst continuous example* of domestic domination as Vietnam is of foreign imperialism'. (Italics in original.)

A further FBI report in the same volume names two people specifically involved in the 'abolish prisons' campaign. One was our 'third man', Arthur Waskow; the other, Joann Malone, was described as a former nun with the Sisters of Laredo and a convicted member of the 'DC Nine', who were responsible for the destruction of the records and property of the Dow Chemical Company, Washington, in 1969.

In yet another FBI report marked 'SECRET' and dated 16 October 1970 (mentioned in Chapter 8), Waskow was described as a supporter of the Black Panther Party, one of a number of terrorist groups that were very active at the time. In an Appendix, the BPP's paper, *The Black Panther*, was quoted as advocating the use of guns and guerrilla tactics in its revolutionary programme to end oppression of the black people. Residents of the black community were urged to arm themselves against the police who are constantly referred to as 'pigs' who should be killed.

It seems fair, in the light of this and other reports about Arthur Waskow, to categorise him as a practitioner of physical, as distinct from intellectual, activism. As a man of 'peace', it could be said, perhaps, that he gave the word a new shade of meaning.

Notes

1.   Better known as MOBE: see *CADRE* pp.36-37.

2.   In *The Coercive Utopians* (Chicago, 1983), Rael Jean Isaac and her husband Eric Isaac deal in detail with the IPSA and related organisations. See also two learned articles by R.J. Isaac, in the New York Jewish review *Midstream*, in June-July 1980 and again in February 1981. The second of these was written to counter a critical rejoinder to the first from Robert Borosage, Director of the IPS. The quotation comes from this second article.

3.   In *Myths and Realities of the 'Soviet Threat'* proceedings of a 1979 IPS conference.

4.   'Ritual Dance of the Superpowers', in *The Nation* (New York), 9 April 1985.

5.   *Washington Times*, 9 September 1985.

6.   Special Forces of Soviet GRU (military intelligence).

7.   For full details, see Brian Crozier, 'Who's Next for Russia's Killer Squads?' in *The Times*, 30 December 1983, based on a lengthy conversation with a senior KGB defector. Since then my unnamed defector,

Vladimir Kuzichkin, has told his own story: *INSIDE THE KGB: Myth and Reality* (Andre Deutsch, London, 1990).
8.   *Midstream*, June-July 1990 (see 1. above).

12. The IPS: The Letelier Affair

In Chapter 6 I dealt briefly with the Letelier affair. This is a fuller version. The date has become a kind of landmark: 21 September 1976. That morning, Detective Stanley Wilson, of the Washington DC Homicide Squad, was first on the scene after a booby-trapped car had exploded on Embassy Row. Inside the remains of the car were two charred corpses and one injured man, who survived.

One of the dead occupants was Orlando Letelier, 44, a former ambassador of the late President Salvador Allende's extreme left regime in Chile which, three years earlier, had been overthrown in a military coup led by General Augusto Pinochet. A married couple were in the car. The husband, who was driving, was the survivor. His wife, Mrs Ronni Karpen Moffit, died.

In Washington, some years later, ex-Detective Wilson told me what had happened. He was now 'ex-Detective' because the investigation he conducted caused embarrassment in places high and low, and he was eased out of the police. The dead ambassador carried around with him a bulky suitcase, containing letters and other documents, including an address book and a diary, all of which Wilson read with fascination.

Much of this material was in Spanish which, as it happened, Wilson spoke fluently through the happy accident of having been brought up in the Panama Canal zone, and having an Hispanic mother. It is interesting to speculate what might have happened if a non-Spanish speaker had been on duty on Embassy Row that day. Quite possibly, nothing further would have been heard of the Letelier documents. Instead, Wilson's curiosity started a *cause célèbre*, more 'celebrated' by far than the assassination of a foreign ex-diplomat would otherwise have been.

Although Stanley Wilson could read the material he had found, he

was in no position to evaluate its significance. His next move, therefore, was to take photocopies of the documents he had found and show
them to a friend of his; as it happens, a man already mentioned more
than once in these pages: Alfonso Tarabochia, linguist and Chief Investigator of the Senate Subcommittee on Internal Security.

Tarabochia whistled as he read his way through and one sensational
find succeeded another. They showed, beyond reasonable doubt, that
the murdered diplomat had been on the secret payroll of Fidel Castro's
Intelligence service, the DGI. That was interesting enough in itself.
What made it several degrees more sensational was that the late Orlando
Letelier had also been on the payroll, openly this time, of the Institute
for Policy Studies, as the first Director of its overseas offshoot, the
Transnational Institute (TNI) in Amsterdam.

I am not suggesting that the IPS was aware of Letelier's DGI connection. Indeed, it would be fair to assume that, in his own interest,
Letelier would have concealed it from his American friends.

According to one of the books which inevitably followed, *Assassination on Embassy Row,*[1] Stanley Wilson also talked to the press attaché
at the Chilean embassy (which, by now of course, represented the
Pinochet government), whose name was Rafael Otero. 'I've got something to show you,' Wilson is quoted as saying. 'And by the way, who
is "Tati"?'

The answer was that 'Tati' was Beatriz Allende, the dead President's daughter, who was now living in Cuba. The 'something' Wilson
wanted to show Otero was a letter from Tati to Letelier.

Of all the Letelier documents, the most sensational was undoubtedly
that letter from Beatriz Allende to Orlando Letelier. The date on it was
8 May 1975, and she wrote it from Havana. A short note of only 12
lines, it contained the following key passage:

> I know that Altamirano[2] wants to be in touch with you to find a
> solution to the problems we have here and he has asked me to let you
> know that, from here, we shall send you, in the name of the Party, one
> thousand dollars (1,000) a month to support your work. For now, I am
> sending you five thousand, to avoid having to make monthly pay-
> ments.

There was a further reference to payments in a later letter from Tati to

Letelier, dated 20 August 1976:

> In addition, I am sending you five thousand dollars, to cover the instalments from August to December inclusive. I know this isn't much in relation to the needs of the work, but it isn't possible to get more out of this poor Party. Wouldn't it be a good idea for you to talk so that others too might contribute?

That Letelier did get monthly payments from Havana, through Beatriz Allende, is not in dispute. What is hotly disputed by the IPS is that these funds came from Cuban Intelligence.

There are, in fact, four competing versions of the origin of the money. Version 1 came from Tati herself, in a letter to *The Washington Post* in April 1977, in which she said the funds had been raised by 'progressive peoples throughout the world'[3]. Version 2 came more than three years later, from another interested party, Isabel Letelier, widow of Orlando, who claimed in a letter to the *New York Times* that the money had been raised in 'Western Europe and the United States'[4].

Version 3, a variation of Version 2, came from Peter Weiss and Robert Borosage of IPS, who claimed that the money had been raised from 'Churches and unions throughout Western Europe'[5].

The first two accounts contradict each other, and neither is very convincing. The phrase 'progressive peoples of the world' is meaningless to the uninitiated. In Communist semantics, however, it meant the 'peoples' of countries living under Communist totalitarian regimes, and thereby denied free expression — for instance, the USSR, the satellite regimes of Eastern Europe, Cuba, etc. As for the claim by Isabel Letelier that the money was raised in Western Europe and the United States, if true, it would make no sense that Letelier's monthly instalments should have been paid from Havana.

The same objection applies to the variant proposed by Peter Weiss and Robert Borosage, which is open to a further objection: that it contradicts Version 4, offered by Borosage alone, in his capacity as Director of the IPS, in a revealing exchange of letters with Edward Leigh, a British Conservative Member of Parliament. Leigh kindly made these letters available to me on hearing of my interest in the matter.

In a letter to the London *Daily Telegraph* of 8 June, Leigh had described Letelier as 'an agent of Cuban Intelligence'. This kind of item tends to cross the Atlantic at its own speed, and in time it was drawn to the attention of Borosage, who wrote to Edward Leigh on 16 August, calling for a retraction. Leigh's reply, dated 9 September, was succinct:

> I have your letter of 16 August to hand. Perhaps you would care to tell me what you think was the precise nature of the relationship between the late Mr Letelier and Mr Julián Toreros Rio [*sic:* the correct name was Julián Torres Rizo — BC] of the Cuban Intelligence service, and what you think Letelier used to make of the regular monthly sum of $1,000 he received from that gentleman?

Responding to Leigh on 15 November 1985, Borosage stated that Beatriz Allende was Treasurer of the Chilean Socialist Party. Without saying so specifically, he seemed to imply that the reference to 'the Party' in Tati's first letter related, not to the Cuban Communist Party, as Leigh seemed to have assumed, but to the Chilean Socialist Party (of which ex-Senator Carlos Altamirano, whom she mentioned, was a leader).

As to the purpose of the payments, Borosage added that the work referred to was hardly espionage; its purpose was to enable Letelier to help other members of the party who were seeking asylum in the United States and Canada. Another purpose was to support his international efforts to put pressure on the military dictatorship in his country to bring democracy back to Chile.

Borosage had enclosed a letter he had received from Clarence Kelley, the then Director of the FBI, dated 8 July 1977, to a Congressman (William Cotter), in which he declined to comment on the Letelier case on the ground that it was under criminal investigation. He also sent Leigh copies of a heavily censored report on Letelier's death, dated 10 January 1977. The whole of the first page of this report was deleted, and most of three paragraphs on the next page. This second page (or what was left of it) summarised the letter of 8 May 1975 from Tati to Orlando Letelier, and made the following comment:

> The FBI is at the present time not in possession of any information developed from investigation in this matter which indicates that Letelier is or ever has been an intelligence asset of the Cuban government.

In receipt of this admittedly impressive documentation, Edward Leigh (a barrister by profession), naturally decided to do some further research. A friend put him in touch with Reed Irvine[6] of Accuracy in Media.

Reed Irvine was, in fact, one of the journalists who broke the story of the contents of Letelier's briefcase.[7] In a letter to Leigh's friend (who wishes to remain nameless), Irvine declared:

> Much as I regret to say it, the FBI was clearly covering up for Letelier. I detailed in the enclosed report the misleading translations and omission of relevant information from the English translations of the Letelier file. The agent in charge had no explanation of these things.

The 'agent in charge' was in fact Carter Cornick, mentioned in Chapter 7. The 'report' he had enclosed for Edward Leigh was the issue of his newsletter dated 1 October 1980. In this he mentioned that he had contacted Cornick who had said that the evidence did not prove Letelier to be a Cuban agent. Reed Irvine was interested to note that Cornick, although a Spanish speaker, had released inaccurate translations of some of the key documents. Incredibly, as he put it, the English translation of Tati Allende's simple letter in the FBI file was so distorted that its true meaning was concealed. The AIM Report quoted the FBI version of the key paragraph, as follows (distorted passage italicised):

> I know that Altamirano wishes to talk to you concerning the problems *we have here and has told me that we will send you $1,000 from the Party* to support your work.

This was evidently more than Borosage could stand, as his reply, dated 14 February 1986 made clear.

If Mr Leigh (he wrote) chose to believe 'the rabid Mr Irvine' in preference to the FBI and the Justice Department, the good sense of the *New York Times, Washington Post* and other establishment journals, then there was no point in continuing the discussion.

Edward Leigh could well have left the matter there, but felt Borosage had failed to deal with the points of substance raised by Reed Irvine. So, on 18 March 1986, he returned to the attack:

It seems to me that your opinion of the character of Mr Irvine is hardly relevant to the accuracy or otherwise of the points he made about Mr Letelier.

You must surely have been aware of the contents of the *AIM Report* of 1 October 1980, and presumably would have prepared an attempted refutation of it at the time.

Your failure to send me any such commentary would seem to suggest an inability on your part to deal with the points raised by Accuracy in Media.

A lengthy gap followed. Then, on 10 July, Borosage wrote again, to say that the FBI and the Justice Department had refuted the *AIM Report*. Borosage and his colleagues joined this refutation, in that Letelier was not an agent of Castro or of the DGI. In fact, he was what he presented himself to be: a Chilean patriot, rallying those who opposed Pinochet's dictatorship. That was why he had been assassinated. Irvine's attempt to slander 'a victim of political terrorism' had failed.

Pressure, even by the right, (he went on) on the Reagan Administration had failed to reverse that conclusion, and it was sad that Mr Leigh should lend his pen to such calumnies. He had written thinking of Edward Leigh as a man of reason, not somebody who would pick Irvine in preference to the FBI and the Justice Department.

In a further rejoinder, Leigh pointed out that Borosage's letter of 10 July 'simply reiterated your *ad hominem* approach to the subject, which doesn't really help anybody. (....) Despite the manful posthumous efforts to excuse them, I cannot help feeling that if Mr Letelier's former contacts with Cuban agents like Julio Rizo [*sic*] had been paralleled by similar ones between right-wing activists and the CIA, the latter would never hear the last of it from the Institute of Policy Studies and indeed, yourself.'

And there, at last, the inconclusive correspondence ended.

It has to be said that Robert Borosage had mustered a formidable, or at any rate formidable-looking, array of forces. And yet, their combined 'good sense' does not stand up to critical scrutiny. Borosage's sins of omission are as weighty and culpable as the real but unstated reasons for the curious reticence of the FBI and the Justice Department.

Let us look at both the sins and the reasons.

The conclusion that Letelier was indeed working for Cuban Intelligence is inescapable from the following circumstances. First, Tati Allende was living in Havana not in her capacity as Treasurer of the Chilean Socialist Party but because she was the wife of Luis Fernández Oña, a section chief of the Americas Department of the Cuban Communist Party, a branch of Cuban Intelligence. Secondly, as a number of the Letelier documents make abundantly clear, his communications with Tati were handled by a senior Cuban Intelligence officer named Julián Torres Rizo.

In his 1982 testimony (see Chapter 10), Gerardo Peraza reported that Toreros Rizo had 'been recruited and prepared as an Intelligence officer at least for two years before he came to the United States'. In fact, he had been identified, notably by Alfonso Tarabochia, in his capacity as Chief Investigator of the Internal Security Subcommittee of the US Senate, as the Cuban DGI's station chief in New York, under official 'cover' as First Secretary to the Cuban mission to the United Nations.

Torres Rizo made his diplomatic bag available to Letelier for this traffic, as the briefcase documents confirm. It is surely highly unlikely that this facility would have been made available to the Chilean if the Cubans had not deemed it to be in the interests of the DGI. Torres Rizo was later expelled from the US for his spying activities. He turned up in Grenada as Cuba's ambassador to the 'Marxist' government of Maurice Bishop.

As for the other Cuban Intelligence man, Luis Fernández Oña, Tati's husband, he had helped to arrange Che Guevara's ill-fated Bolivian expedition, and played a key role in Santiago during the Allende years. It is important to note that the advent of the extreme left Allende government in Chile enabled Fidel Castro to shift his Intelligence operations in Latin America from Paris to Santiago: a move that was followed by a massive increase in terrorism in neighbouring Argentina and Uruguay. In the jargon of the American Intelligence community, Letelier was undoubtedly a major Cuban 'asset'.

Another detail: in Tati's later and longer letter to Letelier dated 20 August 1976, she mentioned problems in conveying certain documents to him, and said she would try to arrange a channel to him via 'the comrades of the USSR and Germany'. This passage, too, as Reed Irvine discovered, had been omitted from the FBI's translations of the Letelier documents. A strange omission, for which Carter Cornick was unable to account when Irvine challenged him. And there were further strange omissions from the FBI file, most notably of a number of the most significant names in Letelier's address book. The names left out included those of Torres Rizo himself, of two Soviet embassy officers, a number of East Germans, and of nearly all Cubans living in Cuba, among them the Cuban Foreign Minister, Raúl Roa, and the leading Communist Party official, Carlos Rafael Rodríguez.

It is clear from the contents of the briefcase that Letelier's activities far exceeded aiding other Chilean Socialists to seek asylum or bringing pressure to bear on the Chilean military dictatorship to restore democracy. To give one example: why did Letelier help to meet the expense of sending a former US Congressman, Michael Harrington, to Mexico? The question is interesting in itself, even though the sum he provided was only $174, but the occasion was more interesting still: the purpose of the journey was for Harrington to take part in the Third Session of the so-called International Commission of Inquiry into the Crimes of the Chilean Military Junta. A worthy, truly Chilean cause, it may be thought; except that the 'Commission' was an offshoot of the Soviet-controlled international front, the World Peace council, based, as was its parent body, in Helsinki.[8]

For that matter, Letelier also played an important role in the Church Committee's witch hunt into the CIA's Latin American operations and in the press campaign attacking alleged CIA operations against Allende in Chile; certainly an interest of the Chilean Socialist Party in exile, but surely of greater interest still to Cuban and Soviet intelligence?

Against this background, Robert Borosage's comment, in his correspondence with Edward Leigh, that Letelier's work was 'hardly espionage' is highly disingenuous. He was in fact an *agent of influence* for the DGI, and therefore for the KGB. Here, then, was a man who had occupied high diplomatic posts, who had been appointed by the IPS to head its overseas activities through the TNI in the Netherlands. I am not suggesting that the Directors of IPS, and Richard Barnet in particular, were aware of Letelier's Cuban Intelligence connections at the time the appointment was made. What *is* clear, beyond all reasonable doubt, is that the Cubans were using the IPS for their own purposes; in other words, that the IPS was indeed a front for Cuban Intelligence, as I had said in my letter to *The Spectator*.

Why did the FBI not investigate the political side of the case? The answer to this question can only be found in the political context of the events.

The first point to grasp is that the assassination of Orlando Letelier raised two entirely separate issues. The first, and most immediately important, was that a serious crime had been committed: the murder, or homicide, of the two victims. The other issue was one of security and intelligence: was Letelier working, or linked, with the Intelligence service of a hostile foreign State? Under its all-embracing charter, the Federal Bureau of Investigation has a dual responsibility — to investigate crime, and to defend the security and integrity of the United States. In the Letelier case, it rightly gave precedence to investigating the homicide and bringing the culprits to justice. Wrongly, it took no action on the other issue: there was *no investigation* of the security and intelligence issues raised by the discovery of Letelier's confidential papers.

The criminal aspect of the case does not concern us here, but for the record, this is what happened. An American living in Chile, Michael Townley, was expelled to the United States in April 1977. A professional assassin for the head of Chile's secret police, DINA, General Manuel Contreras, he was indicted but not extradited. Contreras had resigned on 21 March, and DINA was dissolved in August. The failure to investigate the security aspects of the case was probably a tacit one, and therefore unrecorded. It was politically impossible, at the time, for any such investigation to be initiated, and even if there had been no political obstacles, a security investigation would have run into legal difficulties.

At the time of the Letelier murder and during the subsequent criminal investigations, the FBI was the defendant in a lawsuit brought by IPS (see Chapter 8) The legal proceedings mentioned were spread over five years between 1974 and 1979. Thus, the case was still *sub judice* at the time of the murder. Letelier was a salaried employee of the IPS, and his papers naturally showed the degree of his involvement with the Institute. It is therefore safe to assume that the Bureau would have been under strong, indeed irresistible, pressure to desist from any investigation which might incriminate the IPS. (In due course, as we noted earlier, the FBI lost its case and thereafter was prohibited from conducting any surveillance of the IPS.)

In the pre-trial hearings, US Attorney Eugene Propper declared that the FBI had found 'no evidence that Letelier was working for any government, either Cuban, Chilean or other'.[9] It should be borne in mind, however, that his statement was made in response to a defence request to be given access to the briefcase papers on the ground that they contained material that might exculpate the defendants. The reason the FBI found no such evidence is, quite simply, that it wasn't looking for any. Instead, it was resolutely looking the other way!

It could of course be argued that precisely because the FBI itself was at the receiving end of an IPS lawsuit, it should have had a strong incentive to delve into the political aspects of the case, in the hope of finding material that would justify its earlier decision to keep an eye on the IPS on the grounds of national security.

Had the political climate and circumstances been more favourable, this might conceivably have happened, but they could hardly have been less propitious. The post-Watergate mood was in full flood. One of the most striking symptoms of it was the presence of the IPS, or people connected with it, in positions of power or influence in the Administration. It would be an exaggeration to say that the IPS was virtually in power under President Jimmy Carter, but not by very much. To give a few examples:

> *W. Anthony Lake*, appointed by President Carter as Director of the State Department's Policy Planning staff, was consultant associate to the Center for International Policy, an organisation closely linked with the IPS. Indeed, Letelier himself had been on the board of the Center.
>
> *David Aaron*, another consultant associate of the Center, was made Deputy to Carter's National Security Adviser, Zbigniew Brzezinski.
>
> *William Miller*, also with IPS connections, played an important role as staff director to the Senate Intelligence Committee.
>
> *Brady Tyson*, appointed Special Adviser to Ambassador Andrew Young at the United Nations. Tyson was a founding member of the North American Conference on Latin America (NACLA), an IPS affiliate closely connected with the Fidel Castro regime. Before joining NACLA, Tyson had been expelled from a teaching post in Brazil for 'disturbing the social and political order'.[10] Shortly after his appointment to the UN post, he publicly apologised for America's role in Vietnam.

As for Richard Barnet himself, although he did not occupy any official post, he was undoubtedly among the most important figures in Carter's policy-making. He was named as a member of 'the New Foreign-Policy Establishment' in the New York Jewish review, *Commentary*, in the summer of 1980.

Against this background, it would have been astonishing if the FBI had wished to tangle with the IPS by launching an investigation, and hardly surprising that Bureau officials should have found little to say when challenged on the issue.

A Parallel Case

In another book on the Letelier affair, *Death in Washington* (1980), the authors, Donald Freed and Dr Fred Simon Landis, alleged that a former CIA officer, David Atlee Phillips, had been involved in the murder. Mr Phillips sued them for libel, but took 4½ years to clear his name. On 15 February 1986, before the US District Court in Washington, the authors agreed to the terms of a published retraction and paid undisclosed damages. Mr Phillips's legal costs were met by Challenge, Inc. a legal action group set up to defend former US intelligence officers.[11]

Notes

1. By John Dinges and Saul Landau. Landau, a Fellow of IPS, will merit a chapter of this book. The (perfectly legitimate) purpose of their own book was to indict the Pinochet regime for organising the assassination of Letelier.
2. Senator Carlos Altamirano headed an extremist faction in Allende's Socialist Party.
3. Rael Jean Isaac, in *Midstream* (New York), February 1981.
4. Ibid.
5. Peter Weiss and Robert L. Borosage, in *Midstream*, February 1981.
6. See Ch.6.
7. Another was my friend Robert Moss, in three issues of *The Econo-*

mist's confidential bulletin, F*oreign Report,* which are of enduring interest (2 March, 6 April and 10 August 1977).

8.   Isaac, *Ibid.*

9.   John Rees, 'Murdered KGB Agent's papers Show Payoffs to Congressmen: Inside the Letelier Briefcase', *The Review of the News,* 27 April 1977.

10.   *Foreign Report* (London), No.1499, 10 August 1977.

11.   *New York Times,* 16 February 1986; *The Washington Post,* 17 February 1986.

13. IPS: The Agee Interlude

It was natural that the most notorious of the CIA's modest handful of defectors at that time should find refuge with the Institute for Policy Studies. For Philip Agee, it was a refuge in more senses than one. An ideological refuge with a naturally sympathetic organisation; and a physical refuge when he was expelled from Britain in 1976. If a man is on the run, he seeks out those who will welcome him, and neither turn him away nor turn him in. It was as natural for Philip Agee to go to the IPS as for Kim Philby to go to Moscow when he was unmasked in Beirut.

Agee has told his own story twice[1]; indeed, obligingly, his second account appeared in London when I was about to write this chapter. This, however, does not make the chapter unnecessary, for his two autobiographies, though very lengthy, omit many relevant names and details. Although the motives of traitors through the ages have been diverse, the act of treachery is a transfer of allegiance from one country to another. Neither Agee nor Philby had mercenary motives; both were ideological defectors.

Philip Agee joined the Central Intelligence Agency in 1957 and spent most of his career in Latin America. He left the service in 1969, stating that he had resigned in order to re-marry and settle down in Mexico. Later, he gave a different version, claiming that he had become wholly disillusioned with CIA policy but had not wished to admit it for fear of being labelled a security risk.

His former employers put the facts in a somewhat different light. At the time of his departure from the Agency he was said to be already under a cloud for heavy drinking and womanising. He had then exceeded all reasonable limits by kidnapping his two children from their mother's home in Virginia and taking them to live with him in Mexico City. Already of course, he had separated from his wife, who thereupon threatened to blow her husband's cover unless he returned the children to her. Indeed, he was ordered to do so by the American Ambassador to Mexico and the CIA chief in the Federal Capital. He declined and the CIA, not unnaturally, asked him to resign. He did so, initially without apparent rancour.

Between the years 1969 and 1972, he studied for an advanced degree at the National University of Mexico, went into business with friends in that country, Canada and the USA, had a long sojourn in Cuba followed by a lengthy stay in Paris. His guiding influence in the period appear to have been the French publisher François Maspéro, who specialised in extreme left material. He wanted to write a book on his experiences and Maspéro encouraged him to do so. In his 1987 book, he gives a fairly full account of his life during this period, and of his relationship with Maspéro.

By the time Agee landed in London in October 1972, his behaviour had attracted the attention of various security services, including of course the French Security Service, the DST.

Was Agee already, in 1972, working for the other side? In *On the Run* (p.29), he is "economical with the truth". He ascribes his ideological conversion to the eye-opening experience of seeing the Cuban revolution for himself:

> Such a contrast with the other Latin America that I knew, where Kennedy's grandiose Alliance for Progress had been a near-total failure. In Cuba they had all but wiped out illiteracy and started enormous investments in educational programs of all kinds. Radical agrarian and urban reforms had changed forever the lot of peasants and renters. The Cubans were trying, at least, to build a new society free of corruption and exploitation. No question that they were still far from their goals, and they were quick to admit it. On balance, though, revolutionary Cuba made the rest of Latin America look like it was in a political and social Stone Age.

To be starry-eyed about the Cuban revolution is an affliction common among the idealistic young, and in no sense an indictable offence. However, the facts not mentioned in his books suggest that Agee may have come under Soviet control not later than 1964, five years before his forced resignation from the CIA. It is known that he met the senior KGB officer, Vitaly Petrovich Semënov, in Montevideo in 1964. After the Soviet take over of the DGI (mentioned several times in this book), Semënov became one of the three KGB officers supervising plans, operations and sensitive projects at DGI headquarters in Havana. He was promoted to KGB General and had an office next door to the DGI Intelligence Chief, José Méndez Cominches. General Semënov was present both in Havana and in Moscow at the exact time of Agee's visits to those places: a fact which may, or may not, be coincidental.

In both his books, Agee is frank about his primary and constant aim: his resolve to damage Western security to the maximum by revealing the names of CIA personnel, giving clues to the identity of others, and exposing details of the CIA operations of which he had knowledge in the Latin American area. His acceptance by the KGB was such that the Soviets granted the DGI permission to allow Agee to make use of their data banks in Cuba to fill in the blanks in his own research, a rare privilege for an aspiring Western author.

Having set up his base in the UK, Agee proved himself a dedicated 'socialist' in the Soviet cause. Clearly well briefed, and with a mission to accomplish, he knew exactly where to go for help. He started with the International Commission for Peace and Disarmament in London. From there, he went on to make contact with the (Trotskyist) Workers' Revolutionary Party and other extremist groups.

In London, as had happened earlier in Paris, he was often seen in the company of known Soviet or Cuban intelligence officers, thereby causing the overworked British Security Service (MI-5) a considerable expenditure of man-hours to monitor his movements. His most frequent contact seems to have been with one Torres Rodríguez, with whom he had at least 30 meetings.

Humberto Modesto Torres Rodríguez, the man's full name, was accredited as a Second Secretary at the Cuban embassy in London, where he arrived in 1975. At that time, the DGI station chief had been identified as Guido Sánchez Robert. When the latter left in 1976, Torres was promoted to First Secretary and became the acting Station chief.

Obviously bothered by the attention he had aroused, Agee made a half-hearted attempt to live secretly. One of his favourite haunts was

the British Museum, but whenever he left he found he was being followed, so he gave up the attempt and stopped trying to elude the men
assigned to tail him.

Apart from such minor inconveniences, however, he was free to carry
on writing. In 1974, two years after his arrival in England, the well-
known publisher Allen Lane issued Agee's *INSIDE THE COMPANY:
A CIA Diary*. As a result of his disclosures, hundreds of CIA agents
and informants had to be recalled or relocated. Those in the know noted
certain teasing passages in the book implying DGI involvement in attempts to hoodwink and confuse American Intelligence. Dates were
altered here and there; portions of one operation were transferred to
another; the years of research had helped the author to lay his booby
traps.

A year later, he reached a mass audience when Penguin Books published a paperback edition with an eye-catching cover picturing a bugged
portable typewriter. Throughout this period, the British government
kept a dignified silence. It knew what was going on, through the Security Service, but so far Agee had done nothing that directly affected
British security, at least as far as could be judged.

Agee's own comments on the British attitude during this first period
are worth quoting. In an introduction to a book published in 1983[2] he
wrote as follows:

> ...by early 1975, when the book came out [in paperback] , there
> was still no way to explain why British authorities had failed to pre-
> vent my use of British research facilities and a British publisher. No
> less mysterious was the seeming acquiescence in Britain to my con-
> tinuous travels in and out of the country for lectures, political rallies,
> press conferences, films and television projects — all dedicated to
> focusing sharp attention on the CIA's presence and activities through-
> out Western Europe, Canada and Latin America.

In the coded language of the professional provocateur, Agee was not so
much complimenting the British on their libertarian values as calling
attention to British indifference to the presence of an active anti-American subversive in their midst. He was, in fact, talking indirectly to the
American government and people, and incidentally poking fun at the
British for their apparent unawareness of what he was up to.

In so doing, he was doubtless well aware that there were stringent limits to what a British Home Secretary could do when faced with reports from Agee's tailing team about his conversations in Spanish with DGI officers posing as peace-loving cultural attachés and the like.

Suddenly, at the end of 1975 Agee found himself at the centre of a storm ultimately of his own making, but the consequences of which he had certainly not planned. On the night of 23 December, the CIA station chief in Athens, Richard Welch, was shot dead late at night when he returned home from a party at the residence of the American Ambassador. The assassin, a masked man, had emerged from a car, shot Welch three times, then been driven off by two masked companions. The killers were never caught. Mingling with the sombre crowd at Welch's funeral were two KGB men who took pictures of the CIA mourners.

It turned out that Agee had been involved in exposing Welch and other Agency officers, through a newsletter named *CounterSpy*, of which he was the original editor. The group behind the newsletter styled itself the 'Organising Committee for a Fifth Estate'. Agee was one of the original members; so was Marcus Raskin, of the IPS. And so, appropriately, was Victor Marchetti, another defector from the CIA. After the assassination of Welch, however, Raskin removed his name from the advisory board of *CounterSpy*[3].

Why 'a Fifth Estate'? 'What the American people need to help focus their massive resistance to techno-fascism is an alternative intelligence community — A Fifth Estate', was the way *CounterSpy* answered the question.

In the edition of *CounterSpy* in which Richard Welch had been identified, Agee wrote an article in which the following passage occurred:

> The most effective and important systematic efforts to combat the CIA that can be taken right now are, I think, the identification, exposure, and neutralisation of its people working abroad .... Having this information, the people victimised by the CIA and the economic exploitation that CIA enforces can bring pressure on their so-often compromised governments to expel the CIA people. And, in the absence of such expulsion, which will not be uncommon, the people themselves will have to decide what they must do to rid themselves of the CIA.

If this is not incitement to murder, it comes close to it. In *On the Run*[4] Agee excused the murder of Welch on the ground that the CIA had helped the Greek colonels set up a repressive fascist dictatorship. However, he added (with some cogency) that his publication had not been the first or only source to reveal the identity of the CIA station chief in Athens. Welch's name had appeared in a *Who's Who in the CIA* published in East Germany in 1968 by one Julius Maders. Agee comments: 'I was in it along with hundreds of other officers and quite a few mistaken names. It was most likely a KGB publication.'

The only critical note in this reference to the East German publication (which he attributes, no doubt correctly, to the KGB) is that it included 'quite a few mistaken names'. Agee evidently decided to make a better job of it; and indeed, if one wants to expose secret Intelligence men, it is surely better to get the names right and leave out the wrong ones.

The news of Welch's murder reached Agee by telephone in Rome where he had checked in at the local YMCA (the C for Christian evidently not considered a cause for boycotting the establishment). The bearer of the news was a compatriot and associate of his in London, Steve Weissman, who reminded him that Welch's name and address had also been published in late November in the newspaper *Athens News*. He warned Agee that the murder had aroused fierce emotions and hostility in Washington, where the offices of Fifth Estate were virtually under siege. Agee's response was that Fifth Estate should not allow itself to be intimidated. Instead, it should: 'Put the blame on President and Congress, and the CIA itself, first, for what the Agency does, and second, for its incompetence in protecting people'.

In other words, if people were killed, that was their fault for belonging to Agee's former service, and the fault of the service for not protecting them. In retrospect, Agee must count himself lucky in not having been at the receiving end of his own philosophy of legitimate exposure.

After an internal dispute, *CounterSpy* was temporarily closed, then re-launched under a new editor. Thereupon, Agee and a group of alienated ex-colleagues decided to start a new magazine, under the title *Covert Action Information Bulletin*[5]. Now Agee and his friends got down seriously to the business of exposing their former colleagues. Over a period, the names of more than 2,000 were given. The technique was simple: consult the official State Department registries. By some lapse of the bureaucratic mind, CIA officers were indirectly identified, by the adjoining abbreviation FRS (Foreign Service Reserve), whereas 'straight' career diplomats were designated FSO (Foreign Service Officer). Wise after the event, the State Department changed it ways, and in 1982, the Intelligence Identities Protection Act became law, providing for the prosecution and possible imprisonment of offenders, including any found living overseas.

One early issue of *Covert Action Information Bulletin* named Mr Richard Kinsman, CIA station chief in Kingston, Jamaica. His house was raked with machine-gun fire, but he escaped unhurt. On a visit to Jamaica in 1976, Agee attacked the Agency in a series of meetings, and named nine American diplomats, whom he accused of seeking to destabilise the island. These remarks were helpful, if not to the CIA and the State Department, then at least to the Cuban DGI which, at the time, was trying to extend its own influence in Jamaica.

Doubtless the Cubans knew that they had a friend in their midst. After all, Agee made half a dozen visits to Cuba while writing *Inside the Company*, one of them lasting six months. He had had frequent meetings with DGI officers from Cuban embassies in Europe[6]. While in Havana, he had been allowed to consult what he called Cuban government 'documentation centres', in reality, DGI data banks. Any such access would have had to be authorised by the KGB General Semënov, mentioned earlier.[7]

It is hardly surprising that an early issue of *Covert Action* drew attention to the role of Cuban counter-intelligence in exposing the CIA, and praised the work of Cuban State Security.

However much the DGI men in Jamaica may have appreciated Agee's efforts, not all Jamaicans took the same view. One who did not was the President of the Jamaica Manufacturers' Association, Mr Winston Mahfood, who accused Agee of 'spouting hatred and antagonism since his arrival'.[8]

Philip Agee's second burst of notoriety came towards the end of 1976. On 15 November, the Home Secretary in Britain's Labour government, Merlyn Rees, informed him that a deportation order was being made against him under Section 3(5) (b) of the 1971 Immigration Act. A similar order was issued against a younger fellow-American, Mark

Hosenball. A letter delivered to Agee by the police stated that the Home Secretary had based his section on the following grounds[9]:

> 1.   He had maintained regular contacts harmful to the security of the United Kingdom with foreign intelligence officers;
> 2.   He had been and continued to be involved in disseminating information harmful to the security of the United Kingdom;
> 3.   He had aided and counselled others in obtaining information for publication which could be harmful to the security of the United Kingdom.

The deportation orders had been approved in advance by the Prime Minister, Mr James (later Lord) Callaghan, and caused a sensation. Inquiring reporters were told by a Home Office spokesman that there had been no pressure from the US authorities to take action against Agee. The decision to deport him was entirely a British decision on grounds of British security.

Mark Hosenball was a journalist working on the London *Evening Standard*. Before that he had worked with *Time Out*, a 'fun revolutionary' magazine aimed at young readers, for which Hosenball had written articles on the operations of the ultra-secret General Communications Headquarters (GCHQ) in Cheltenham and on alleged CIA activities in Britain[10]. Compared to Agee, he was a minor figure; or perhaps, more accurately, he was junior to Agee in the latter's loose revolutionary hierarchy in exile.

Mr Rees, by common consent, belonged to the decent, moderate midstream of the Labour Party, a social democrat to his marrow, a patriotic Welsh Briton who was probably appalled, although it would have been politically very difficult for him to say so, at the extremist penetration of the party of Attlee and Bevin in which he had started his career.

The Home Secretary made a statement on the Agee-Hosenball affair in the House of Commons on 18 November. He reminded his fellow MPs that, under the Immigration Act, the government had powers to remove people from the country. There was no statutory right of appeal where the ground for deportation was that it was in the interests of national security, and therefore conducive to the public good. However, representations could be made to an independent Home Office advisory panel.

Mr Rees added that his decision had been taken 'solely in the interests of the security of this country and of the personal safety of individuals in the service of the Crown' and that he was 'not prepared to go into greater detail...about the grounds for my decision'.

As might have been expected, the storm broke immediately above the Home Secretary's head, and over the months that followed, it gathered further strength and virulence. Had the deportation order taken immediate effect, the storm might have been even greater. it might even have endangered the Callaghan government. But there is nothing like the finality of an accomplished fact. The deed would have been done, not to be undone. As it was, by allowing representations to the advisory panel, Mr Rees invited the subversives to do their worst. And they responded.

Within 24 hours, Agee's ideological allies had set up an 'Agee-Hosenball Defence Committee' and various left-wing MPs and organisations were protesting vociferously. One of the protesting groups was the National Union of Journalists (NUJ), which described Merlyn Rees's decision as 'smacking of a police State'.

Not all journalists, however, considered themselves bound to toe the line set by their left-wing union leaders. A number of them, indeed, wrote objective articles about the affair. Thus on 17 November 1976, the day before the Home Secretary's statement in the House, Hosenball's employer, the *Evening Standard*, editorialised:

> Philip Agee is an agent who became disillusioned, turned extreme Socialist and resigned in protest against US policies in Latin America. He was a CIA man for 12 years and served nine of them in Ecuador, Uruguay and Mexico. After he resigned in 1969 he went to live in Cornwall and it was there that he wrote his book *INSIDE THE COMPANY: A CIA Diary* in which he shocked his former employers by disclosing the identities of dozens of serving CIA men and women. He did it with the help of left-wing extremist groups in Britain, including the International Socialists, the Workers' Revolutionary Party and the International Marxist Group. He is connected with the 'Fifth Estate', the American organisation which has named the CIA Athens chief Mr Richard Welch who was later murdered by Greek extremists.

In a long article in the *Sunday Telegraph*, the well-known journalist

Christopher Dobson, assisted by a team of investigative reporters, wrote:

> Questioned after Welch's death, Agee said: "I do not think there
> will be any further deaths because I think the people exposed will
> heed the demands of prudence and go home. And writing in
> *CounterSpy*, he called the CIA a sinister force and argued that the best
> way to defeat it was the 'identification, exposure and neutralisation of
> its people working abroad. (....)
> There are files on his activities among the dossiers of nearly every
> Western security service, and it is on this material and that gathered
> by Britain's own security services that Mr Rees had based his decision
> to deport Mr Agee. In June of this year he travelled to Germany to
> give evidence on behalf of the Baader-Meinhof gang who were trying
> to 'politicise' their defence in their trial for bombings, murder and
> bank robbery. The following month he went to Moscow to discuss the
> publication of his book.
> He has conducted a series of anti-CIA lectures under the auspices
> of a variety of militant left-wing organisations in this and other coun-
> tries. It was, however, Mr Winston Churchill, speaking in the House
> of Commons last Thursday, who hinted at the real charges being made
> against Mr Agee. Mr Churchill who, like his late grandfather, has his
> own sources of information, said: 'There will be particular concern to
> learn that individuals have been maintaining contacts with Cuban and
> Soviet bloc intelligence services. Agee vehemently denied that he
> works for the Russians or the Cubans. However, he agrees that he
> maintains close contacts with the Cubans. And, from the security
> services' point of view, it must be remembered that the Cuban secret
> service, the DGI, is completely controlled by the Soviet Union's KGB.

On the same day as Christopher Dobson's article appeared, Barry Powell
wrote in the mass circulation *News of the World*:

> The man leading a campaign to stop Philip Agee and Mark
> Hosenball being deported from Britain yesterday spelled out why they
> have gone to war on America's secret service and not Russia's. Phil
> Kelly, who works for a news agency called Interpress News Service,
> based in the Middle East, told me:
> 'Like Agee and Hosenball, I believe the CIA is intrinsically evil
> and its aims do not coincide with the people's choice.'
> I asked Kelly whether, in working with Agee and Hosenball, they

had considered also identifying other countries' secret services including Russia's infamous KGB. he said: 'That's just not the same. There is nothing wrong with Russian foreign policy. And anyway, the KGB only operates internally to repress subversive elements. It isn't designed as a counter-espionage system, unlike the CIA which is the biggest threat to the freedom of the world.[11]

Agee, who has denied any subversive links with Communist States, said yesterday that he had had frequent meetings with both the Russian and Cuban embassies in London. He also said he spent much of July and August in Russia discussing future revelations about the CIA and plans to expose another 500 agents throughout Europe.

Agee said he plans to publish a new book, called 'Who's Who and What They Do' in the New Year in Russia and eventually in Britain.

In mid-February 1977, Agee sent a final submission to Mr Rees in a letter delivered through Mrs Judith Hart, one of the group of concerned MPs in Mr Callaghan's party, not all of whom could be described as 'extremists'[12]. In it, he complained that he had still not been told of the substance of the allegations against him except that the Prime Minister had said privately that 'lives are at stake' because of his activities. He went on: 'I urge you to consider that my work on balance is serving the vital interests of people vastly greater in number and worth than any lives of the CIA employees.'

By then, both Agee and Hosenball had made their representations to the Home Office advisory panel, which had rejected them. On 15 February, Mr Rees announced in the Commons[13] that he had reached 'the clear conclusion' that in both cases his original decision must stand and that therefore he had made a deportation order against each of them. Amid the standard uproar from left-wing Labour MPs, Mr Rees said there was information in the case 'that can't be brought out without risking the lives of people who work for the State'. He added that he could not disregard the advice of the independent panel that had considered the matter. 'The people who shout,' he went on, 'are not the people who have had access to the papers. I have put the information which I have before an independent panel which I have not spoken to. The decision is mine at the end of the day. No Home Secretary could lightly disregard the advice that comes from the panel. I am not prepared to say any more than that.'

Agee's allies were prompt to respond. On 17 February 1977, in an editorial across the top of its front page, the *Morning Star*, organ of the Communist Party (CPGB), said the decision 'should be opposed by the entire Labour and trade union movement'. 'Today,' it went on ominously, 'a picket is to be held by the Agee-Hosenball Defence Committee outside the Home Office'.

On 23 February, the London *Daily Mail* reported that 'Mr Agee has not named any British agents in the many lectures and interviews he has given. However, British intelligence believes that Mr Agee could start naming British agents in future. It has been hinted that he would get the British names from his Cuban contacts who in turn are totally controlled by the Soviets and their secret police thugs, the KGB.'

That day, *The Guardian* recorded that Mr Agee had sought a declaration in the Scottish courts that the Home Secretary's powers did not extend to Scotland, but the Court of Session, meeting in Edinburgh on 22 February, had rejected this somewhat desperate plea. Agee had also failed in an attempt to persuade the European Human Rights Commission in Strasbourg to block the British government's move to deport him. The Commission decided that the claim was 'manifestly ill-founded', a decision it reached without even calling on the British government to reply to Agee's claim.[14]

The grand climax was a debate in the House of Commons on 3 May 1977, duly reported in Hansard for that day. Merlyn Rees opened with these words:

> The decision to deport has been mine and mine alone throughout and it was taken solely in the interests of this country. It was taken neither at the behest of nor after consultations, with the government of the United States or its agencies, including the CIA.[15]

Mr Rees went on:

> Those who believe that this is the way that the government of this country takes place [sic] are talking with great naivety. It is more than six months since the original notices of intention to deport were served so there has been no unseemly haste. The courts have reviewed the cases and have seen no reason to interfere with the way I have acted.

There were, of course, impassioned denunciations of the Home Secretary, and of the United States, from left-wing Labour Members, and more sober voices in defence of the government's actions. By far the most interesting speech was contributed by Mr (later Sir) Stephen Hastings, a Conservative backbencher who made his early career in MI-6. He said:

> What has emerged in our debates is what the security services are up against. They are up against an organisation which has not met one word of criticism yet in this debate: the KGB, a vast instrument of internal oppression and external subversion (....)
>
> There was a press conference at the end of last year when a question was put to Agee: 'Why do you not attack the KGB as well as the CIA?' That seems to be a perfectly reasonable question. He replied: 'Because Russia long ago had its Socialist Revolution. Russia is safe.'

Stephen Hastings went on to mention the known facts of Agee's contacts with the senior KGB man Semënov. He added:

> It has been alleged publicly on more than one occasion that Agee frequented the KGB and had contacts with them in London. He denies it, but he admits frequent meetings with Soviet and Cuban embassies. Last summer he said that two years ago he spent some days in Russia to discuss his plans to expose CIA agents. Some people, certainly in the United States, would call that treachery but never mind. With whom does he imagine he was discussing these plans? The Russian Ballet? Moscow Dynamo? I hardly think so. He must have known perfectly clearly with whom he was discussing them.

In the division at the end of the debate, there was a government majority of 138 votes to 34; all those against were Labour backbenchers. That was it. Agee and his friends had lost their battle, and Agee was going to have to leave Britain and seek refuge elsewhere. He records[16] that at the height of the agitation by the Agee-Hosenball Defence Committee, he had had a call from Saul Landau in Amsterdam. Landau had taken over from the murdered Orlando Letelier as acting Director of the Amsterdam-based overseas branch of the IPS, the Transnational Institute (TNI). Landau was authorised to offer him a fellowship and help in persuading the Dutch government to grant him a residence permit. He had gratefully accepted the offer. He sailed for Holland on 3 June 1977.

In fact, for about a month Agee slept in the dormitory at the TNI building, 'a five-storey red brick turn-of-the-century house facing the Vincent Van Gogh Museum'[17]. He also had office space there. The respected Dutch newspaper *De Telegraaf* reported that Agee would continue his work at TNI, most of it consisting of gathering and publishing confidential material relating to Western intelligence services[18]. He gave the impression that he would be working in the public domain. Later, however, he told *Newsweek* in an interview that he would be exposing *secret* CIA operations, to make them ineffective.[19]

Since Agee no longer worked for the CIA, it is hard to see how he could gain access to such secret material except from hostile intelligence services. The only real source would have been the KGB; if, for good reasons, his direct contacts were with the DGI, he could still have been getting KGB material through the Cubans. The real point is that the IPS obviously approved of Agee's work, or it would not have harboured him at the TNI premises.

Although the TNI was said to wield much influence in Dutch official quarters, the Dutch security service soon had Agee expelled, and in short order he was also forced to leave France, Belgium and West Germany. In Britain, he had lived with a Brazilian woman who had taken his name, although they were not married: Angela Agee. She was a member of her country's Revolutionary Communist Party and had vowed to return one day to take part in an armed revolution.[20] After his successive expulsions Agee parted company with her, and married a German ballet dancer about half his age (he was then 43) named Giselle Roberge. This matrimonial contract entitled him to German residence and he settled down, for some years, in Hamburg, where a left-wing Land government made him feel welcome.

The revolutionary associate he had left behind in London, Steven Weissman, had married a British woman. Unlike Agee and Hosenball (a bachelor at the time), he was not expelled from the UK.

Notes

1.   *Inside the Company* (1974); and *On the Run* (1987). The first

is tedious to the point of being unreadable. The second is very lively, the author's skills as a communicator having vastly improved during his years "on the run".

2.   The book, entitled *British Intelligence and Covert Action*, was published in Dublin as well as London, to avoid any possible official action to prevent it from appearing.

3.   Steven Powell, p.66, records Raskin's withdrawal from *CounterSpy*.

4.   Pp. 130-134.

5.   *Ibid*. p.255.

6.   William F, Parham, 'Cuban Intelligence gave Agee help to expose, discredit CIA', in the *Norwich Sunday Bulletin* (Connecticut) 23 August 1981: an authoritative account, presumably based on information provided by Agee's former colleagues. The dateline is Washington.

7.   In the British edition of *Inside the Company* Agee wrote of the debt he owed the Cuban government and to certain people who had given him information. One of these was Michael Locker, who became the Director of the IPS offshoot, the Corporate Data Exchange, and a member of the IPS *ad hoc* Working Group on Latin America. Nicole Szulc, who collaborated with Agee in writing the book, was a member of the Center for National Security Studies, the President of which was Peter Weiss, Chairman of the IPS Board.

8.   *Kingston Daily Gleaner* (Jamaica), 16 September 1976.

9.   *Evening Standard* (London), 17 November 1976.

10.   *Sunday Telegraph* (London), 21 November 1976.

11.   The remarks about the KGB by Agee's leading British campaigner, Phil Kelly, were perhaps the most striking aspect of Barry Powell's piece in the *News of the World* indicating either a quite astonishing naïveté, if sincere, or if not, a no less astonishing brazenness. Somebody in the Agee camp must have made a remark to this effect, because Kelly wrote to the Editor to the *News of the World* to complain that he had been misreported. Barry Powell produced his verbatim shorthand notes and was duly vindicated by his employers. — BC

12.   *The Guardian*, 15 February 1977.

13.   *Hansard*, Vol. 926, No.50.

14.   *Sunday Times* (London) 20 January 1977.

15.   In *On the Run* (pp 195-196), Philip Agee quotes State Depart-

ment documents he obtained under the Freedom of Information Act (FOIA) purporting to show that the then Secretary of State, Henry Kissinger, made secret trips to London on 30 September and 8 or 9 October 1976, presumably to discuss his case with the British government. Honesty and objectivity cause me to say that the inference he draws from two classified cables may well be justified, in that each cable was addressed 'the Secretary of State in London', although neither the *New York Times* nor the London *Times* reported that Kissinger had gone to London at the relevant times, nor indeed that he had been elsewhere. Agee does not, however, prove that the US government put *pressure* on the British to deport him, only that, as he himself says, 'enough was said in the index to conclude that the British had informed the CIA of the action they were about to take against me. Another secret document mentioned in the index is one called 'Contingency Press Guidance concerning Mr Agee''. That document was dated 11 November, five days before delivery of the deportation notice'. It has to be said that it would have been surprising if the two governments had not consulted on the matter, even if Merlyn Rees was technically correct in saying there had been no pressure from Washington.— BC

16.   *On the Run*, p.169.

17.   *Ibid.*, p.201.

18.   *De Telegraaf*, 22 August 1977.

19.   *Newsweek*, 22 August 1977.

20.   The Dutch academic and journalist, J.A. Emerson Vermaat, in an important article, 'The Transnational Institute: The Cuban Connection', in *Midstream* (New York), February 1986. See also *7 days* (London), 28 March 1977.

14. IPS: Landau, or Services Rendered

The passenger lists of the fateful Cubana Airlines flights from Mexico City to Havana in July 1969 are revealing documents. Al Tarabochia had mentioned them to me at the start of my IPS investigation (see ch.8), and later found them and sent them to me.

The first of the two flights took place on 4 July. The passengers included 13 American citizens, among them three of interest to this story, listed as follows:

DOHRN, Bernadine Rae
FAGEN, Richard Rees
LANDAU, Saul Irwin

Bernadette Dohrn was involved in the terrorist activities of the Weather Underground (with which the IPS founding member Arthur Waskow had close links); Richard Fagen had been involved from time to time in the pro-Castro activities of the IPS; Saul Landau, an IPS Fellow, had a long history of collaboration with the Castro regime, often in areas of special interest to Cuban intelligence.

Three days later, on 7 July, another Cubana flight from Mexico City landed at Havana. This one carried 34 US citizens, among them two more Weather Underground terrorists: Diana Oughton and Theodore Gold.

In their minor way, these two flights made history, by setting up the first Venceremos Brigade. In American political semantics, all 47 of the young Americans who flew to Cuba that July were 'radicals'; that is, they were committed to fundamental change in the society of the United States, if necessary by violent means. What most of them, perhaps indeed all, were unaware of is that they were about to be recruited for a major intelligence operation of the Cuban DGI, the ultimate beneficiary of which would be the Soviet KGB. Conceivably, many of them might have been repelled by such knowledge. Doubtless that was why the true purposes of the expedition were, at least initially, kept from them. As far as they knew, the Brigade was to help the Cuban people with the sugarcane harvest and other meritorious deeds. At least, that was what their hosts had told them.

The stated purpose of the trip was apparently not connected with its ultimate goals. The meeting Landau attended in Havana, had been called, ostensibly, at the request of the Communist government of North Vietnam and of its Vietcong guerrillas in South Vietnam. The object was to secure a united front of the American Left in support of the Communist side in the Vietnam War.

There was of course a fundamental unity on objectives among those on the trip. The unifying factor was Moscow: the Vietnamese Communist leader, Ho Chi Minh, trained in Moscow as a Comintern agent; Fidel Castro, a Communist leader, only recently brought under Soviet control; the DGI, instrument of the KGB. (As it happens, Ho would die on 3 September 1969, a couple of months after the Venceremos flights; but the war he had launched went on to a victory he never saw.)

We know from the DGI defector Gerardo Peraza that the Venceremos Brigade was a DGI/KGB operation, in which Julián Torres Rizo, Orlando Letelier's contact man for communications with Tati Allende in Havana, was involved.

As Peraza put it, Torres Rizo had been active in the Venceremos Brigade camps: 'His first intelligence job was to recruit members of the Venceremos Brigade. He had also connections with many North Americans, preparing himself to come to the United States. And he continued directing the work of his agents in the United States[1].

The best summary of what is known of the Venceremos Brigade appears in an official report[2], published in February 1975. Investigation of the VB had begun in 1969, on a continuing basis. Here is a key passage:

> The involvement of the DGI in the genesis of the Brigade was so blatant that one of its UN Center officers was openly mentioned in a

letter to the leadership of the SD Weatherman faction.

From this report, and from another published some months later[3], some interesting details emerge. A letter quoted therein was from a Puerto Rican Communist, Julie Nichamin, one of the Americans used by the DGI to set up the Venceremos Brigade. It was addressed to Bernadine Dohrn, the Weatherman terrorist who was on Landau's flight to Havana in July 1969. And the DGI officer mentioned was identified simply as 'Jiménez'. Alfonso Tarabochia named him as Jesús Jiménez Escóbar, who was expelled from the United States on 19 February 1969, for espionage activities against the United States.

The earlier report goes on:

> When active recruiting of the Brigade began in the Fall of 1969, the DGI had to rely on a cadre formed mainly by New Left activists who had made one or more trips to Cuba. The results of the interviews were then reviewed by the United Nations Center, which gave final approval....Those selected for the Brigade undergo preliminary indoctrination at the hands of the cadre who, under the guise of assessing the involvement of the recruit, elicit information on a variety of subjects that are of great interest to the DGI and the KGB.

On p.13, the report mentions Orlando Castro Hidalgo's revelations about the Soviet oil embargo which brought the Cubans to heel. It goes on, in a parenthesis: '(Evidence of this is to be found in a lengthy Philippic delivered by Raúl Castro on January 24, 1968, during a secret session of the Cuban Communist Party.)'

The true significance of the Brigade comes to light in these further passages:

> Ironically, the details of the whole affair are contained in a booklet published by the Cuban government and brought to the United States by a returning member of the Brigade. The booklet is entitled "Information from the Central Committee of the Communist Party of Cuba on Microfaction Activities" Instituto de Libro Ediciones Políticas, Havana 1968.

> As a result of a new agreement, the DGI was ordered to collect intelligence which was of little intrinsic value to Cuba but of very

great interest to the Soviet Union. Immediately afterwards, the number of DGI personnel stationed in Cuban embassies in Western Europe was increased sharply.

It is in this context that the KGB advisor to the DGI, Vitaly Petrovich Semënov, insisted on the priority of establishing a good network of illegals in the United States, instead of confining the Directorate's interest to the activities of the anti-Castro exiles. The DGI was eager to comply. (Emphasis added)

In fact, as the February 1975 Hearings revealed: 'The Venceremos Brigade was brought into being through the clever manipulation of a small group of US Leftist radicals, prominent among whom were some of the leaders of the SDS "Weatherman" faction.'[4] The Brigade made it possible for the DGI to infiltrate Cuban 'illegals' into the US, in response to pressure from the Soviets. But it also served specifically Cuban aims in helping to destabilise American society and in establishing links with American and Third World terrorist groups.

(Some months after the Havana meeting, on 6 March 1970, the terrorists Diane Oughton and Theodore Gold, with another named Terry Robbins, met a fate only occasionally meted out to their kind. While working at the Weatherman bomb factory on West 11th Street, New York City, they blew themselves up.)

Against this background, it appears to emerge that Saul Landau, a long-serving Fellow of the Institute for Policy Studies, was involved in a Cuban Intelligence operation on behalf of the KGB. Was he aware of the fact? I have seen no evidence that he was personally involved in the VB operation, although he helped to pave the way for it[5]. In any event, it is clear that Cuban intelligence was using the IPS for its own, and Soviet, purposes.

In later years, Saul Landau often said that he considered himself a personal friend of Fidel Castro. Name-dropping? Reflected glory? It matters little. Even if he acted initially out of idealism and was unaware that he was indirectly working for the Soviet KGB, it is on record that he did not recant in any way after it had become public knowledge that the KGB had taken over the Cuban DGI.

Just as Orlando Letelier used the DGI officer Torres Rizo as in effect his 'post box' to Havana, so did Landau use Letelier himself as a courier for letters to the same destination. He took advantage of Letelier's access to the diplomatic bag. In one such letter, found in Letelier's briefcase, Landau wrote: 'At age forty the time has come to dedicate myself to narrower pursuits, namely making propaganda for American socialism.'

Although 1969 was a crucial year for Landau, in fact his Cuban involvement had begun at least eight years earlier, indeed as long ago as 29 July 1961, in the early days of the Castro regime. That day, Landau spoke for the student branch of the Fair Play for Cuba Committee at a meeting sponsored by the Youth Wing of the Communist Party USA.

Landau would not necessarily have known that the CPUSA was funded annually by the KGB and that it received its policy directives from the International Department of the Soviet Communist Party. (Incidentally, the Committee dissolved itself when one of its members assassinated President John F. Kennedy in 1963. The assassin's name was Lee Harvey Oswald; trained in Russia and with a Russian wife.)[6]

In those heady early days of the Cuban revolution, Saul Landau often spoke in support of it. On 22 October 1962, for instance, he was a speaker at a big rally on Cuba, under the slogans: 'No war! No invasion! No blockade!'[7] The date is of some interest, for it was on that very day, 22 October 1962, that the late President Kennedy made his dramatic broadcast to the American people, in which he revealed that his government had unmistakable evidence of the installation on Cuban soil of Soviet missiles capable of delivering nuclear warheads to large areas of the United States and Central America.

This was indeed the start of the Cuban missiles confrontation, at the end of which the Soviet leader, Nikita Khrushchev, was forced to back down and remove the nuclear installations. (I am not here concerned with the price Kennedy also paid to end the crisis, except to recall that he gave a pledge that the US would make no further attempts to bring down Fidel Castro by force, after the failure of the Bay of Pigs expedition.)

It is surely interesting that at this time of national and international crisis, Saul Landau was making speeches in support of Fidel Castro's regime, which had made the missile sites available to the Soviet Union.

My files bulge with documentary evidence of Saul Landau's apparently unconditional support for Fidel Castro's régime. It would be tedious to reproduce it all. One major service does deserve mention, however: his propaganda film *With Fidel*. An earlier film, *Report from Cuba*, was perhaps of transitory value, but *With Fidel* has enjoyed a continuing vogue. It had its first showing in San Francisco in December 1969, at the close of Venceremos year. Later, Saul Landau was the co-producer of a film on President Allende of Chile — another example of the Chilean-Cuban connection.

I have already quoted the views of Landau's former friend and colleague of the New Left and of *Ramparts* magazine, David Horowitz (see Ch.9). In common with a number of other disillusioned early enthusiasts, Mr Horowitz held the view that Fidel Castro betrayed his own revolution by turning it into a Soviet-style dictatorship, indeed into a Soviet satellite. As he put it in his signed Statement of 4 September 1986:

> Castro declared himself a Communist and turned Cuba into a Soviet mini-State....and just as Fidel completed his betrayal of every principle to which he had once been committed, and by which our 'New Left' defined what it was, Saul Landau appeared as the dictator's principal apologist with his propaganda 'documentary' *With Fidel*.

For saying just that, as we saw earlier, Fidel's former companion in battle, Huber Matos, was gaoled and tortured for 20 years; which Saul Landau refused to condemn.

One hesitates whether to pay Saul Landau the dubious compliment of concluding from his behaviour that he is innocent but stupid; or drawing the alternative conclusion that he has always known what the true situation was, and rendered services to Castro's revolution in the full knowledge that he was also servicing the KGB and the Communist Party of the Soviet Union. What is certain is that the IPS never publicly rebuked Landau for his involvement in, and support for, Cuban operations. On the contrary, his Fellowship with the IPS continued undisturbed.

The influence of the IPS naturally began to wane with the landslide victory of Ronald Reagan at the Presidential elections of 1980. But the IPS did not relax its efforts. When President Reagan formed a Bi-Partisan Commission on Central America, headed by Richard Nixon's former Secretary of State, Dr Henry Kissinger, the IPS set up its own project in early 1982, calling it PACCA (Policy Alternatives for the

Caribbean and Central America). Three years later, PACCA issued a report running to 116 pages, which was immediately acclaimed by the Communist guerrillas in Guatemala and El Salvador, backed by the KGB and DGI.[8]

As is usual with Communist-backed guerrilla groups, those in El Salvador were supported by a political apparatus. This one was known as CISPES, which stands for Committee in Solidarity with the People of El Salvador. Much the same applied in Vietnam, where the Communist Vietcong guerrillas had a political front called the National Front for the Liberation of South Vietnam (designed, successfully in this case, to confuse the innocent).

The point of interest about CISPES, however, is that the IPS was involved in setting it up, along with the Cuban DGI. Isabel Letelier, widow of Orlando, and a Fellow of the IPS, met a Salvadoran Communist agent and introduced him to others potentially interested in the project. Also involved was a DGI agent named Alfredo García-Almeida, whose cover was as Counsellor (Political) at the Cuban mission to the UN.

The Salvadoran Communist agent was named Farid Handal, brother of the Salvadoran Communist Party Chairman, Shafik Handal[9], Shafik was also on the five-man directorate of the Farabundo Martí National Liberation Front or FMLN, the Soviet-backed paramilitary organisation which enjoyed political support from the IPS.

In the mid-1970s, Farid Handal was receiving $2,000 a month 'from the Russians'. That, at any rate, was his boast at a meeting of the Salvadoran Cotton Growers' Association. He added that this stipend was for 'work' in Central America. While Farid was in America organising CISPES, his brother Shafik was in the Soviet bloc obtaining military aid. Farid's diary of the trip was captured by the Salvadoran military forces and made public by the US State Department in 1981. It specifically mentions meetings he had at IPS.

One of the leaders of the Soviet-funded Communist Party USA, Sandy Pollack, was also involved in setting up CISPES. In 1982 CISPES, by then in existence, helped create a wider World Front in Solidarity with the People of El Salvador, with headquarters in Mexico. On the board of this World Front there sat a Cuban agent, Jorge Gallada Fernández, representing the Cuban Institute for Friendship with the Peoples (ICAP from the initials in Spanish), long identified as a DGI front.

I have mentioned PACCA and its 116-page report. This report, entitled 'Blueprint for Peace in Central America and the Caribbean', was widely distributed by CISPES. The Blueprint, in line with other IPS reports, blamed 'US militarism' for the wars in that area, while ignoring or minimising military aid to local guerrillas from the Soviet Union, East Germany, North Vietnam, Cuba and Nicaragua.

It — the Blueprint — was unveiled at the home of the radical multi-millionaire and General Motors heir, Stewart Mott, a major financial supporter of the IPS. An interesting detail: an attaché at the Soviet embassy was present on this occasion. His name was Viktor Taltz. His conversation with a companion was tape recorded by a journalist, also present. He said: 'I read this book last night. It was very good and accurate.... We are grateful to the IPS to be brave enough to tell the truth.'[10]

These words constituted, in effect, a Soviet endorsement of an IPS report.

This same man, Viktor Taltz, attended an IPS seminar on Nicaragua and Cuba, which was addressed both by the director of IPS, Robert Borosage, and by the ubiquitous Saul Landau. Other Soviet officials, including Valeriy Lekarev and Sergei Rogov, were regular visitors to the IPS.

Once again, I have mentioned Saul Landau. It would be a mistake, however, to give the impression that he is the only member of the IPS network to have identified uncritically with the Communist regime on Cuba. Another is Michael Locker, a staff member of NACLA (the Northern American Congress on Latin America), founded in 1966 by SDS (Students for a Democratic Society), that cradle of young American revolutionaries, to which, like Landau, Locker belonged.

Another champion of the Castro regime was Michael Klare, a member of the IPS European subsidiary, the TNI's Ad Hoc Working Group on Latin America. He, too, learned his revolutionary ways and skills in the SDS. Both Locker and Klare have contributed to *Tricontinental*, official organ of the Havana-based and Soviet-supported Organisation of Solidarity of the Peoples of Africa, Asia and Latin America, known as AALAPSO.

The genesis of AALAPSO is also worth recalling. Essentially, it was a joint Soviet/Cuban front organisation to cover the activities of

Communist or pro-Communist groups in the Third World, including guerrillas and terrorists. It was set up at a major conference in Havana in January 1966, at which there was a large Soviet delegation consisting of personnel from the Asian Republics of the USSR. Klare wrote the cover story of the 18th issue of *Tricontinental*. He had also lectured at the University of Havana, an honour normally reserved for supporters of the Castro régime.

TERRORIST LINKS

Let us now take a closer look at the terrorist links of the IPS. There is ample documentation for the fact that the SDS was at the heart of the so-called New Left.[11] SDS sent delegations to North Vietnam, Czechoslovakia and Cuba. The hero of the New Left, and of the SDS in particular, was Fidel Castro. Disillusionment set in when Castro publicly supported the Soviet occupation of Czechoslovakia in his much quoted speech of 23 August 1968.

In due course, and especially after it became known that the KGB had asserted total control over the Cuban DGI, some of the New Left's former leaders, including Peter Collier and David Horowitz, gradually detached themselves from the organisations they had previously supported or led. The difference between them and Saul Landau of the IPS and the TNI, and other IPS figures, was that Landau and his associates continued their support of Castro's Cuba.

The Weatherman, in fact, was born of a split in the SDS. The term Weatherman emerged from a paper prepared by its leaders and entitled: 'You don't need a Weatherman to Know Which Way the Wind Blows'.[12] At the June 1969 National Convention of the SDS, the Weatherman faction won all three leading positions in the SDS and took over the SDS national office.

As for the Black Panthers Party (BPP), one of its leaders (later disillusioned) was Eldridge Cleaver, who urged that the masses be spurred towards 'revolutionary temptation to kidnap American ambassadors, hijack American airplanes, blow up American pipelines and buildings, and to shoot anyone who uses guns or other weapons in the bloodstained service of imperialism against the people.' In 1969 alone 348 Panthers were arrested for serious crimes, including murder, armed robbery, rape and burglary. And this was the terrorist organisation supported in various ways by members of the IPS.

The height, or depth, of urban terrorism in the US, in which the Black Panthers and Weatherman were heavily involved, was the period between January 1969 and the end of April 1970. During that period there were more than 40,000 bombings, attempted bombings or bomb threats, averaging more than 80 a day. Forty-three people were killed and damage to property was estimated at more than $21 million. It was not until 1977 that the *New York Times* reported that the FBI had evidence showing that the Weatherman was receiving direct support from Cuba and North Vietnam. Cuban military instructed them in 'practical weaponry'.

CUI BONO?

Although I have devoted five chapters to the story of the IPS, I don't claim to have given it exhaustive treatment. For a fuller picture, interested readers may wish to consult the remarkable work of Steven Powell, already mentioned: *COVERT CADRE: Inside the Institute for Policy Studies* (1987).

Before closing this account, however, there is an important point to be made: the activities of the IPS and its affiliates concentrated, to a degree unique in the history of American Leftist groups, on weakening US Intelligence and counter-Intelligence operations and defence establishments. Other such groups had campaigned against the police, or denounced informers, or attacked 'capitalism', but the systematic and sustained effort mounted by the IPS and its subsidiaries was of a different order of magnitude. To these ends, the IPS mobilised not only its own staff and associates, but also the Government Accountability Project, the Center for National Security Studies and such subordinate organisations as the Project on Intelligence and Covert Action, the project on National Security and the Constitution, the Citizens' Projects on National Security, the Campaign to Stop Governments Spying, the National Lawyers' Guild (a Soviet-funded front group, launched in 1936, which followed a consistent line thereafter), and the publications *Counterspy* and *Covert Action Bulletin*.

It is surely apposite to put the question: *cui bono*? The argument that defence spending was excessive does have validity; but it is clear that systematic attacks on the defences of the United States did benefit the KGB and Soviet military intelligence, the GRU, and their surrogate services such as the Cuban DGI.

One point should not be forgotten in this context. The governments of the Soviet Union, Cuba and Nicaragua are (or were at that time) *totalitarian*. That is, all power and all authority were vested in the ruling party. In all such countries, in all Communist regimes, the secret intelligence and security organisations were charged with recruiting not only espionage agents, but agents of influence. It does not greatly matter whether such agents of influence were conscious or not; in other words, whether or not they realised that they were being used by, say, the KGB and the DGI. What matter are the final results.

To substantiate my charge that the IPS was a 'major front for Cuban Intelligence, itself controlled by the KGB', it would not, in my view, have been necessary to show that people like Saul Landau or Richard Barnet or Robert Borosage were actually recruited or paid by the DGI or KGB. The important thing was that their own work, even if unintentionally, served the purpose of both organisations. As for the late Orlando Letelier, he was actually receiving money through the DGI, even if the IPS disputed this.

Did the work of the IPS serve the Soviet and Cuban policy interests? Despite occasional mild criticisms by Richard Barnet, he himself and other Fellows or Associates of the IPS did in fact often defend Soviet and Cuban policies. This was so over the Vietnam war; over the Allende and Pinochet regimes in Chile; over disarmament and arms control; over Cuba, Nicaragua, the Caribbean and Central America. Stalin's prosecutor in the terror trials of the 1930s, Vishinsky, used to call the Soviet secret police 'the naked sword of the Revolution'. The interests of the KGB and the DGI were in substance indistinguishable from those of the Soviet and Cuban States.

Notes

1.   *The Role of Cuba in International Terrorism and Subversion.* Hearing before the Subcommittee on Security and Terrorism of the Committee on the Judiciary United States Senate: second session, 26

February , 4, 11 and 12 March 1982; p.15.

2.   Report of the Subcommittee to Investigate the Administration of the Internal Security Act and other Internal Security Laws of the Committee on the Judiciary, United States Senate; first session, February 1975; pp 12-13.

3.   *Terrorist Activitiy: The Cuban Connection in Puerto Rico: Castro's Hand in Puerto Rican and US Terrorism.* Hearings (Internal Security Act), 30 July 1975.

4.   See Note 3. This report mentions that one of the leaders of the Weatherman, Larry Gratwohl, was recruited as an FBI informant (p.8).

5.   See Ch.8

6.   I am not concerned here with the protracted conspiracy theories later aired in the American media. — BC.

7.   Signed Statement by J. Michael Waller (Council for Inter-American Security), Washington DC, 3 August 1986.

8.   Letter to Brian Crozier from J Michael Waller (see note 5), 12 September 1986.

9.   *CADRE. op.cit.,* p.331.

10.   See, for instance, 'Another "Low Dishonest Decade" on the Left, an important article by two former editors of the widely read organ of the New Left, *Ramparts*, Peter Collier and David Horowitz, in the New York monthly, *Commentary*, of January 1987. There was much additional evidence in the FBI files released to the author.

11.   See *New Left Notes*, 18 June 1969.

12.   Nicholas M. Horrock in *New York Times*, p.1, 9 October 1977.

15. Victory by Default

The legal battle raged on, as in the *Spiegel* case. As I knew from the start, it was in the truest sense a war of nerves. The Plaintiff wants to intimidate the Defendant by making him believe that he will take the case all the way to trial. The Defendant professes confidence (perhaps more than he really feels), by affecting indifference to the implied threat. It is in the Defendant's interest that the date set for the trial be deferred, to give him time to collect cast-iron evidence, if possible with the unexpected key witness 'in the know' in reserve to surprise the Plaintiff and sway the judge and jury.

Since the Plaintiff has the initiative, there are virtually no limits to the amount of sheer labour he can impose on the Defendant. However, 'discovery' can work both ways.

On 9 May 1985, Alasdair Pepper wrote to inform me that 'Barnet has now paid the sum of £5,000 in security for your costs into a Deposit Account'. In addition, he went on, 'Barnet has now issued a Summons for Directions for trial....The Directions sought are that the parties to the action serve on others a List of Documents within 21 days'. And Pepper concluded that 'it appears to me that Barnet seriously intends taking this action to Court'.

Certainly this was what Barnet wanted us to believe. Jimmy Goldsmith took a different view. In a letter to me on 24 May 1985, he said: 'Personally, I don't believe that Barnet will go through with it. At this stage I think he is playing chicken. However, we must not count on that, and I am sure the case should be prepared assiduously.'

Indeed, there was little choice. I prepared a truly formidable list of documents we should require Barnet to produce. In due course he replied on a somewhat whining note, telling us how busy he was and that he didn't know where a lot of the required material could be found.

One weakness was that there were two Defendants on our side, and only one was determined to see the matter through. The other was *The Spectator*, which had published the letter that had triggered off the Barnet/ IPS lawsuits, but which had absolutely no interest in winning. It was only natural that Barnet's lawyer, Geoffrey Bindman, should exploit this patent lack of unity on the defending side.

In July 1985, when I was writing at my second home in Shoreham, Alasdair Pepper telephoned to say that Bindman had been in touch, dropping hints that his clients might not, after all, insist on an apology from me for what I had said about the IPS; although he did think I should pay Barnet's costs. Clearly, Bindman's tactic was to get an apology from *The Spectator,* then put pressure on me to join in. The full implications of the Bindman manoeuvre emerged in stages. Here are some of them:

> 13 August 1985
> Richard C.M.Sykes, Solicitor, for *The Spectator*
> To Bindman and Partners
>
> WITHOUT PREJUDICE
>
> My clients have asked me to inquire as to the possibility of their settling the Plaintiff's claim.
> No pun is intended when I say that they feel themselves to be on-lookers in this dispute which is essentially one between your client and Mr Crozier.
> My clients would be willing to publish a retraction in agreed terms and to make a contribution to Mr Barnet's costs.

There was a triumphant note in the reply from Bindman and Partners, dated 20 August 1985. The letter welcomed the willingness of Richard Sykes's client to publish a retraction in agreed terms. If this were done, he would gladly waive his claim to damages but would require to be indemnified in respect of the whole of his costs.

There followed a proposed form of words for a retraction.

> *The Spectator* would be required to point out that the Institute for

Policy Studies, which was a respected research organisation, had no
link whatever with either Cuban intelligence or the KGB. There would
then be an apology to Mr Barnet for any embarrassment 'this unfortunate mis-statement' had caused him.

It added that I would be required to join in this settlement and that,
accordingly, they were sending a copy of the letter to Peter Carter-Ruck
and Partners.

Alerted by a telephone call from Alasdair Pepper, I said immediately
that while I couldn't stop *The Spectator* from agreeing to this abjectly
apologetic form of words, I could not in any way be associated with it.
Accordingly, Peter Carter-Ruck and Partners sent me a draft letter to
Richard Sykes, from which I cull these excerpts:

> You are correct that at present there is no possibility of Mr Crozier
> joining in any settlement as he is confident of successfully defending
> the action.
>
> (....)
>
> If your client agrees to publish an apology along the lines sug-
> gested by Bindman and Partners it would be likely to seriously under-
> mine our client's position in these proceedings and gravely discredit
> him.
>
> We urge your client...to allow our client the opportunity of com-
> menting on the terms before he proceeds to settle.

In a further telephone exchange, the line I had taken with Pepper had
been less emollient. 'Tell *The Spectator*'s lawyers,' I urged, 'that if
they apologise for something I wrote, and if I then win the case, I shall
have no alternative but to sue them.' On 30 August, I wrote to Sir
James Goldsmith to bring him up to date. From this letter, I quote: '...if
The Spectator went ahead, it would seriously prejudice my own case.
Moreover, if my case gets to court and if I win it, *The Spectator* will
quite seriously have defamed me.'

Tactically, I won this battle in the protracted conflict. Nearly a year
passed without any further talk of a separate settlement by *The Spectator*. Meanwhile, the relative lull was helpful to our side.

On 28 July 1986, Alasdair Pepper wrote to say that he had obtained
a Court Order that:

1.   Barnet do on or before 1 October 1986 make and serve on you a Further and Better List of Documents which are or have been in his possession, custody or power relating to any matter in question in this action and that the costs of the application be paid by Barnet in any event.

2.   Barnet do pay into Court or into a joint account in his Solicitors and our name, within 28 days the sum of £40,000 by way of Security for your costs and that in the meantime the action be stayed.

3.   Barnet do pay your costs of applications in any event.

I believe that the above constitutes a substantial step forward in the action and will test Barnet's resolve to continue with it. You will note that if Barnet does not pay the sum into Court or into a joint account the action will be stayed pending such payment. This is important.

The order for a Further and Better List of Documents is also important as it should involve Barnet in a substantial amount of work. If he does not comply with the Order it will be possible for me to apply to strike out the action at a date in the future.

This would test Barnet's resolve and also the depth of the purse at his disposal.

He stood firm, however. Bindman later rang Carter-Ruck to hint that Barnet might be prepared to drop the action without an apology from me, on condition that I met at least part of his costs. He was evasive when asked whether *The Spectator* would be required to apologise and just what proportion of the costs I would be expected to meet.

In the event, Alasdair Pepper's Court initiative did bring Richard Barnet's intentions into the open. On 20 August 1986, Alasdair wrote to say he had received 'an encouraging "without prejudice" telephone call from Barnet's solicitors'. Barnet, it emerged, saw little point in continuing with the action, particularly in view of its enormous expense. He would be content with an apology and £4,000 towards his costs from *The Spectator*. He also required an unspecified contribution from myself, again towards the costs; but he would not require damages.

As instructed by me, Pepper reiterated, in conversation with *The Spectator*'s lawyers, that I considered any apology from them would be seriously damaging to me. Meanwhile, Barnet had paid the £40,000 into Court, which seemed to show that he intended to proceed, although our formidable Further and Better List of Documents might deter him.

He strongly advised me to consider settling on the basis of a modified apology, and added:

> You should be in no doubt that if you proceed with this action it remains my view that you are unlikely to be successful in defence, unless one or more DGI or KGB defectors can be persuaded to assist and give evidence and that, additionally, the defence will be hugely expensive. It is, of course, conceivable that Barnet will withdraw before trial but you must appreciate the substantial chance that he will not.

In retrospect, I have to say that this professional pessimism was probably justified. We had built up a massive portfolio of documentary material, including signed Statements. Yet we did lack that essential element under England's adversarial system of justice: the witness who knew, and was prepared to tell all. The temptation to negotiate acceptable terms was certainly there, but I couldn't yield to it. Moreover, the notion of contributing even a penny to Richard Barnet's expenses in his action against me was repugnant. It was in a state of gloomy defiance that I sat down and drafted my first 'Speech for the Defence'.

I had sent a copy of Pepper's letter of 20 August to Jimmy, who was in Paris at the time. On 4 September, he replied by Telex:

> My dear Brian,
>
> I must say that I disagree wholeheartedly with his [Pepper's] advice. I think that the proposed wording of the apology by *The Spectator* would be immensely damaging to you in Court.
>
> If *The Spectator* are too ignorant to know of the links between the IPS and Cuba, then you should inform them and let their lawyers see part of the evidence.
>
> It is essential that only part be shown to them because in view of the softness of *The Spectator*, they will undoubtedly leak. That is why you must be revealing but not revealed.
>
> I will [*sic*] put *The Spectator* on formal warning that you will sue them and I would record in writing through the lawyers that you are willing to be revealing of the facts.
>
> I am perfectly happy that a copy of my letter be forwarded to Peter

Carter-Ruck. This is obviously an important case which has to be fought tooth and nail.

Yours ever,

Jimmy Goldsmith

I did as Jimmy suggested, and further legal warnings went out. But they fell on unreceptive minds. For their part, Algy Cluff and *The Spectator* were quite determined to quit, with or without me. This attitude had been made clear from the start (see Ch.6)

Although I couldn't share their attitude, I understood it. Indeed, Cluff had explained it to me over lunch at Wilton's; ironically, Sir James Goldsmith's favourite London restaurant.

Immensely tall and with a voice of grave beauty, Algy Cluff was understandably a worried man. He was one of the defendants in another libel case which at that very moment was coming to trial. It involved the well-known Greek journalist Taki (Theodoracopulos), author of the entertaining column, 'High Life' in *The Spectator*. The case attracted wide media coverage when it ended unfavourably for the defending side some weeks later, and Mr Cluff emerged from the ordeal poorer, it was reported, by about £300,000.

I therefore listened sympathetically but resolved not to capitulate. I made it clear that for my part I intended to fight all the way, and therefore reserved the right to sue *The Spectator* for libel if their proposed apology for what I had written in effect accused me of lying. But all told, it was an agreeable lunch.

Early in October 1986, I learned from Alasdair Pepper that Cluff and *The Spectator* had indeed decided to publish a letter of apology. On the 7th, I wrote to Cluff to say that I was 'surprised and disquieted' by the news. I recalled how, many years earlier, the well-known journalist Honor Tracey, had successfully sued Kemsley Newspapers for apologising over something she had written. My recollection was that she had been awarded £3,000 damages, which in 1954 was a considerable sum. I spelled out the implications:

> Even in the modified wording suggested by my solicitors, Peter Carter-Ruck, an apology by *The Spectator* would amount to calling me a liar and thus seriously impugning my professional integrity. Any such apology would obviously be widely publicised by the IPS, not

only in the United States but internationally and the effects would thus be multiplied. Moreover, in the event that the case should actually come to trial (which I still consider unlikely), an apology of this kind would prejudice any jury against me as the main Defendant.

You will remember that I touched on such possibilities over lunch with you some months ago, and indicated that an apology by *The Spectator* would leave me with no alternative but to sue your side.

(....)

I can well understand your desire to avoid further involvement, especially after the somewhat disastrous case of Taki. However, I do want to make it clear that if an apology is printed, I shall cause a writ to be issued. Meanwhile, I have instructed my solicitors to apply for an injunction to restrain *The Spectator* from any such action.

I should perhaps add that by now we do have a vast amount of evidence tending to substantiate the statements made in my letter to *The Spectator*. Moreover, more material is still reaching me, and I am confident that we can sustain my case.

Should you wish to gain at least some access to my material, that is a matter for discussion.

I have no idea whether these arguments were seriously considered by Algy Cluff. What is certain is that they did not prevail over his own counter-arguments. My threat was a contingent one, a hypothesis. The £300,000 he had lost over the Taki case was reality, painful and recent. The evidence I had assembled would have been useful, but only if he had been interested in winning. But he was not. His choice — an understandable one — was to get out, saving what he could.

Having struck my blow, I entered the Middlesex Hospital the next day, 8 October 1986, for further surgery. I emerged a few days later, and allowed myself a short convalescence, caught up with pressing commitments, then on Friday 31 October had a two-hour meeting with Alasdair Pepper and his firm's Counsel, Mr Richard Walker. They professed themselves favourably impressed by my draft speech, but still put my chances 40-60 against.

I reported to Jimmy Goldsmith, saying: 'I do not share this pessimism, but cannot ignore their advice.' I went along with the lawyers on one suggestion: that we should now take up Bindman's suggestion (since it had come from his side) that the action should be dropped, but on the basis that each side should pay its own costs. This seemed a good time, psychologically, because my letter to Cluff (although he had not replied to it) appeared to have had an intimidatory effect, and his lawyers were now saying they would take no further action for some weeks.

It looked at that stage as though the case would come up for trial in March or April 1987, but (I wrote): 'I still think it is highly unlikely that Barnet/IPS, for the sake of destroying me, will in the final analysis, run the risk of destroying themselves.'

But Bindman's position was stronger than we knew, since Algy Cluff's determination to capitulate was unshakeable. I created legal history (or so Alasdair Pepper assured me) when I appealed against the decision of the High Court, Queen's Bench Division, to allow *The Spectator* to settle on the basis of an apology for what I had said in its columns.

Judgement on my appeal was given on Thursday 11 December 1986, in the Court of Appeal in the neo-Gothic Law Courts, a stone's throw from Peter Carter-Ruck's offices.

I listened in mounting amazement to the lengthy judgement read out by Lord Justice Ralph Gibson, in the presence of his colleague Lord Justice Nourse. My intimidatory letter to Algy Cluff, and the warnings from my lawyers, had had some effect, in that the proposed apology from *The Spectator* did not mention me by name. Yet the judgement, as delivered in open court, mentioned me repeatedly — 14 times by my count; thus nullifying any advantage I might have gained from *The Spectator*'s judicious reticence. Unless the trial was postponed for a long period, and not a mere four or five months, and possibly less, one or more members of the jury would surely be prejudiced against me by knowing that my Appeal had been rejected. Even if they did not, it would have been easy enough (whatever the rules might say) for one of them to be tipped off.

There was another reasons for my amazement. Judge Gibson described me as 'a journalist of distinction and a writer on international affairs'. But, he said, 'none of the parties was famous or notorious' (myself, of course, included). Therefore, he 'did not think that a statement made in open court in November 1986 [a reference to the agreement to settle the case against *The Spectator*] would have the slightest effect on a trial taking place in March to May or June 1987. Potential jurors would be unaffected. Any publicity resulting from such a statement would have passed out of their minds long before the trial'.

This seemed to me to imply that there is one justice for celebrities and another for the merely 'distinguished'. I was no Jeffrey Archer or Joan Collins.

Months after the judgement of 11 December 1986, it became fair to say that in some respects the judge was right; although it is impossible to be definitive on this point, as the lawsuit against me never did come to trial. With one weighty exception, the press ignored the rejection of my Appeal. The exception was *The Times* (no less) which, in its issue of 30 December 1986 (nearly three weeks after the event, and with Christmas intervening) carried a massive Law Report of the proceedings: 45 column inches of it.

On 30 December, the day of *The Times* report, Pepper wrote to me, drawing my attention to the fact that *The Spectator* would not be mentioning my name in its agreed apology, so that the impact of it on my reputation should be to that extent diminished. He went on:

> An additional and, in my view, important consequence of your strenuous efforts to prevent the Statement in Open Court being read is that it should cause Barnet considerable concern over your intentions in the proceedings and as to the evidence you have supporting your defence of justification.

The Spectator went ahead with its apology, which described the IPS as an 'independent and respected centre in Washington DC, devoted to research on public policy issues'. The grovel came at the end:

> *The Spectator* accepted that neither Mr Barnet nor the Institute was a front for Cuban intelligence and that neither was controlled by the KGB. It apologised to Mr Barnet and agreed to pay his legal costs.

It soon became clear that Barnet's morale, and Bindman's, had been boosted by *The Spectator*'s apology. On 13 April 1987, I wrote to Jimmy Goldsmith to report that Bindman had rejected a proposal for a straight withdrawal on both sides, each to pay its own expenses. However, the enemy was not asking for an apology from me, being content with the one from *The Spectator*. Pepper had concluded from this that what they were really after was for me to pay their expenses. I was still determined not to do this, as it would look like an admission of guilt on my part.

He had put an alternative proposal to me: that I should offer to pay a portion of the other side's expenses — say £10,000 — it being made clear in a confidential covering letter that I was doing this strictly for financial reasons and that it did not constitute an admission of liability on my part. In response I had made the point that even assuming that Barnet personally observed the confidentiality of such a settlement, it could easily be leaked to publications elsewhere.

By this time, Harriet's important primary material was pouring in and I had embarked on the major task of redrafting my proposed 'Speech for the Defence'. Having read the outcome, the lawyers enjoyed a brief period of 'conditional optimism' before relapsing into professional pessimism.

Jimmy's support continued, unwavering. In a terse note, dated 'Paris, 13 May 1987', he said: 'I agree with everything you say. If anything, they should pay your costs. I can see no reason for being soft.'

On 21 May, after another long conversation with Alasdair Pepper (who in turn had been conferring with our new leading Counsel, David Eady, QC, and with Richard Walker), I fired off two more letters: one to Jimmy, the other to Alasdair.

In the former, I complained that the lawyers still believed that, in the absence of a 'smoking gun' witness, I stood to lose, at least if the case came to trial as early as the next month. For that reason, they were applying for a further postponement, until January 1988, I went on:

> If the lawyers are right, then I might face the ordeal of a trial lasting three or four months and costing in the region of £600,000....I do think, however, that the knowledge that we now do have this powerful stuff may well cause the other side to drop out.

In my letter to Alasdair Pepper, I allowed my bitterness and dismay to show in these paragraphs:

> What surprises me most in your views and the views of your senior colleagues is that you should incline to the less likely of the alternative explanations for the line taken by the IPS and people like Saul Landau — that they simply belong to an American version of the 'loony Left' and are basically simply expressing their own views.

> With people of their obvious intelligence and ability, this is a most unlikely explanation. It does not stand up, in my view, in the face of the numerous examples of support for the Cuban government in defiance of the facts. The most glaring example, clearly, is that of the Matos case, but there are lots of others.
>
> Having said that, I do agree that a 'smoking gun' witness would make the case unassailable. But it does seem to me that the mass of documents now assembled makes my interpretation of the facts the only valid one

On the day I was dictating these lines, Alasdair Pepper was drafting his long and closely argued missive, explaining in explicit detail the reasons why, on balance, I seemed likely to lose my case. The views he expressed were those of Eady and Walker, and they urged me to reopen negotiations with Barnet and Bindman.

I sent the letter to Jimmy, with my comments, and he replied, saying: 'I have no particular comment except that I feel that Agee is "the smoking gun". It is perfectly clear who and what Agee is, and also the fact that he worked for Transnational, a subsidiary of IPS.'

I had no intention of reopening negotiations with Barnet. And now, just when I needed it most, potentially good news reached me in a letter dated 27 May from the New York law firm, which was moving into high gear. They had learned of a witness with first-hand knowledge of a Cuban-IPS connection. The man was Arturo Cruz, Jr., (see Ch. 8) formerly the coordinator of intelligence for Nicaragua's Sandinista government with the Cuban DGI. They were now setting up an interview with Cruz. They also had three former Cuban intelligence officers to interview in Florida.

In line with Jimmy's suggestion, I set Ron Baxter the task of gathering all the material he could on the Agee connection. I mentioned this in a letter to Jimmy on 11 June, and also gave him the good news that the Clerk of the Court had just granted us a deferment for a whole year: until June 1988.

As it turned out, we didn't need the deferment. On 9 July 1987, Alasdair Pepper wrote to say that Allan Altman had now made contact with Arturo Cruz, who apparently knew Saul Landau, and from first-hand knowledge was aware that he and IPS colleagues were helping Sandinista intelligence, which was closely connected with the Cuban

DGI.

At last, the 'smoking gun'! There was only one snag. Quite suddenly Cruz said he was willing to help and to give evidence for me, but not until his involvement in the Iran-Contra hearings, then in progress, was concluded.

Pepper's letter ended with a PS:

> Since dictating this letter I have heard from Barnet's solicitors that they are prepared to withdraw the action with no order as to costs. Great news. My congratulations to you.

Great news, indeed....

Confirmation took the form of a letter from Bindman and Partners, dated 7 July 1987, the key passages of which read:

> As you are already aware, our client's purpose in bringing this action was not to recover damages against your client or anyone else but to vindicate his reputation by obtaining public acknowledgement that he had no link with Cuban intelligence or the KGB.
>
> Our client has achieved his objective by the giving of such acknowledgement by *The Spectator* both in their paper and in open Court. He therefore has no interest in pursuing the action against your client save that he has naturally hoped that your client would be prepared to indemnify him for his legal costs.
>
> Since your client has declined to do this our client has instructed us that, rather than pursue an extremely expensive and lengthy action solely for the purpose of determining the issue of costs, he will accept your client's offer that on withdrawal of the action your client will agree to there being no order as to costs.

This prolix statement of good news was made official by a Court order dated 11 August 1987. It was all over. We had won by default, just as Sir James Goldsmith had won in the *Der Spiegel* case three years earlier.

Greatly relieved, I went down to Shoreham. For some weeks, I pondered the pros and cons of suing *The Spectator*, as I had threatened I would if they apologised for what I had said about IPS. I decided, instead, to write this book and tell the story in detail.

On 25 August, Allan Altman sent me a massive collection of memoranda he and his colleagues had prepared for the trial that never took place. It included an interesting though incomplete statement by Arturo Cruz, Jr., taken in the open air in Washington DC. He had said that he preferred not to talk in his apartment for fear that it was being 'bugged'. (See Appendices.) He confirmed that he had worked in the Sandinista government's intelligence division in Managua. His immediate superior, named Julio López, had been receiving intelligence reports from a woman who had been working for the IPS but now worked for the American government. He declined, for the time being, to name the woman, who had sent intelligence information to the Sandinistas, instructing them on how to proceed, and through which channel, in lobbying their cause with the US people and government.

He had also seen her several times with Saul Landau in Managua and Havana, in meetings with top Sandinista and Cuban Intelligence officers. Her material had been very useful in producing disinformation on Central America, which he defined as 'perhaps the most important aspect of Intelligence gathering' for their purposes.

On one point, I had misjudged Barnet and IPS. I had assumed that they would make widespread use of the apology from *The Spectator*, and indeed had feared that such adverse publicity would gravely prejudice my trial. In the event they did nothing of the kind. Interestingly, some months after the 'end', a short item appeared in the Fall 1987 issue of the IPS newsletter *In Progress*, under the title 'Spectator Sport!'. Readers were told that a blow for media justice had been struck by Richard Barnet. It recalled, accurately, the circumstances of the lawsuit. It went on to state, inaccurately, that 'the affair was concluded in September [read July] having been delayed by Crozier's attempts to prevent *The Spectator* from settling.' Next came the text of the apology followed by these two paragraphs:

> The purpose of the lawsuit was not to win large damages. The action was brought to show that reputable journals should not condone the libels of ideologues like Crozier, and to offer encouragement to progressives elsewhere in their struggle against such attacks.
>
> The case was handled by Geoffrey Bindman, a well-known progressive British solicitor, instructed by Peter Weiss, former Chair [sic] of the IPS Board of Trustees.

How many readers, I wonder, savoured the historical overtones of the last sentence, with Peter Weiss, son-in-law of Moscow's man Sam Rubin, instructing a 'progressive' British solicitor?

The IPS account of the settlement, apart from the slight inaccuracy of the month, was not untrue, but it was not the whole truth. For some reason, it neglected to tell its readers that I had refused to settle or to apologise or to contribute to Barnet's expenses. The truth of the 'progressive' thus differs from the truth of the 'ideologue'!

By Way of Epilogue

Straight face. In reply to a reader asking for information about the American Institute for Policy Studies, the Soviet ideological monthly *New Times*, in its issue of July 1984, ran a boxed column saying (truthfully) that 'the IPS seeks to influence not only the minds of ordinary citizens but also Administration policy'. Two other passages suggested a party hack's tongue in the cheek: 'The IPS is believed to reflect the views of the liberal-minded circles of the New Left movement'; and: 'The IPS is financed chiefly by the Samuel Rubin Foundation, which provides money for programmes in the fields of education, medicine and culture. Its annual budget is estimated at two million dollars.'

16. Birth of a Nation

To Ethnos means 'The Nation' in Greek. It is also the title of a sensational, and sensationally successful, tabloid newspaper launched in Athens in September 1981. There was one peculiarity about its news coverage and editorial opinions: both favoured the Soviet interests to a quite extraordinary degree.

Was this by accident or by design? Was it because the publisher and editor just happened to feel that way about the Union of Soviet Socialist Republics? Or because the KGB had been involved in setting it up and had some kind of hold over its contents?

To this day, it is impossible to give absolutely clear and unchallengable answers to these questions. Allegations of a Soviet connection sparked a number of legal actions, not only in Greece, but also in France and Britain. By my definition, therefore, these actions qualify for inclusion in *The KGB Lawsuits*.

As with the other cases dealt with in this book, though to a lesser, more indirect, degree, I was involved in the *Ethnos* affair. So was Sir James Goldsmith. But for one Greek investigative journalist, the affair meant years of trauma and battle; from which, I am happy to report, he emerged at last, if not unscathed, then considerably the wiser for his brave stand.

Paul Anastasi, who sometimes wrote as 'Paul Anast', was born in Cyprus, but had spent most of his life in Greece. His father was a Greek Cypriot, but his mother was British, and he was perfectly bilingual. After graduating from Southampton and London, he settled in Greece, where he became the Athens correspondent of the *New York Times* and the London *Daily Telegraph*.

He was 30 when he embarked on an investigation of the *Ethnos* affair which lasted 14 months, and yielded a book, ingeniously entitled *Take the Nation in Your Hands*. That was when his troubles began. He was well aware that there would be problems, for he was taking on an influential, indeed a powerful, figure in Greek public life: George Bobolas, the publisher of *Ethnos*.

The choice of a publisher for Anastasi's book wasn't easy, but George Tsiveriotis Publishers took it on. The conditions, however, would have been impossible in, say, Britain or the US: there would be no imprint, no indication of who had done the typesetting or the distributing. In Greece, such conditions were not illegal; and Tsiveriotis valued his anonymity. One point in choosing him was that Anastasi wanted to bring the book out in English as well as Greek, and this facility was on offer.

Distribution, however, did present real problems. There were two big agencies distributing books in Greece. One of them ruled itself out, as Bobolas had a substantial stake in it. The other was in effect controlled by one Christos Lambrakis, and the publisher sounded him out, through his representatives. The answer was a flat No. Lambrakis saw no special advantage in tangling with Bobolas, especially since he himself had originally held the same publishing and commercial agreements with the Soviets that Bobolas was to acquire.

This was not the end of the story, but only the start of Anastasi's problems. Despite its glorious literary heritage, Greece has few bookshops by West European standards. What it does have, in vast numbers, is newspaper kiosks: hardly a street corner is without its newsstand. There was no other way: the publisher started approaching them all, one by one. There was a further obstacle to be overcome: the Union of Greek Book Vendors had good reasons to avoid handling publications likely to offend the Greek Communist Party (KKE).

In the face of all these obstacles, *Take the Nation in Your Hands* duly appeared (in Greek only), on 22 June 1983 and, against the odds, topped the best-selling list for the next two months. Strong though the KKE was, in influence if not in numbers, it was not strong enough to stifle the entrepreneurial spirit of the Greeks. Sensing an opportunity, a piratical publisher rushed in with a cheap, unauthorised version which flooded the market with 15,000 copies; and remained unmasked.

What, then, did the book say which has caused so many Greeks to rush out and buy it?

To answer my own question, let me first fill in some of the background. One name dominates recent Greek politics: Papandreou. Like father, like son. In February 1964, after years of democratic turbulence and a succession of caretaker governments, the veteran politician George Papandreou was elected to power with a solid majority for his Centre Union Party. He was 75. His son, Andreas, born in 1919, had spent much of his life in the US, where he held various academic posts and acquired American citizenship. Sensing victory, his father had persuaded him to come home in 1964. Back in Athens, he renounced his US citizenship. Political power in his native Greece beckoned the younger man.

George Papandreou brought Andreas into his cabinet, first as Minister to the Prime Minister, then as Deputy Minister of Co-ordination. Through never, in a formal sense, a Communist, Andreas was partial to Communists. During his second cabinet stint, starting in April 1965, a number of fellow travellers of the KKE were appointed to positions in the Greek Central Intelligence Service (whose duties covered domestic as well as foreign Intelligence).

The dark shadow of the Greek Civil War (May 1946 to October 1949) still hung over the political scene. The Communists had lost and the party had been outlawed, in December 1947. After their military defeat in 1944, many party members took refuge in the Soviet bloc.

The Papandreou team was going to change all that. Without actually lifting the ban on the KKE, Papandreou senior freed any gaoled Communists or sympathisers. This surprised nobody. The Papandreous had given much encouragement to the legal 'front' party known as the United Democratic Left (EDA), behind which the banned KKE had sheltered since 1951. While the Papandreous were in power, the EDA's membership soared to 90,000, an increase of nearly 100 per cent. In the spring of 1965, there was a kind of 'pre-Watergate' atmosphere in Greece, with widespread complaints that the security and intelligence machinery was being used to spy on ministers considered to be less than loyal to the Papandreous. Private telephones had even been bugged. Similar charges of harassing opponents had been made against previous conservative governments.

What happened next was the so-called Aspida affair. Aspida, meaning 'shield' in Greek, was the name of a secret political group within the Army said to be plotting to overthrow the monarchy and set up a Nasser-type republic. Andreas Papandreou was rumoured to have links with the plotters, but was protected by parliamentary immunity and never brought to trial. Others were less lucky: 28 Army officers found themselves in dock, of whom 15 were gaoled for terms of up to 18 years.

Chaos reigned. The King sacked his Prime Minister. The EDA, professionally manipulated by the KKE, staged anti-monarchist and pro-Papandreou marches. In parliament, the Papandreou faction howled down its opponents. No one was able to form a government; strikes paralysed the country. It was against this background that Col Papadopoulos and his fellow officers struck on 21 April 1967. Greece, they said, not entirely untruthfully, had become a 'pit of political corruption' and the Communists were about to launch an insurrection. This was untrue, and indeed the KKE was taken by surprise, but thousands of its members were rounded up and interned. The seven years of the Greek colonels followed, and Andreas Papandreou resumed his exile, which he spent in professorial Chairs in Sweden and Canada.

Back in Athens when the military regime collapsed in 1974, he founded the Pan-Hellenic Socialist Movement (which became the Party of the same name PASOK). Three years later he became leader of the Parliamentary opposition. His time came with the elections of October 1981, which brought him to power with a comfortable PASOK majority.

One month earlier, and hardly by coincidence, *To Ethnos* was launched. In more ways than one, it broke new ground. The Editor, Alexander Filippopoulos, had studied the tabloid press, especially in what used to be Fleet Street. He hit upon a winning Greek equivalent formula, with gossip and pictures, crime, cartoons and racy sports coverage. With remarkable speed, it was selling 180,000 copies a day, a record for Greece.

Popular tabloids don't usually bore their readers with turgid political propaganda, nor did *Ethnos*. Instead, it peddled a consistently anti-Western line in its international coverage. Any reader whose eye strayed from the more lurid bits of paper would unconsciously absorb the message: the US was bad, the USSR, good. For the party hacks, this was a lesson.

One of the constant readers, of course, was Paul Anastasi, who belonged to the small minority more interested in the paper's treatment of the Polish Solidarity crisis, for example, than in who the current pop idol was, or who was tipped to be the next world heavyweight champ. Lech Walesa, he learned from *Ethnos*, was a CIA stooge, and the Agency, along with the Vatican, was blamed for the mounting unrest. Jaruzelski, though, was presented as a noble and dedicated patriot, battling to save his people from evil outside influences.

One article, in particular, made an impression on Anastasi. It appeared in the issue dated 14 April 1982, and was signed by one I Andronov (the KGB man from *Literaturnaya Gazeta*). The heading told him what he wanted to know:

THE CIA TRAINS MOSQUITOES TO POISON POPULATIONS
The Secrets of the CIA's Biological War

Surely, his intelligence told him, this was a good example of what was meant by 'disinformation'. His investigative antennae were alerted. He would look into the origins of this popular daily which just happened to side with Moscow and which indeed was going still further by telling its readers that the philosophers could henceforth call off the Platonic search for what Sir Thomas More called 'Utopia'. For Utopia already existed: in the Soviet Union. True, this was before Mikhail Gorbachev had lifted the veil in his book *Perestroika*.

What he uncovered made his heart beat faster. History is made by men (and at times by women). The men who played the key roles in this particular bit of history were: a senior KGB man named Sitnikov; a Greek millionaire named Bobolas; and a KKE party hack, Yannikos, who brought them together.

Colonel Vassily Romanovich Sitnikov was a well-known figure in the shadowy spy world of the Soviet regime. He was identified as such by John Barron in the first of his two books on the KGB, and in greater detail by various KGB defectors mentioned in this book: Levchenko, Deriabin, Golitsyn and Dzhirkvelov. In the 1960s, he rose to Deputy Director of the KGB's Department D, and in 1974 was appointed Deputy Chairman of the Soviet Copyright Agency, VAAP, which is responsible for Soviet publishing interests abroad, and therefore provides a perfect cover for developing ties with foreign media and book publishers.

His willing instrument in Athens was Yannis Yannikos. During World War II, Yannikos had served with the Communist-led ELAS guerrillas. In keeping with the image of the rugged fighter in rugged mountains, he had grown a splendid moustache, which he had kept. For his activities, especially during the Civil War that followed the defeat of the Nazis, he had served a ten-year gaol sentence. Emerging, he had resumed his work for the Moscow-line KKE, at first in clandestinity, latterly in the open. The Soviet apparatus had looked after this devoted servant, giving him a well paid job as the main publisher of Soviet material in Greece.

His boss, in fact if not in title, was Sitnikov. One day in 1977, Sitnikov gave him a special job; to find a publisher for a Greek language edition of *The Great Soviet Encyclopaedia*. Dutifully, Yannikos approached several 'possibles', who turned him down. Eventually, agreement was reached with the publishing tycoon Lambrakis, but the deal fell through over the publishing agreements the Soviets wanted to set up.

But Party professionals never give up. Yannikos turned to a most unlikely prospect. George Bobolas had made his fortune in a manner hardly likely to earn him praise from Moscow: by public works during the rule of the colonels. But what would normally be a black mark against a capitalist with right-wing connections became a qualification for the job. Nobody was going to accuse Bobolas of being a fellow traveller. At least, that was the way they reasoned.

There was a more practical negative consideration, in that he had no experience of publishing. As it happened, Bobolas found Yannikos both congenial and persuasive. In March 1978, Yannikos signalled that Bobolas was responding as planned, and Sitnikov summoned him to Moscow. There, after exhaustive discussions, Sitnikov gave Yannikos a personal letter to Bobolas, which Yannikos delivered by hand. In gushing tones, the letter said the negotiations had been going very well. He referred to 'fruitful meetings' in Athens with his 'colleagues, Mr Pokhomenkov and Mrs Smirnova' and added: ' Your partner and our friend Mr Yannis Yannikos spoke to us particularly warmly of you....'

Bobolas lost no time. His reply, dated 30 March, written in flowery English, said:

I want to assure you that my collaborators and I will spare no efforts to make a success of this edition [of *The Great Soviet Encyclopaedia*] in an exemplary manner to be a milestone in the publishing annals of our country, and to render honour deserved by your Great Country and the Soviet scientists who contributed to the making of this brilliant work. I am confident that in our endeavours to bring to a success this enormous undertaking we will have the full assistance from VAAP and from you personally.

Agreements were duly signed. Business had come first; now was the time for pleasure. June 1978 was to be party time in Moscow. With Bobolas on the flight to the USSR were Yannikos, Alexander Filippopoulos (the future editor of *To Ethnos*), and Bobolas's lawyer, Costas Rondiris.

Ten days of red carpet treatment followed. Bobolas was received by the Soviet Minister for the Press and Publishing, Boris Stukalin (later to become Andropov's Head of Propaganda); by Sitnikov's immediate boss, Boris Pankin, head of the KGB's Department DI[1]; and by Sergei Kovalev who, after World War II, headed the Agitation and Propaganda (Agitprop) Department of the Ukrainian Communist Party. It is fair to assume that apart from Stukalin, Bobolas would not have been given the job descriptions of the other personalities he met on that occasion.

A number of agreements were signed. The grand climax came when Bobolas and Filippopoulos (but not Yannikos) were received in the Kremlin by Konstantin Chernenko who, some years later, would succeed Brezhnev's successor Andropov in the most powerful office in the Politburo. A dazzling honour for the Greek businessman; a snub for the humble Greek Party hack.

It was the beginning of a fateful rift between Bobolas and Yannikos. In mid-August, Bobolas was host to a luxury cruise. His principal guests were the Soviet Ambassador to Greece, Ivan Udaltsov (identified by former associates as a senior KGB officer who played a key role in the Soviet occupation of Czechoslovakia in 1968), and his press attaché, Evgeny Chistiakov (who, soon after, was expelled for spying on Greek naval headquarters). Yannikos was not invited.

By then, Bobolas had decided that Yannikos, with 50 per cent of the shares in his Akadymos Company, was about to do too well for himself out of the deal. Back from the cruise, he called a Board meeting and demanded that Yannikos should hand over half of his shares. The battle was on.

Yannikos soon found he was fighting alone. He looked to Sitnikov for help, and none was forthcoming. Chistiakov was told to rebuke him for 'creating problems'. Under pressure, Yannikos did hand over the shares; then had second thoughts and sued for their return, alleging chicanery and fraud. Bobolas counter-attacked through the courts. Yannis Yannikos was in a 'no win' situation. He was also an embittered man, let down by the people whose cause he had served all his working life.

All this, and much more, was in Paul Anastasi's book. A mere book rarely makes front-page headlines; this one did. Stunned at first, *To Ethnos* ignored the story, but only for 24 hours. Then came the first counterblast, with a nine-inch banner headline on the front page:

SATANIC FAIRY-TALE OF THE RIGHT AND THE USA

A first attempt by Bobolas to ban the Anastasi book failed in court, with the judge ruling:

> 'The author's presentation of the actual facts in this book is thorough, accompanied by documents, letters and pictures which are not disputed by the petitioner.
>
> 'The petitioner appears in these documents, obviously by reason of his commercial transactions with the Soviets for the publication of the aforesaid Encyclopaedia, as having close ties with representatives of the USSR, some of whom were at certain times accused of being agents of the KGB.'

The respite was brief. *Ethnos* reacted with a full-page 'open letter' calling on the Minister of Justice and the Supreme Court to intervene. Pending a response, the paper, while not disputing the facts in the book, started a classic smear campaign against the author. Here is a selection of headlines:

SHADOW OF McCARTHYISM OVER THE PRESS
FREE-LANCE JOURNALISTS, ORGANS OF THE CIA

THE ACTIVITY OF THE MERCENARIES AGAINST
THE FORCES OF DÉTENTE

HOW NEO-McCARTHYISM PRODUCES
AGENTS AND SPIES

THE CIA FILES AND THE RATS OF SUBVERSION

The stories below the headlines were inventively vicious. Anastasi was described as 'a pseudo-journalist' and a 'remnant of society'. Cartoons showed him as a puppet dancing on a CIA string and as a 'clockwork CIA writer' typing in the shadows. One particularly nasty one showed him as a foreign spy being strangled by the Greek people.

One date that Paul Anastasi would never forget was 28 July 1983. On that day, *Ethnos* published a word-for-word transcript of a telephone conversation between Paul Anastasi and his lawyer, Panayotis Zatos. It was described as a dialogue 'between Anastasi and a CIA agent'.

The two men had been plotting, it seemed, to carry out terrorist attacks on the premises of *Ethnos*. Selected staff members were to be murdered, and in general, democracy was going to be destabilised in Greece and elsewhere. The paper went on to claim that 'tens' of tapes had reached it anonymously through the post, from one of Anastasi's disenchanted agents. A voice (anonymous of course) had telephoned to draw particular attention to one of the tapes; which was the one they had published (with their own embellishments).

Paul Anastasi was not aware that he had been plotting to destabilise democracy, still less to order murder and terrorist outrages. But his friends or acquaintances didn't know what to believe, and seem to have decided collectively that they had better refrain from talking to him in case what they said turned up on a tape. By this time, Anastasi too was becoming unnerved — the purpose, after all, of a war of nerves. He photocopied all the documents in his possession and hid them in a derelict house.

A tense and protracted period of trial and counter-trial followed. Sued for criminal libel and defamation, Anastasi was found guilty on 16 December 1983, and sentenced to two years' gaol. The experience must have been traumatic for him, because at the last minute his two key witnesses had opted out.

The main one was Yannis Yannikos, the Communist who had initiated the deal with Bobolas. His son Christos, not himself a member of the KKE, rang and asked to see Anastasi. Over lunch, he said his father had reached a compromise deal with Bobolas, so was not prepared to appear in court. For Yannikos, senior, it was the kind of compromise that turns a poor man into a rich one: $650,000 (in drachmas) changed hands.

The other witness, Alexander Athanasiades, also decided not to turn up. He had told Anastasi and his lawyers about Soviet plans to use Bobolas's commercial companies to cover transfers of Western technology to the USSR; but had come under 'serious pressure'. Earlier, Anastasi had also been abandoned only ten hours before a hearing by one of his lawyers, Takis Pappas. Being a government legal adviser, Pappas admitted that he had been officially ordered off the case.

One man, however, did not let Anastasi down. Christos Yannikos testified on his behalf. He was able to confirm all that his father had said about the Soviet involvement. He also revealed that as part of the financial settlement with Yannis Yannikos, Bobolas had asked him to sign a statement retracting the evidence he had given Anastasi. To his honour, Yannikos declined.

The son's evidence, however, was secondhand, and did not carry the same weight as the father's would have done. Hence, the finding of Guilty.

The defence lawyers appealed immediately, so their client walked away free, with the judge's words ringing in his ears: 'Until then, you all have lots of time to compromise.'

But victory, not compromise, was the end Anastasi had in mind. One by one, emissaries from the *Ethnos* camp came to see him with proposals for a settlement. He sent all of them away, telling each to forget it.

The appeal hearing began on 18 May, and opened with a big and heartening surprise: under pressure from his family, Yannis Yannikos had changed his mind, and reluctantly turned up to give evidence in Anastasi's defence.

In the event, what Yannikos had to say was somewhat less than decisive. At critical moments, he seemed smitten with amnesia. His son was there, too, and battled nobly on the side of truth. So did a lawyer named Athanasios Thanos, who had made the ideological journey from pro-Soviet to disillusioned. Both men had been present at meetings between Sitnikov and Yannikos, at which the KGB man had put pressure on Yannikos to accept a financial settlement from Bobolas. At one point, Yannikos had reminded him of his ten-year sentence, of spending much of his life 'hunted like a goat from mountain peak to mountain peak' in pursuit of Communist goals.

'You speak of principles and ideology,' he exclaimed, 'but how can you side with a capitalist instead of me, who has served the cause so long?'

Sitnikov, a big, assertive man, had been stopped in his tracks. Embarrassed, he had tried to explain:

> 'I don't doubt any of the things you say, Yannis. and I can assure you that there will be more publishing work for you. But Bobolas now owns *Ethnos*, and you know how important that paper is to us.'

Significantly, Bobolas's lawyers had not contested this remarkable evidence of KGB interest in *Ethnos*.

Seven days after the appeal hearing had begun, it ended, less than satisfactorily. Anastasi's sentence was reduced from two years to one. Under Greek law, this meant that, instead of going to prison, he could buy his freedom for a fine of about $1,200 in drachmas. The evidence about the KGB and other official connections of Sitnikov and others involved in the negotiations with Bobolas was upheld, as was the evidence of the overwhelmingly pro-Soviet stance of the newspaper. But the court rejected the contention that Bobolas and Filippopoulos were therefore agents of influence, on the ground that they would not necessarily have known about the KGB's interest in launching *Ethnos*.

On a further appeal to the Supreme Court, the original sentence of Paul Anastasi was ruled invalid, on a technicality. However, he was denied the right to a retrial on the actual evidence he had presented in his book and the one-year sentence remained on the record.

As for Bobolas the plaintiff, he fared less than brilliantly at his own trials. Between 1984 and 1991 he repeatedly claimed illness to avoid appearing in court on the embarrassing charges of phone-tapping the offices and home of Paul Anastasi. On 24 April 1985, with only Filippopoulos in court and Bobolas absent, the two men were found guilty of the illegal use of such tapes and sentenced to five months' imprisonment. But they were acquitted of the charge of actually doing the phone-tapping themselves, for lack of first-hand proof. The sentence was imposed despite the shock appearance in court, as defence witnesses for *Ethnos*, of the Press and Public Order ministers of Andreas Papandreou's Socialist government.

In October 1987, at their appeals trial (with Bobolas again absent), the two men were again found guilty but their five-month sentence was reduced by two. Finally, the guilty verdict was confirmed irrevocably by the Supreme Court.

Earlier, on 30 June 1986, Paul Anastasi was cleared of threatening terrorist action against *Ethnos*. He countered with perjury and defamation charges against them, but they in turn were also acquitted on the ground that their misunderstanding of his intentions was 'understandable'.

In a bruising, long distance fight lasting eight years, with more than 40 court confrontations, the lone journalist had lost one case and won another. He publicly claimed victory, citing the mounting evidence of *Ethnos*'s involvement in the KGB's disinformation mills, even after the court feuds ended. Indeed, the most impressive vindication came in October 1991 when defector Victor Gundarev, the Deputy Director of the KGB mission in Greece between 1983-86, told an international conference in Athens that the KGB did in fact make more use of his country. He also admitted that one of the operations launched by the KGB during his period in Greece was a defamation campaign to present Anastasi as a Western agent trying to destabilise Greek democracy and discredit the 'progressive press'. 'We had no doubt that Anastasi suffered considerably as a result of this campaign,' Gundarev said.

Paul Anastasi would be the first to say that he could not have pursued his fight to its victorious end without the moral support and the prize he had won from Sir James Goldsmith. There had been black moments, moments of despair, with mounting debts and further trial looming. By October 1984, his debts were touching £13,000 and he had had to part company with his journalistic assistant and his secretary. His one asset was an acre of barren land on the sea front in

Epidaurus in southern Greece, which he thought was worth rather less than the sum of his debts.

He had heard on the BBC World Service of Sir James's offer of a major prize for investigative journalists exposing Soviet disinformation and wrote to my office for further information. As mentioned (in Ch. 5), Jimmy Goldsmith did award him one of the prizes for his 'outstanding courage'.

Others involved, indirectly, were Melvin Lasky, Editor of the influential monthly, *Encounter* (now defunct), and his long-time colleague, the late Polish-born Leopold Labedz, Editor of the quarterly *Survey*. They came to my Regent Street office one day in May 1985, bearing a major article by Anastasi, about the *Ethnos* case, asking me to help as an intermediary to Sir James. They also brought a massive libel report on the article by Peter Carter-Ruck and Partners. By then, *Ethnos* had issued further writs, against *L'Express* in Paris, and *The Economist* in London.

I was about to go to America again. Before going, I rang Jimmy, who asked me to write my own report, commenting both on the article and on the lawyers' libel report. I therefore took the material with me and travelled over the week-end so that I could study it undisturbed. On a silent Sunday, high up in the Madison, I hired a typewriter from the hotel and wrote a detailed memorandum for Sir James. My concern was different from that of the lawyers. Their suggestions, running to 18 pages, were aimed at deleting offensive passages or making changes of wording that would either eliminate or greatly reduce the risks of a libel action from *Ethnos*. My aim was to advise Sir James on the expert evidence that might be mustered to defeat Bobolas, should he issue a writ.

In the end, Lasky felt insufficiently confident of victory to risk publishing the article, upon which (with the author's consent) I have drawn freely in this chapter.

Apart from points of detail, my key suggestion was that the KGB defector Ilya Dzhirkvelov, whose evidence had proved decisive in the *Spiegel* case, should be invited to appear for *The Economist*, should Bobolas press his case. There was good reason for this. In my office, Ilya had disclosed that, before his defection, he had been working closely with the KGB disinformation specialist, Vasily Sitnikov. They had even discussed a plan to set up a daily newspaper in Athens.

I deal with the actions against *L'Express* and *The Economist* in the next chapter.

Notes

1.   After the failed hard-line coup of August 1991, which he condemned, Boris Pankin, who had been the Soviet Ambassador in Czechoslovakia, was promoted to be Foreign Minister. He was later appointed ambassador to Britain.

17. Another, and Another

Paul Anastasi was not the only writer to give offence to George Bobolas. A fellow Greek, writing in Sir James Goldsmith's Parisian news magazine, *L'Express*, also provoked his litigious instincts. And so did the anonymous writer of an item in *The Economist*'s confidential weekly bulletin, *Foreign Report*. Two more lawsuits followed: one in Athens, the other in London. The lawyers did well out of both; the truth was less well served.

The article in *L'Express* undoubtedly caused major embarrassment to Bobolas and to his Communist contacts, for its author was a former member of the Greek Communist Party (KKE), named Ilios Yannakakis. Under the title 'Papandreou's Greece', the article ran to ten pages and was published on 13 April 1984. An Egyptian-born Greek, Yannakakis had joined the KKE in his adolescence. The Party judged him old enough at 17 to bear arms for the Revolution and sent him to Greece when the Civil War broke out, to join the ELAS guerrillas. Yannakakis was one of the 100,000 Greek Communists who took refuge behind the Iron Curtain.

Eventually, he settled in Czechoslovakia, where he joined the Czech Communist Party. He greeted the Prague spring of 1968 with enthusiasm, and fled to France when the Soviets invaded Czechoslovakia and (literally) carted its deposed leader Alexander Dubcek off in handcuffs. An adaptable man, Yannakakis was at that time an Assistant Professor of Modern History at Lille University. In his article, he described what he saw as a Soviet effort to 'Finlandise' Greece, and quoted at length from Paul Anastasi's book on the KGB's involvement with *Ethnos*.

It is one thing when a 'bourgeois' journalist, such as Anastasi, writes such things; quite another when the writer is an ex-Communist who fought with the KKE's comrades in the Greek mountains. Bobolas's advisers claimed that Professor Yannakakis had written for publications with 'Nazi tendencies'. Bobolas then issued a writ for defamation against Yannakakis and *L'Express*, and its then Editor, Yves Cuau.

From the correspondence files in my possession, the legal wrangle that followed had its farcical moments. The hearing was set for 8 January 1985. Ilios Yannakakis was duly present, along with the Parisian barrister retained by *L'Express*, Maître Raoul Castellain. Yves Cuau was not there, because no summons had been served on him.

In distant New York, Jimmy Goldsmith was trying to follow what was going on. He had his own sources, of course, and one of them sent him a disquieting message by telex. The gist of it was that Castellain, whatever his qualifications as a lawyer, seemed to be making a mess of the defence.

The key passage read:

> Castellain seems to have demoralised Yannakakis, telling him that he is 'anti-Soviet and narrow-minded' and that *To Ethnos* does not contain Soviet Disinformation. He has refused to pay the expenses of bringing witnesses to the trial, and at the first hearing Yannakakis was alone in court.

On 23 January 1985, Goldsmith dictated a memorandum for his man of confidence at *L'Express*, the Managing Director Tom Sebestyen, saying:

> I must admit that his message leaves me very puzzled. Maître Castellain is perhaps a good lawyer, but he doesn't seem very committed on the ideological side. There are some things on which compromise must be ruled out. Fortunately, in life, there is black and there is white.

He went on to suggest that it might be necessary to dismiss Castellain and transfer the case of L'Express to the law firm handling the case of *The Economist* (Allen and Overy, in London).

Replying on 28 January, Sebestyen rejected Goldsmith's information. The key paragraphs were:

The contents of the [Castellain's] telex is a curious mixture of true and false, which might be said to recall the disinformation techniques we denounce.

[He and Me Castellain had in fact gone to London on 21 December for exhaustive exchanges with Allen and Overy.]

As for the suggestion that Castellain may have 'demoralised' Yannakakis, by reproaching him for his 'anti-Sovietism', for anybody who knows Castellain and his opinion, this is absurd. What is true, on the other hand, is that several times, Castellain found it necessary to underline that we face specific allegations, with which we have to deal, and that a global denunciation of Soviet policy doesn't help our case at all.

Meanwhile, Me Castellain had made a (strictly non-ideological) complaint of his own, in a letter to Tom Sebestyen, dated 10 January. He described the Greek courts in these words:

Without wishing to importune you with my impressions, I feel I have to tell you that I was dismayed to find that such a sensitive trial should take place in such unlikely surroundings. This tribunal is a tribunal in name only. It reminds me rather of a caravanserai where everybody talks at once. There is no Bar for the lawyers. True, one takes the oath on a Bible which (one never knows) is screwed to the witnesses' Bar ... I must say I am puzzled in the face of this unusual conception of justice, in such an ambience and in such conditions....

Altogether, there were seven adjournments, plus two appeals. Yves Cuau never appeared. On 2 July, a lengthy summons was delivered to his home at 61 Avenue Hoche in Paris, through the Greek Consulate, and via the French Ministry of Justice. Marked 'URGENT', it spelled out in detail the charges against him and ordered him to appear before the Correctional Court in Athens on 17 July 1985. The familiar material about Bobolas and Sitnikov was duly regurgitated, plus a passage in which the Yannakakis article was quoted as alleging that the Greek Communist Party had insisted on imposing upon the founding team of *Ethnos* the presence of Maria Beiku, described as the widow of a Greek Communist leader who had died in Moscow. In the same passage (according to the summons), Cuau was accused of having allowed the publication of allegations that the Soviets had used a Luxembourg company, Jean Monitor, with links to East Germany and the Soviet Union, to launder Soviet money, thus allowing the Greek Communist Party to acquire an ultra-modern printing plant.

Under Article 166 of the Greek Penal Code, the summons should have been delivered one month before the date of the trial; so Cuau ignored it. The same thing happened with a further summons for a hearing scheduled for 18 September. The Greek lawyers told Me Castellain that under Article 49 of the Press Law, only 12 days' notice was required. Castellain replied that even if this law was held to be applicable, the notice given was too short. Besides, he added (in a letter dated 9 September), Monsieur Cuau was in China.

In a further hearing on 30 September, the Court decided to separate the lawsuit against Cuau from that against Yannakakis, who was sentenced (in absentia) to a year's imprisonment. On appeal, heard on 7 March 1986, the case against Yannakakis was dropped. In Cuau's case, the procrastinating tactic worked. On 26 March 1986, the Tribunal dropped all charges against him.

It was a technical victory, though hardly a victory for the truth. But at least it was a frustrating defeat for George Bobolas.

The sheer logic of England's eccentric libel laws turned the *Ethnos v. The Economist* into an altogether more formidable battle. As it happened, I was in Jimmy Goldsmith's favourite club in Curzon Street, having tea with him and Ilya Dzhirkvelov, when I learned that Bobolas was suing *The Economist*. The news came through a telephone call from the then Editor of *The Economist*, Andrew Knight, asking Goldsmith's advice.

I had only met Knight once at a splendid canapé lunch on a bright day in June 1984, when three generations of *Economist* alumni had gathered at his invitation. Our relations, by letter, had been less than cordial. 'Tetchy', was Knight's word when my old colleague, Brian Beedham, the long-time Foreign Editor, had introduced us on that day. We had agreed to be more cordial in future.

The key witness was in the room when Jimmy told me what Knight had been saying. Having worked with Sitnikov, Dzhirkvelov had knowledge of the KGB's plans for Greece. With him, *The Economist* had a good chance of winning; without him, none.

The offending article had appeared in *Foreign Report* in April 1982.

It said that *To Ethnos* had been started with a Soviet subsidy of $1.8 million, and claimed that the newspaper was running at a loss which was being met by the Russians.

As with Anastasi's book, and Yannakakis's article, Bobolas acted on the standard procedure recommended by his KKE advisers: vilify and discredit the author (in this case, the source). An imposing set of articles appeared in *Ethnos*, presenting *Foreign Report*'s allegations as a CIA campaign. Then somebody had a bright idea. Hadn't that anti-Communist fanatic Robert Moss made a pile of money out of a novel called *The Spike*, which he had written with (Arnaud de Borchgrave) about Soviet manipulation of an American Institute which bore a striking resemblance to the IPS in Washington? And wasn't Moss a former editor of *Foreign Report*? Come to think of it, didn't a character in *The Spike* bear a more than passing resemblance to the CIA defector, Philip Agee (although the latter had been mentioned separately in the book)? Well, then, how about interviewing Agee?

Such hypothetical suggestions were presumably made, for *Ethnos* did indeed send a reporter to Hamburg to interview Agee. Agee obliged, duly attacking Moss and *Foreign Report*, and of course his former employers of the Central Intelligence Agency. Thereupon, Ethnos ran a series of articles, supposedly based on the interview, and presented to give the impression that Agee had blamed the CIA for the story that the KGB had financed *Ethnos*, and in general for interfering in Greek politics and waging a campaign against Papandreou and PASOK. Asked by a left-wing Greek magazine, *Ami*, about the interview, Agee angrily denied that he had said such things and demanded that *Ethnos* publish a correction; a request which *Ethnos* ignored.

I obtained a transcript of the Agee interview, which he had taped, and studied it carefully. He did not say that the CIA had invented the story about KGB financing of *Ethnos*. What he did say was that this was the kind of thing the Agency did.

He went on to comment that if it was being suggested that the KGB provided $181 million, this did seem an awful lot of money, but he did not say that the CIA invented the story. (The sum mentioned in the transcript was indeed $181 million, although it is not absolutely clear whether this was the sum mentioned by the *Ethnos* interviewer; the sum mentioned in the *Foreign Report* story was in fact a far more plausible

$1.8 million.) As for the charge that the CIA was interfering in Greek politics, he merely recalled that this was what had happened in Greece at the time of the Civil War and immediately afterwards. (I have to add that the transcript was incomplete, as Agee stopped the tape-recorder. But he is unlikely to have said the things attributed to him, as the *Ethnos* reporter repeatedly fed leading questions to him, which he countered with speculative answers.)

Since Dzhirkvelov had defected (from his post in Geneva) in 1980, he would not have had direct knowledge of the actual negotiations that led to the creation of *Ethnos*. What he did know, however, about Sitnikov and his plans would probably carry sufficient weight on its own to sway a jury.

Andrew Knight came to my Regent Street office on a hot afternoon in July 1985. Tall and handsome in his white tropical suit, and self-composed, he explained the problem as he saw it and asked if I could help. I offered to introduce him to Dzhirkvelov, and did. The affair had come at a bad time for Knight who was about to accept an offer from the Canadian magnate, Conrad Black, to be Chief Executive of the *Daily Telegraph*, which Black had bought. Three days later, on 11 July, he came again to meet Dzhirkvelov in my presence, then bowed out of the affair. Brian Beedham took over and he, too, met Dzhirkvelov in my office. Some tough Georgian haggling went on, about Dzhirkvelov's time and the problem he had over parting with some of the material before the book he was writing could appear.

At a subsequent meeting with one of the partners of Allen and Overy, Dzhirkvelov identified the various Soviet officials who had conducted the original negotiations with Bobolas and Filippopoulos.

With Dzhirkvelov's evidence in reserve, *The Economist* felt it had a strong hand to play. With help from Paul Anastasi, it soon had ammunition for a counter-attack as well. In June 1982, *Ethnos* had published an article alleging that *Foreign Report* was controlled and financed by the CIA. On close examination, this turned out to be an unusually blatant piece of distortion. The article was headed: 'Now the big revelation: the method of fabricated information. CIA and *Foreign Report*.' As presented by *Ethnos* the article was a reprint of a piece that had appeared in an American journal in 1976, dealing with two London-based newsletters, one was *Foreign Report*; the other, *Soviet Analyst*.

The writer, a Cypriot diplomat named Marios Evriviades, had declared that both newsletters had carried material from the CIA. But, he added: '...I by no means suggest that either of the two publications are CIA controlled or funded.' Neatly inverting the original, the *Ethnos* version was: 'Personally, I maintain that both these publications are controlled and financed by the CIA.'

Another round of potential ammunition lay in the distortions and insertions *Ethnos* had made in the interview with Philip Agee. Thus armed, *The Economist* counter-sued.

The two lawsuits came to trial before the Queen's Bench Division in London, on 9 February 1987, and ended, most unsatisfactorily, on 8 April, with a hung jury. The usual practice in such cases is for the judge to ask the parties to the dispute to accept a simple majority decision, the actual voting having been kept secret. *The Economist* declared itself ready to accept a majority verdict, but *Ethnos* was not. With costs approaching £1 million, *The Economist*, for its part, was against a re-trial. Its Executive Editor, Dudley Fishburn, conferred with George Bobolas in neutral Switzerland, where a compromise settlement was agreed.

In a Statement in Open Court, *The Economist* admitted that two statements in *Foreign Report* in April 1982 were untrue: *To Ethnos* had not been started with a Soviet subsidy of $1.8 million; nor was the newspaper running at a loss that was being met by the Soviets. *The Economist* apologised to *Ethnos* and to George Bobolas 'to restore his honour and reputation'.

On their side, *To Ethnos* and George Bobolas unreservedly withdrew the allegation that *Foreign Report* was controlled by the CIA, and apologised to *The Economist*. Neither side paid damages to the other.

As I had suggested, *The Economist*'s chief witness was Ilya Dzhirkvelov. Speaking behind a screen which hid his face from the public and the press, he said he had worked regularly with Vassily Sitnikov, his KGB colleague, between 1960 and 1965, with the aim of making contacts with non-Communist foreign journalists. He said: 'I worked with Mr Sitnikov on specific projects designed to manipulate non-Communist, liberal and even rightist newspapers so as to promote Soviet interests. It was realised by us that identifiable Communist publications had little credibility.' He added that during his period of service, 'Greece was the primary target'. He had known many of the Soviets who had met Bobolas or had worked for *Ethnos*. These included: Boris Pankin, head of the copyright agency (VAAP), who was not KGB but worked closely with it; Boris Stukalin, who succeeded Pankin and later became head of the Agitprop department with responsibility for external propaganda; Ambassador Udaltsov, when he was Director of Novosti press agency; Genrikh Borovik, a KGB colleague in the Second Chief Directorate, responsible for foreign journalists; and Iona Andronov (see Ch.4) of *Literaturnaya Gazeta*. Bobolas and Filippopoulos admitted that they knew these men, but declared they knew nothing about their covert roles.

In his evidence, Dzhirkvelov also stated that he had been personally involved in using several journalists and newspapers in the West as channels for 'planting propaganda, often without the publications being consciously aware of it'. As examples, he cited the *Washington Post*, the *New York Times*, *Le Monde* and *Libération*. He added that he had personally participated in financing and setting up *The Patriot* newspaper in India.

Another witness, Costas Mavropoulos, had worked for 15 years for Moscow Radio. He declared that he had been a Communist but had become disillusioned. He now lived in Greece. He, too, had known Sitnikov and the other Soviet officials mentioned by Dzhirkvelov. His evidence was very valuable in demonstrating that the propaganda he was trained to broadcast to Greece was identical to the contents of *Ethnos*.

In cross-examination, Gilbert Gray, a barrister for *Ethnos*, suggested that Mavropoulos was a fascist because he was wearing a black shirt. He returned to the point repeatedly, until the witness explained that he was in mourning after the death of his son.

Back in Athens, Mavropoulos sued *Ethnos* for alleging that he was a fascist. He won. On 21 April 1988, Bobolas, his daughter Maria, Editor Filippopoulos and the paper's London correspondent were sentenced to six months' imprisonment each (which they bought off). Mavropoulos was awarded £5,000 damages.

One of the most interesting points that emerged during the trial was the exposure of the claim by *Ethnos* that it would maintain impartiality in presenting world events, by providing the Eastern bloc viewpoint through Soviet writers, and the Western viewpoint through an American, Carl Marzani, and a Briton, Stanley Harrison. It had not disclosed, however, that Marzani had been sentenced in 1947 to three years' gaol for not declaring his membership of the Communist Party USA while employed by the State Department; as for Harrison, he had joined the British Communist Party in 1938 and was still a member.

In its issue of 18 April 1987, *The Economist* presented a full and illuminating account of the trial. In preparation for it, the paper analysed all the commentaries that had appeared in *Ethnos* during its first six months: all, not a selection. This was the period to which *Foreign Report* had referred. During that time, the newspaper had carried 71 such articles, only five of which had been written by Greeks. *The Economist* drily commented: 'Decidedly odd...for paper that claimed to represent to its readers the Greek national interest and the PASOK line of the Papandreou government.' The remaining 66 articles were contributed either by one or other of the KGB or other Soviet officials, or by the two Western Communists, Marzani and Harrison.

The Economist, therefore, did not propose to retract its general line, which was that *Ethnos* was 'a Soviet mouthpiece'. In fact, *Ethnos* continued to be just that.

However, the trials in Greece and abroad, and the ensuing revelations, did seem to have taken their toll. The circulation of Ethnos dropped to 150,000 — a fall of 17 per cent; though the appearance of another pro-Communist tabloid, *Proti*, may have been partly responsible.

The Greece of Andreas Papandreou, though nominally a member of NATO and the EEC, had little in common with its allies and partners. The *Ethnos* case was merely the most visible example of a massive, long-term Soviet subversion operation which began during the dictatorship of the Colonels, when Moscow was able to exploit Greece's moral and political isolation from the West. This process intensified in the wake of the Junta's collapse through Moscow's encouragement of the notion that the West had been responsible both for the dictatorship and for the Turkish occupation of northern Cyprus.

The evidence strongly suggests that these impressive results were obtained primarily through the infiltration of the Greek press and the dissemination of disinformation on a scale unmatched in any other Western country since the end of World War II. Once again, it should be understood that the covert activities of the KGB, known as 'Active

Measures', are usually unknown to those being manipulated. In a book published in 1984 and entitled *The Soviet Infiltration of Greece* Yannis Dimitriades gave details of Soviet Active Measures in Greece. The author estimated that no less than 65 per cent of the country's total newspaper and magazine circulation offered a platform for Soviet disinformation. Likewise, the State-run radio and television were heavily penetrated.

As *The Economist* put it, this kind of thing 'sits ill alongside Mr Gorbachev's *glasnost*, symbolising as it does the exact opposite to openness'. The paper added, presumably more in hope than expectation:

> Leaving aside *Ethnos*, the sort of exposure that the propaganda apparatus has had in this trial could be one factor that might encourage Mr Gorbachev to dismantle it.

Of this, however, there was no sign a year later. Far-reaching through Mikhail Gorbachev's reforms undoubtedly were, there was no evidence, at the time of *The Economist* hearing, that the 'Active Measures' apparatus of the KGB had been disbanded or even significantly reduced.

All this, of course, was before the collapse of the Soviet régime.

EPILOGUE

'Legal Terrorism'

While this book was being written, several other cases, apparently similar in nature, came into the news. With one exception, I do not cover them, as I was not directly involved in them. The exception is possibly the strangest of all: the case of the Christic Institute, in which several of the defendants are known to me

The Christic Institute is a self-styled 'interfaith and public law and policy centre' originally based in Washington, DC. In May 1986, in a suit filed in Miami, the Institute charged 29 people with engaging in a conspiracy alleged to involve political assassination, gun running and drug trafficking. On 23 June 1988, Federal Judge James Lawrence King, is a 45-page judgement delivered in the same city, dismissed the suit. His judgement cited gaping holes in the logic of the Christic Institute's case and set aside nearly every item of the evidence it had offered.

'It was legal terrorism,' said Theodore Shackley, a very senior former CIA officer — one of the 29. 'They create this thing, tie you up for two years, and use the Big Lie technique to destroy your reputation.' Shackley, one of the defendants known to me, had by then spent well over $100,000 on his own defence, and went on to spend a further $300,000 before winning the final appeal. Another, General John K. Singlaub[1], said he had spent nearly $500,000. The case had been 'all consuming' for two years. It had wrecked his finances and diverted him from other causes[2]. Total costs of the action were estimated at $22.5 million. The plaintiffs in the lawsuit were a husband and wife named Tony Avirgan and Martha Honey, who were living and working in San

José, Costa Rica, as stringers for various newspapers, magazines and television networks. The essence of their complaint was that in the course of an assassination attempt against the Nicaragua Contra leader Eden Pastora (also known as 'Comandante Zero') the defendants were responsible for the construction of a bomb, the explosion of which had grievously injured Avirgan and deprived Honey of her husband's support.

There were about two dozen reporters present when the bomb exploded in Pastora's headquarters in La Penca, Nicaragua. The Christic Institute became involved in the case and provided Avirgan and Honey with a list of names of people who later became the defendants in the lawsuit. In a deposition, Avirgan and Honey stated that they did not even know many of the names supplied by the Institute.

In a detailed account of the case, sympathetic to the defendants, the conservative *Journal of Defense and Diplomacy*[3] analysed the effects of the Christic Institute's action as:

- Influencing the Congress to deny aid to the Nicaraguan anti-Communists (Contras).
- Hamstringing private organisations working to support the Contras.
- Denigrating the work of the Central Intelligence Agency.

These are general, not specific, matters, and therefore not capable of precise measurement or assessment. Undoubtedly, however, the lawsuit contributed to such ends.

A further effect was that the case attracted enormous media coverage, thus keeping the Christic Institute in the news and helping its organisers to raise funds. The *Journal* recorded what happened.

Beginning in 1980 with four founding members, by 1987 Christic personnel had increased to twenty. By early 1988, the staff had risen to 60 employees, assisted by about 50 professional trial lawyers, working on a *pro bono* basis.

In his summary judgement, Judge King declared:

...the plaintiffs have made no showing of existence of genuine issues of material fact with respect to either the bombing of La Penca, the threats made to their news sources, or threats made to themselves. Plaintiffs, therefore, cannot show that their injuries were proximately caused by the defendants...

ORDERED and ADJUDGED summary judgement is hereby entered for and on behalf of each of the defendants in this case.[4]

This costly and unnecessary case ended in 1992, six years after it had begun.

On 18 June the United States Court of Appeals, Eleventh Circuit, in hearing the appeal of the Christics that the United States District Court of the Southern District of Florida should not have dismissed this case, concluded that:

> a.   (the) journalists failed to present evidence that defendants were responsible for their injuries.
>
> b.   evidence showed that journalists and (their) attorneys knew before filing suit that they had no competent evidence, and thus sanctions were warranted.

The Supreme Court on 13 January 1992 refused to review the decisions of the lower courts and let stand the $1.1 million sanction against the Christic Institute. This was the largest Rule 11 sanction ever slapped on plaintiffs for bringing frivolous litigation.

The Christic Institute had to mortgage assets, engage in fund raisers, and obtain loans to pay off the $1.1 million to the defendants. This resulted in the Christics closing their Washington office. The defendants had won, but there was a further Epilogue.

In August 1993, Juan Tamayo, an enterprising reporter for the *Miami Herald*, in conjunction with police officials in Argentina and Panama, established that the La Penca bombing had been carried out by Vital Roberto Gaguine, a member of the Argentine People's Revolutionary Army (ERP). Other reporting indicates Gaguine was under the instructions of the General Department of State Security (DGSE) of the Sandinista-controlled Nicaraguan government. The Cuban DGI in turn is known to have significant influence in the DGSE and as the KGB basically controlled the DGI, it is not hard to reach a conclusion about KGB knowledge of the matter. A Costa Rican congressional commission issued a report in April 1994 which confirmed Gaguine as the La

Penca bomber.

Was this strange and costly case a 'KGB lawsuit'? All that can be said with certainty, in the light of the evidence assembled in this book, is that the effects that followed Christic actions coincided with standing Soviet policy aims during the period under review. The known facts are thus consistent with such an interpretation. Theodore Shackley, a professional specialist in the work of secret intelligence agencies (and now, in private life, a political risks consultant) has no doubts on this score.

I end with a reminder of a point I made in the Author's Note. We were dealing with a one-way traffic. It was open to the KGB, or other such agencies, to use Western law courts, or cause them to be used. No such facility was available to Western plaintiffs in the Soviet Union at the time of the lawsuits considered here.

Notes

1.   Gen. Singlaub was removed as chief of Staff of the US forces in South Korea on 19 May 1977 for publicly criticising President Jimmy Carter's decision to withdraw all American ground forces from that country. The following year, he was 'permitted to request retirement' when he described as 'ridiculous' President Carter's decision not to produce the so-called neutron bomb. Constitutionally, the President was within his rights, as indeed President Truman had been when he dismissed Gen Douglas MacArthur in 1951 for advocating the use of atomic weapons in the Korean War. The correctness or otherwise of each general's stand was another issue.

2.   Christic's "Fairy tale" lawsuit called "legal terrorism", in *The Washington Times*, 28 June 1988

3.   THE CHRISTIC INSTITUTE: Enforcing the Brezhnev Doctrine in Central America' Study Series No.3 (1988),*Journal of Defense and Diplomacy* (Washington, DC). This study opens with a quotation from L.I.Brezhnev, General Secretary of the ruling Communist Party of the Soviet Union from 1964 to 1982:

> The ever more extensive Catholic forces and the representatives of other Christian religious communities and believers of other faiths play an important role in the struggle for the rights of the toilers, for

democracy and peace. The communist and workers' parties realise the need for a dialogue with these forces and for joint action.

4.   Tony Avirgan and Martha Honey, Plaintiffs, vs (29) Defendants: Opinion Granting Summary Judgments, James Lawrence King, Chief US District Judge, Southern District of Florida, 23 June 1988.

Other Sources consulted include:

J. Michael Waller, 'CONTRAS' ACCUSERS FALL APART UNDER SCRUTINY: A Look Inside the Christic Institute', in *West Watch* (Council for Inter-American Security), November 1987.
Cliff Kincaid, 'The Christic Institute's Legal Terorism', in *Human Events*, 28 November 1987.
James Traub, 'Contragate: It's Not Over Yet', in *Mother Jones*, March 1988.
David Brock, 'CHRISTIC MYSTICS AND THEIR DRUG-RUNNING THEORIES: An obscure Washington Institute if filling America's head with nonsense and making a killing', in *The American Spectator*, May 1988.
THE CHRISTIC INSTITUTE vs. GENERAL JOHN K. SINGLAUB; A Case Study in Character Assassination, A White Paper, The Friends of General Singlaub, Washington, DC (undated).
Theodore G.Shackley, 'Legal Terrorism', in *Journal of Defence & Diplomacy* No.9, 1988

APPENDIX I (*Spiegel* Case)

The texts that follow are a selection of Statements by expert witnesses who had offered to appear for the defence in one or other of the first two 'KGB lawsuits': *Spiegel* and IPS. Each one is identified accordingly.

Ilya Dzhirkvelov (*Spiegel*)

I joined the KGB in 1944. In September 1945, I was sent to the KGB Top School (Vysshaya Shkola, then in Bolshoi Kiselny Lane, Moscow). Normally it takes 5 years to graduate from the Top School but, due to the post-war political reorientation, there was an urgent need of trained operatives for foreign intelligence and counter-intelligence. Therefore, we were given intensive training and the 5-year course was crammed into two years. On graduation in 1947, I became an operative in the Soviet Foreign Intelligence: the First Chief Directorate of the KGB.

In September, 1947, "in connection with the aggravation of international situation", the decision was taken to merge political and military intelligence into one supraministerial organisation. The new organisation was named "The Committee of Information attached to the Council of Ministers of the USSR". The First Chief Directorate of the KGB and the Chief Intelligence Directorate (GRU) of the Soviet Armed Forces General Staff merged in the former Comintern buildings in Moscow (Textilshchikov Street). The head of the Committee became Vyacheslav Molotov (the Foreign Secretary and Politburo member), his deputies were Andrei Vyshinsky and Yakov Malik (both Deputy Foreign Secretaries). From the military there were also two deputies, the present head of the Chief Political Directorate of the Armed Forces, Gen Yepishev, and Adm Rodionov of the Naval Intelligence.

From the KGB the deputies have been, in succession, Lt-Gen Evgeny Pitovranov (later Chairman of the All-Union Chamber of Commerce), Gen Alexander Panyushkin (former Soviet Ambassador in Washington; deceased) and Lt-Gen Serenko who afterwards was appointed Chairman.

At that point, in 1947, the first centralised Directorate for Disinformation (*dezinformatsia*) came into being. Disinformation has always been an important part of both foreign and internal policy of the Soviet Union. But before 1947 there was no central office to analyse the political events and general situation in each country of the world, to store information and documentation and to fabricate disinformation material of highest possible plausibility. Now within the Committee of Information such an office was created: the Fifth Information Directorate with Col Grauer as its first head. It was, numerically, the biggest directorate in the whole Committee. Along with professional intelligence operatives, it used the services of diplomats, scientists, economists, lawyers and journalists. Among the most famous journalists were Daniel Kraminov (now Chief Editor of the magazine *Za Rubezhom* which means 'abroad') and Georgy (Yuri) Zhukov, later *Pravda* political observer.

Of course, the word *dezinformatsia* (disinformation) is never used by the KGB or any Soviet officials in describing their own activity or planted material. Disinformation is a derogatory term, always ascribed to the Western media. Even between themselves, the KGB operatives conducting disinformation invariably refer to 'our material' or 'our work' or 'counter-propaganda' or, less frequently, 'Active Measures'.

The main aims of disinformation activity remained the same through all my period of involvement in it (1947-1980): to discredit certain actions of Western and other governments in political, economic or military area; to influence public opinion in a target country (or countries) in the desired direction; to destabilise target governments; to compromise certain politicians whose activity was seen from Moscow as dangerous or embarrassing.

My disinformation work, after an initial period as a KGB operative, was conducted under various guises. First, still in the KGB itself, I worked for the Foreign Journalists' Development Department ('development, *razrabotka*, is a peculiar KGB euphemism for surveillance, influencing, misinforming and possible recruiting). The head of the Department was Maj-Gen Norman Borodin. Later, Gen Borodin, with whom I was in friendly relations, was put in charge of a special disinformation group (again, called simply 'special information group') at the Novosti Press Agency (APN). The group worked not in the APN building but had its own, separate offices in Kutuzovsky Avenue. To this group belonged, for example, the APN political observer, Mikhail Bruck who, due to his perfect English, often appeared on American and British TV. Gen Borodin, however, died several years ago,

The KGB, APN and other organisations involved in disinformation (the CPSU International Information Department created in 1978, the Foreign Office, TASS, etc) are allowed initiative as far as methods, ways and means of disinformation are concerned. However, the political contents of disinformation, the target countries and personalities are determined only by the CPSU Central Committee International Department headed by CPSU CC Secretary Boris Nikolaevich Ponomarev. The KGB coordinates all efforts of other organisations in their work abroad.

My next position, from 1957, was Deputy Secretary-General of the newly created Union of Journalists of the USSR. Officially, I handled international relations of the Union. Unofficially, I was responsible, among other things, for cultivating foreign journalists and feeding them information given to me by the KGB.

Then, from 1965, I worked as a TASS correspondent in Tanzania and the Sudan. From 1977 to 1980 (when I defected to Britain) I was working for the Public Information Department of the World Health Organisation in Geneva, Switzerland, for which purpose I was given a Soviet diplomatic rank of Counsellor.

In 1974 the book called *KGB* appeared in the West. In the Appendix of that book, written by an American journalist, John Barron, there was a list of KGB foreign intelligence operatives known to the Americans. My name was there, but I have never been told by my superiors about it. Apparently, the World Health Organisation, which accepted my appointment in 1977 without a hitch, also did not know or did not want to know that I was on the known KGB operatives' list.

To give an example of disinformation conducted personally by myself, I may recall the discreditating of the US Peace Corps in East Africa. I was then working in Tanzania as a TASS correspondent and had been in close touch with the KGB local Residence. One of the Residence agents, Colonel Arkady Boiko (my old pal since 1947), would supply well written articles 'revealing' scandalous connections between the Peace Corps and the CIA. Using my journalistic contacts and simply paying some local pressmen, I managed to plant several such articles into Tanzanian and Uganda newspapers signed, of course, by popular native names. This has played a certain role in the fact that the Peace Corps found East Africa unfriendly, even hostile, and was finally forced to leave the region.

I know for certain that West German press, and particularly *Der Spiegel*, had been used by the KGB, under direct instructions from the CPSU CC ID Chief Ponomarev, in a disinformation campaign to compromise Herr Franz Josef Strauss. Here is my specific evidence.

In 1957, on the decision of the CPSU Central Committee, the Orgburo (Organisational Bureau) was formed for the launching of a new creative organisation: the Union of Journalists of the USSR. One of the purposes of this action was to acquire a convenient vehicle for feeding disinformation to foreign mass media.

Gen. Norman Borodin, for whom I used to work under the cover of a Soviet Informburo correspondent (Soviet Informburo was the predecessor of Novosti Press Agency, APN), recommended that I was co-opted into the Orgburo as Deputy Secretary-General. My candidature was approved by the CPSU CC in October 1957. In 1959, at the First Congress of the Union of Journalists, I was duly 'elected' Deputy Secretary-General of the Union.

In that capacity, I attended many private and secret meetings, held mostly in the CPSU Central Committee building at Staraya Square. In fact, such meetings and briefings at various levels took place almost daily at the International Department, or Agitprop.

I also had my own sources of inside information. One of the most valuable was Leonid Zavgorodniy, my old KGB colleague. In 1958, he was appointed a secretarial aide to Khrushchev. Thus, at secret briefings and from private sources I usually learned of most major disinformation actions while they were still in the planning stage.

At the beginning of 1960, a top level secret meeting was convened by the ID. I attended it. In the Chair was Boris Ponomarev himself and two more CC Secretaries, the late Mikhail Suslov and Leonid Ilyichev, were present. Ponomarev said that 'not enough attention' had been paid to West Germany. He spoke also of some other countries and pointed out that much could be done to prevent politicians undesirable to the USSR from coming to power. Although he mentioned, apart from West Germany, also Turkey, Iceland, Netherlands and Japan, the only name he gave as 'undesirable' was F.J Strauss. We were instructed to work out, urgently, practical proposals to 'improve the situation'.

Soon afterwards, I discussed possible measures to be taken by the Union of Journalists with Alexei Adjubei, Khrushchev's son-in-law and the powerful editor of *Izvestia* newspaper. He told me to forget Turkey and Japan for the time being and to concentrate on Federal Germany. 'With West Germany in our hands we would control the whole of Western Europe and could be able to liquidate NATO, because West Germany was NATO's striking force', said Adjubei. He then added that there were two most dangerous and influential persons in West Germany, both strong opponents of 'the coming together' with the USSR. One was Strauss, the other Axel Springer. The former, stressed Adjubei, wielded military power, the latter mass media.

Finally, we decided to invite to Moscow a group of West German journalists and to see what could be done through them.

After that, I was summoned by the KGB General Ivan Agayants who was then in charge of the whole disinformation service. (His next position and the last, as he died at the end of the 60s, was Deputy head of Glavlit, the Soviet censorship HQ.) Agayants knew me since Information Committee years: we worked there together. He said the Union's 'work' with foreign journalists who were to come would be of great importance. Naturally, said he, in two weeks it would be impossible to recruit a serious journalist — only a fool, and we did not need fools. But some preliminary approach could be made. Therefore he would like to place 'one of our experienced boys' Pavel Gevorkyan, in the Union of Journalists as, say, deputy head of its international department. There was no such position? No problem: 'We would create it and provide necessary funds'. In one month's time Gevorkyan joined the Union; I was, of course, loudly arguing that we needed him urgently.

Finally it was decided that our invitation would be extended to 10-12 editors of West German Social Democratic papers. Such a choice was made to show that Moscow preferred the SDP and ignored the CDU although the latter was in power. To welcome the guests and to escort them throughout the visit, a special group was appointed by Ponomarev. Apart from myself, there was Pavel Naumov, a German specialist, former Deputy Editor of *Za Rubezhom,* now (1984) in charge of the Novosti Press Agency (APN). Gen Agayants had managed to include into the group another KGB man, Lt-Col Yuri Tregubenkov, also a German specialist.

Just before the arrival of the German delegation (it seems to me that it was early in the spring of 1961 but I find it difficult now to recall the exact period of the visit), our group and, for some reasons, Daniel Kraminov (mentioned above) had been summoned to the ID to finalise the programme of the visit. This procedure is routine on the eve of the arrival of any important group of foreigners. That particular briefing, however, was very far from routine. We gathered in the office of the Head of German Desk; but I was shocked by the presence of Ponomarev in that modest office. After the more or less usual discussion on details, he started talking at length.

He first warned us of our great responsibility for the good results of the visit. On our professionalism in handling the Germans might, to a certain extent, depend our relations with West Germany in future, when the SDP came to power. Our treatment of Social Democrats was 'critical' but we had no choice. And besides, we had to use this opportunity to compromise not only the CDU policy as a whole but, particularly, F.J Strauss who, contrary to the interests of both Western and Eastern Germans, pushed his country closer and closer to the US, which was totally unacceptable to the USSR. 'Tell them openly,' said Ponomarev. 'that we view Strauss as a revanchist and a Hitlerite who was very harmful to Europe. Don't be shy, tell it just like that.'

I cannot be sure of the exact words but the end of Ponomarev's speech I remember quite well. He said: 'In talking to them, do not use our traditional propaganda. Try to display as much openness and frankness as you could and they will believe that you are genuinely concerned with the grave consequences of people like Strauss coming to the top of political power in West Germany.'

Right after the ID briefing, I was again invited by Gen Agayants.

That time in his KGB HQ office I found Col Sitnikov (I remembered him as another Information Committee old hand) and Lt-Col Yuri Tregubenkov who, it was decided, would accompany the German delegation under the guise of a *New Times* magazine journalist. Sitnikov has always been a KGB German specialist and his presence was no surprise to me.

Characteristically, Gen Agayants first rehashed almost precisely the remarks I heard from Ponomarev. And then he came to the point: what to do about Strauss. I was ordered to hint to the Germans at every opportunity that we had evidence of Strauss's link with the US intelligence which allegedly recruited him while he was a POW. I had to tell them privately that the Americans were still paying Strauss large sums of money for his services and that therefore he was primarily interested in getting from them more and more, while the future of Germany meant nothing to him in comparison to self-enrichment. Asked what kind of evidence there was, I had to reply that there were convincing documents in our possession and that I would even be able to produce them but under one strict condition: that they should be published in German papers without any reference to the source. This condition (I had to say) would be possible to observe in West Germany where journalists had the right not to disclose their sources.

At this point Sitnikov took over. He gave us the list of the coming Germans and made several suggestions. First, we had to avoid discussing matters related to Strauss in the presence of one member of the German group. He mentioned the name but, regrettably, I fail to recall it. That man from Bavaria, said Sitnikov, although an SDP journalist, was suspected of being a secret Strauss sympathiser. He also understood Russian rather well, so we had to be doubly cautious.

Second, Tregubenkov would be ready to supply further material at short notice if any of the Germans showed initial interest. Third, it would be extremely useful and timely if a Social Democratic paper came forward now with accusations against Strauss along the lines spelled out by Gen Agayants. This was because we were presently conducting 'an operation' to compromise Strauss through non-SDP papers and other West German outlets, and the wider range of accusation the better.

It was firmly decided that if I sensed susceptibility in the head of the delegation, Herr Von Puttkammer, I would immediately tell Tregubenkov who had to take the matter into his hands. At the same time, Tregubenkov would explore similar possibilities in private talks with other members of the German group, while I had to concentrate on Von Puttkammer, working on him together with Pavel Naumov who spoke perfect German but was not present at our meeting with Gen Agayants because he was not a KGB officer.

The Germans duly arrived. The head of the group indeed was Herr Von Puttkammer, the Editor of *Vorwaerts*. I was given a full dossier on him. It appeared that his father was a high-ranking Hitlerite. Herr Von Puttkammer himself, however, was taken prisoner by the Soviet Army at Stalingrad and 'turned': He became a member of the 'Free Germany' committee formed in the Soviet Union from POWs under the chairmanship of Walter Ulbricht who later became the ruler of East Germany.

The hospitality extended to German guests was extraordinary even by Soviet standards. To give only one example: the Germans were the first foreigners ever taken on a VIP trip to Siberia, Sverdlovsk, Novosibirsk, Irkutsk, initially prepared for Eisenhower when his visit was planned in 1960.

I spent most of the time with Herr Von Puttkammer, almost always in the company of Naumov. As instructed, I offered the following line: Adenauer's rule was bad for Germany and we would much prefer an SDP government; but Adenauer was very old and soon would inevitably leave the political arena; the worst that could happen then would be the ascent to power by a dangerous and ambitious man, an American agent, Strauss. Persistently, I hinted at the evidence that could be produced against Strauss.

Herr Von Puttkammer was a good listener but he never asked to be shown our 'evidence'. In that respect my efforts had not met with any success. But very soon after their departure I learned from Gen Agayants that the SDP leadership held two meetings at which Von Puttkammer's findings were discussed; and that some SDP right-wingers criticised Von Puttkammer allegedly for his 'gullibility'. Agayants obtained this information from KGB agents in Germany.

I do not know to what extent Tregubenkov was successful with other members of the delegation. He was not my personal friend and at an official level such matters are never discussed. But I do know from excellent sources listed below that 'an operation' to compromise Strauss, mentioned by Col Sitnikov, was certainly successful.

Chronologically, my first definite proof came from Boris Ponomarev early in 1963. At a secret ID meeting under his chairmanship the work of the so-called 'front' organisations was discussed. Somebody said that to achieve the desired goals in our ideological struggle versus the US propaganda machine, we needed large amounts of hard currency. Without it, on a purely ideological basis, it was very difficult to find good collaborators. To this, Ponomarev rather angrily retorted that 'ideological work can never be materially profitable, it is an investment into the future'. He claimed that money would be always available, provided there were good and productive ideas as to how to use the funds. We never spared foreign currency, continued Ponomarev, when real possibilities emerged. Thus, we successfully used *Der Spiegel* and (he then named another publication) to undermine such a big figure as Strauss.

This claim was repeated in the spring of 1963 by the Politburo member and CPSU CC Secretary, Mikhail Suslov, at the confidential meeting of chief editors of central Party newspapers at which I was also present.

My second, and more detailed, proof came years later. As I mentioned before, I worked in Tanzania with Col Arkady Boiko, my close friend. In 1970, he was recalled to Moscow and I lost contact with him till late 1974. When I met him again, in Moscow, he was in distress because the KGB sacked him from a very important job apparently due to his drinking problem. What he told me about that job was quite a revelation.

Having been recalled from Tanzania, Boiko was sent to Dresden in East Germany, to take charge of a top secret 'special Residence' established by the KGB in the late 1950s. That 'special Residence' was deliberately not located in East Berlin to attract minimum attention. The sole purpose of the Dresden Residence was to conduct 'active measures' against West Germany and Austria. It worked independently of anybody except the Moscow Centre and specialised in planting disinformation material into respectable media of German-speaking Western countries.

No Soviet national, said Boiko, would ever go from Dresden to West Germany or Austria. The material was always carried by Westerners, 'routed' via Switzerland or Italy or France. Subsequently local German journalists would be discreetly offered sensational stories not by strangers, only by their known and trusted friends or colleagues.

Boiko named several publications and cited various success stories but, he said, the biggest coup was well before he went to Dresden, when the Residence succeeded in using *Der Spiegel* to compromise Franz Josef Strauss. In his years, said Boiko, they always tried to emulate that great achievement and they pulled many good ones, too. And yet, complained Boiko, he was sacked...

I later learned that after Boiko the Dresden Residence continued under Evgeny Biryukov. He used to be my acquaintance in Moscow and, incidentally, prior to his Dresden appointment had also worked in East Africa.

Apart from those two direct proofs, I heard the *Der Spiegel* affair mentioned as a great success by Pavel Gevorkyan, Alexei Adjubei and Leonid Zavgorodnij. With Gevorkyan we travelled to Prague on a special mission to the International Organisation of Journalists HQ (the IOJ is one of the Communist front organisations) to look through the dossiers compiled there on Western newsmen with the view to using them for disinformation purposes. We also instructed the Soviet Deputy Secretary-General of the IOJ Alexander Yefremov to widen IOJ contacts with foreign publications and individual journalists, to develop them into friendly ties and to report on new disinformation opportunities.

Naturally, in the course of such a mission we discussed successes and failures of the past, and he mentioned *Der Spiegel* as one of the best jobs ever.

As for Adjubei, I was in almost daily touch with him in the course of my Union of Journalists duties. In the late 1950s and up to 1964, he was one of the most powerful men in the land. What is more, he was sent on a very delicate mission to West Germany to offer the reunification of Germany on Soviet conditions. He maintained that it was in preparation for that offer that the Berlin wall was erected in 1961, more than for any other reason: Khrushchev wanted to show the Germans that their fate was firmly in his hands and the West Germans would be better advised to rely upon the USSR if they desired to be reunited with East Germany.

Therefore, Adjubei's word about the success with *Der Spiegel* against Strauss was a very good corroboration indeed.

I also heard the same expression of satisfaction with the *Der Spiegel* affair from my friend Leonid Zavgorodnij who, as I mentioned before, was Khrushchev's secretarial aide and a former KGB officer.

There could be no doubt at all that the anti-Strauss campaign in *Der Spiegel* was launched on the basis of KGB-planted material. But this, of course, does not imply any collaboration between the KGB and *Der Spiegel:* many respectable and politically impeccable publications fell victim to the KGB 'active measures' without knowing by whom they had been used.

APPENDIX II

Tomas D. Schuman (*Spiegel case*)

(Yuri A Bezmenov)

Tomas David Schuman was born in Moscow in 1939, under the name Yuri Alexandrovich Bezmenov. His father was a high-ranking military officer of the Soviet Army's General Staff. At the beginning of the World War II his family, together with many other military families, was evacuated from the front line to the Asian part of the USSR (Kazakhstan) There at the age of three Yuri was exposed to the Oriental way of life and, living in one house with many other kids of various ethnic origin, learnt to speak Ukrainian, Kazakh, Yiddish, Tatar and of course Russian. The 'multiracial' environment and frequent absences of his parents gave him the opportunity to compare the Asian life-style (especially the strong family ties and traditional respect for elders) with the Russian/European way of life in an industrial environment. Yuri preferred the former.

Returning to the Moscow suburb of Mytishchi (20 miles North from Moscow) after 1943 to join his father, Yuri entered school. At the age of 7 he started to learn English, initially from his eldest sister Vera, a student of Philology at Moscow State University. Due to his early exposure to both Western literature and media (the Bezmenovs had a short-wave radio set, allowed to senior military officers), he developed a fascination for Rudyard Kipling's novels and stories about India. Against his father's wishes, Yuri entered the Institute of Oriental Languages of Moscow State University (MGU); his father wanted him to go to a military school.

Upon graduating from secondary school in 1957, Yuri successfully passed the entrance examinations and became a student of MGU. The post-Stalin period of relative liberalisation under comrade Khrushchev allowed Yuri to study in depth the nature and practice of Soviet 'Socialism' and he became less than enchanted with the cumbersome ideology of Marxism-Leninism. On the other hand, Khrushchev's policy of expansion in the Third World required more qualified and highly educated translators and experts on Asia. That promised Yuri a chance to travel abroad and see the exotic Orient he had dreamt about for many years. Skilfully pretending to be a loyal Communist, Yuri successfully mastered Hindi and Urdu, literature, political science and many other related disciplines — all the necessarily qualifications to become a Soviet diplomat, foreign correspondent or spy for his Motherland, good or bad.

Even before graduating from the University, Yuri began working as guide/translator with various foreign delegations in the USSR. In 1960 he was employed by the KGB as an interpreter at an International Trade Fair in Sokolniki Park, Moscow, and was attached to the stand of a British delegation representing the British Thermo-Plastic Corporation. KGB Major Comrade Bobrov instructed Yuri to carefully watch if any of the British became too interested in befriending Soviet technicians and scientists from various defence research bureaux ('post box' experts, as they are called in the USSR *'pochtovyi yashchik'*) and to prevent them from revealing to the British their addresses and the nature of their research. This was Yuri's initiation into the murky world of technological espionage: the British obviously were playing their own game of 'cat and mouse'. On their stands they would display samples of high-temperature- resistant rubber and plastics essential for the production of aircraft tyres, interspersed with innocent pieces of ordinary rubber and watch the Soviet guests' hands reaching for the 'secret' samples, thus betraying their knowledge of the subject. British representatives would then instruct Yuri to invite them for an informal chat and a glass of whisky back in their office. Playing his own risky game, Yuri tried to serve both masters: he tried to warn the Soviets to be careful, yet at the same time he wanted to facilitate the efforts of the British to establish better contacts with the Soviet technicians. Yuri managed to satisfy both the KGB and the British. Mr Lowe, the head of the group, and Mr Joe Frampton, a representative of the company, rewarded Yuri with a case of Scotch at the end of the exhibition. The KGB also noted Yuri's 'diligence' and recommended him for future assignments.

In 1962 Yuri was assigned to work as an apprentice for a newly established Department of Political Publications (GRPP) of the 'Novosti' Press Agency (APN), founded a year earlier as an 'independent, non-government public information agency to promote peace and understanding between the nations'. Very soon Yuri discovered that almost everyone in the department was also working for the KGB. Yuri's job was to scan through volumes of foreign publications to prepare reference backgrounders on various Western 'conservative propaganda' organisations, such as the American Peace Corps, Moral Re-Armament, the John Birch Society, etc. Later, on the basis of Yuri's reports, such prominent Soviet journalists as Yuri Zhukov and Spartak Beglov would write their commentaries, denouncing 'Western imperialist propaganda'.

On graduating from the Oriental Languages Institute — a small elitist school with no more than 400 students (and then only the children of the Soviet 'nomenklatura') at any one time — in 1963 Yuri was immediately assigned to India as a translator with the Soviet Foreign Aid Committee (GKES), building oil refineries in Gujarat and Bihar states. At the same time, he was acting as a propagandist for 'Novosti', working in close cooperation with the Information Department of the Soviet embassy in New Delhi.

Fascinated with India, Yuri was secretly thinking of leaving the USSR and staying. He even dreamed of marrying an Indian girl, a student of Baroda University, whom he attempted to befriend and date, strictly in accordance with Karl Marx's motto: 'Proletarians of all countries unite!' But the Communist Party had a different plan for Yuri. When a local Party supervisor suspected Yuri's intentions, noting his unusually warm 'friendship' with Indians, Yuri was reprimanded and offered a chance to extend his assignment in India after the regular two years on condition that he marry a Soviet girl, a translator on the same construction project. Yuri reluctantly accepted.

By the end of the first assignment Yuri was offered a position with the Information Department of the USSR embassy in New Delhi. In December 1965 Yuri returned to Moscow for a short training period and was immediately hired by 'Novosti' as an editor-translator in their

Asian department .

From 1965 onwards, Yuri was actively involved in various APN-KGB operations in the USSR, particularly with various foreign delegations and groups of prominent guests, such as politicians, government officials, journalists, publishers, intellectuals, businessmen, military and civil servants.

Very soon Yuri was formally recruited by the KGB as a co-opted agent complete with code-name: Musafirov (chosen by himself, dangerously joking about his secret intention to take the KGB for a ride: 'Musafir' means passenger in Urdu).

The KGB overlooked or did not grasp the sarcasm and it was Yuri who was eventually taken for a ride. The Domestic branch of the intelligence service postponed Yuri's assignment to India on the grounds that he was needed in the USSR in the field of Active Measures such as disinformation among the diplomats and foreign correspondents stationed in the USSR.

Between 1965 and 1968 he played an active role in such operations as monitoring the feelings of foreign diplomats on issues such as the Soviet invasion of Czechoslovakia; planting the story of the forthcoming invitation to President Johnson to visit the USSR when Nixon had already been elected; accompanying the Indian Defence Minister, Swaran Singh, to Moscow whilst concealing his knowledge of Hindustani so that he could report the Indians' private conversations during their negotiations to purchase Soviet-made military equipment and to identify the military experts in the delegation; attempting to manipulate Mohan Kumaramangalam, then director of Air India and brother of the Indian Chief of Staff of the Armed Forces, General Kumaramangalam, into buying Soviet-made Tupolev jets instead of US Boeings (to the great displeasure of the KGB, he failed). Three years later whilst assigned to the Soviet embassy in Delhi, on KGB instructions, he again approached Kumaramangalam. Several years later the 'uncooperative' Kumaramangalam died in an air accident in mysterious circumstances.

Yuri's most successful operation was with a group of American journalists and editors representing *Look* magazine who were invited by the APN to cover the 50th anniversary of the October Revolution. Working under the guidance of KGB officer and former Novosti editor, Valeri Neyev, Yuri was assigned to manipulate *Look* photographer Phillip

Harrington during his trip across the USSR. The result surpassed both Yuri's and the KGB's expectations: the Americans were very cooperative and printed a solid package of propaganda lies for the American people. Yuri's bonus was a two-week free trip to Italy with a group of Soviet technicians negotiating a deal with Fiat to build a car plant in the USSR.

Yuri was so alarmed at the efficiency of the Soviet manipulation of the foreign (American) media, that he initially wanted to defect in Italy and to reveal to the Western public the danger of Soviet ideological subversion. However, he changed his mind for two reasons: his first marriage was a total failure and he did not want to embarrass his unsuspecting wife by defecting before he had obtained an official divorce; he also wished to accumulate more data and documentation on the Soviet APN-KGB operations so that when he did defect he had a more convincing mass of evidence. (Little did he realise that the era of détente was looming on the horizon and that no one in the West would either believe him or be willing to listen for fear of antagonising Moscow!)

Towards the end of 1968 Yuri married the daughter of a designer in a Tupolev factory; and an expert in foreign languages in her own right. She was employed as an interpreter with Intourist and was 'security-cleared' and able to travel abroad. Although a marriage of convenience for the KGB, their relationship developed into one of deep love and respect. She was a person of high integrity and realism with no thought of defection. She was too well off as she was to risk the culture shock and initial drop in her standard of living. Again, Yuri postponed his defection plan. He was promoted to USSR press officer at the Soviet embassy in New Delhi.

Once in India, Yuri was 'activated' by the KGB and was involved in a number of serious operations. Within a year he was appointed a deputy-chief of a newly created secret section of 'Research and Counter-propaganda', under KGB officers Valeri Neyev, Alexander Gornov and a faceless Major Badin. It was not long before Yuri concluded that his job had nothing to do with either research or propaganda but rather the collection of information of a very private nature on influential Indian personalities: editors, publishers, Members of Parliament, university professors, radical politicians and even potential 'student' recruits for Lumumba University in Moscow to be trained as future leaders of '*Mukti*

Fauwj' in East Pakistan in readiness for the Bangladesh crisis. Those who cooperated with the Soviets were promoted to positions of power through bribery, corruption, publicity and prestige-building 'Nehru Friendship and Peace Prizes' (sometimes given as rather large sums of money). Some were regularly invited to the USSR for various 'international conferences' and 'forums' orchestrated by the KGB through Novosti and affiliated ideological fronts such as the World Peace Council, World Council of Churches, Union of Friendship Societies etc. Yuri's role was to give character assessments and recommendations that such individuals should be listed and filed for further 'cultivation' and invitation to the USSR.

Those who persistently resisted Soviet efforts were marked down for character assassination, blackmail and worse. Yuri was disgusted when he realised that even some of his close Indian friends, such as Nihal Singh, political correspondent of *The Statesman*, were listed for 'destruction'. His impulse was immediate defection to reveal the impending danger.

However, defection in India was a risky business after Stalin's daughter Svetlana defected to the West. The Soviet embassy pressurised Indira Gandhi into introducing a new law which stated that 'No defector from any country has a right to political asylum in any foreign mission in India', which in Yuri's mind was pure hypocrisy since only a Soviet defector would need asylum; a US citizen would not.

Although defection for Yuri and his wife and new born baby was almost impossible, his impatience grew. He found it increasingly difficult to conceal his revulsion against Soviet colonialism in India. He thought he detected a certain nostalgia among some of his Indian friends for the British Raj: Soviet 'sahibs' were no match for the British who were forced from India by the nationalists Nehru and Gandhi.

A plan to defect materialised with the unprecedented influx of American 'counter-culture' to the Indian subcontinent: thousands of hippies were roaming India in search of 'enlightenment', smoking hashish and generally annoying the Indian police. Yuri planned to disguise himself as a hippy and to join them; several hours before his planned defection, he revealed his plan to a US embassy official whom he hoped was a CIA agent. After two weeks travel with the hippies, he contacted the CIA in Bombay and was smuggled out of India to Athens. There he was debriefed. He changed his identity to that of Tomas D. Schuman and, with the help of the Americans, obtained a visa to Canada where he landed in July 1970.

In Canada he studied Political Science at the University of Toronto, lectured at McGill University in Montreal, took Journalism at Carleton University, Ottawa, and worked as a farm help, a truck driver, a proof-reader for the *Globe & Mail*. From 1972-1976 he worked as an announcer/producer for the overseas service of the Canadian Broadcasting Corporation but was forced out of the job when Soviet Ambassador Alexander Yakovlev personally complained to the ever-appeasing Canadian 'Trudeaucrats' in the External Affairs Department that Tomas Schuman was 'ruining the friendship between Canada and the USSR by his belligerent anti-Communist propaganda programmes' beamed to the USSR by the CBC-International. Finally he became a freelance writer and journalist

After about five years, the KGB discovered Schuman's real identity and in 1976 they blew his cover and conducted a smear campaign in the Canadian media branding him a 'traitor of the Motherland'. Schuman's Russian wife had no chance of joining him and they were formally divorced. Tomas finally fulfilled his old dream by marrying an Oriental girl from the Philippines who was also an immigrant to Canada. To date, the Schumans have two children. Tomas has written two as yet unpublished books detailing his experiences of Soviet Active Measures; the books have been rejected by at least a dozen Western 'liberal' publishers as being 'too belligerent to the Soviet Union'.

Currently[1] Tomas Schuman is a freelance columnist for a Russian American weekly *Panorama* in Los Angeles. He lectures extensively and writes on his favourite subject propaganda and is a publisher of his own newsletter *Schuman's File*.

Notes

1. In 1987.

APPENDIX III

Resignation Letter from Huber Matos to Fidel Castro (IPS Case)

Camagüey, 19 October 1959
Dr Fidel Castro Ruz,
Prime Minister,
Havana.

Comrade Fidel,

Today I sent to the Chief of the General Staff, through the official channel, a radiogram about my dismissal from the Rebel Army. To make sure that this incident shall be brought to your attention for a solution and because I believe it is my duty to inform you of the reasons I had to request my departure from the Army, I shall now suggest the following conclusions to you:

First: I have no wish to become an obstacle to the Revolution and I believe I had to choose between adapting myself and withdrawing myself to avoid causing harm, and decided that the honourable and revolutionary thing was to leave.

Secondly: For reasons of conscience, I have to renounce all responsibility within the ranks of the Revolution, after learning of certain commentaries you made on the conversation you had with Comrades Agramonte and Fernandez Vila, Provincial Co-ordinators of Camaguey and Havana, respectively; although, in this conversation, you did not mention me by name, I happened to be present. I also believe that after the replacement of Duque and other changes, all who frankly discussed with you the Communist problem should also go before being discharged.

Thirdly: I can only conceive the triumph of the Revolution on the basis of a united people, ready to endure the worst sacrifices — because a thousand economic and political problems loom ahead — and this united and militant people cannot be found or sustained except on the basis of a programme that would satisfy both its interests and its sentiments, and of a leadership that would deal with the Cuban problems in their true dimensions and not as a matter of tendencies or clashes between groups.

If one's aim is the triumph of the Revolution, tell us where and how we are going, paying less attention to gossip and intrigues, and do not accuse anybody who brings up such matters in an honourable spirit of being reactionaries. On the other side, to resort to insinuation to besmirch clean and disinterested people who did not suddenly materialise on January 1st, but who in fact were present on the hour of sacrifice and had taken on their responsibilities in this task out of pure idealism, is also a disloyalty, an injustice, and it is good to recall that great men begin to decline when they cease to be just.

I want to make it clear that none of this is intended to wound you or other persons; I am saying what I feel and what I think within my rights as a Cuban citizen ready to be sacrificed for a better Cuba. For although you refrained from mentioning my name when you were speaking about those who had fought and are fighting next to you, what is certain is that I did all I could for Cuba now and for ever. I did not organise the expedition of Cienaguilla, which was so useful in the resistance to the spring offensive, so that you would thank me, but to defend the rights of my people, and I am content to have accomplished the mission which you charged me with at the head of one of the columns of the Rebel Army which took part in the most combat. Similarly I am very happy to have organised a province as you ordered me to. I believe that I laboured enough and this gives me satisfaction because it is independent of whatever respect I earned from those who saw me at close quarters, the men who know how to direct their efforts to the achievement of the collective benefit, enjoying within their weariness the fact of having devoted themselves in the service of the common interest. And this labour which I am describing is not mine alone, but the product of the common efforts of those who, like myself, knew how to carry out their duty. However, if despite all this I am considered to be motivated by ambition and if it is insinuated that I am plotting, there are good reasons not only to withdraw but also to regret that I was not one of the many comrades who fell in battle.

I also want you to understand that I have carefully thought out this determination, which is irrevocable, and I appeal to you not as Major Huber Matos, but simply as any one of your comrades of the Sierra (do you remember?) among those who were ready to die to carry out your orders, to agree to my request as soon as possible, and allow me to go back to my home, as a civilian so that my children will not have to learn later, in the street, that their father is a deserter and a traitor.

Wishing you all possible success for yourself in your revolutionary projects and ambitions, and for the fatherland — agony and duty of all of us — I remain for ever your comrade,

(Signed) Huber Matos
Castro letter

This letter and the ensuing statement were translated from the Spanish original by the author. The translations are literal, i.e., no embellishments, such as improved punctuation or other editing.

APPENDIX IV

Huber Matos (IPS Case)

(former political prisoner in Cuba)

My name is Huber Matos Benítez. I was born in the village of Yara, in Oriente Province, Cuba, on 26 November 1918. In the month of June of the year 1940, I graduated in the Normal School for Teachers (Escuela Normal para Maestros) of Santiago de Cuba and later, in 1944, obtained a doctorate in Pedagogy of the University of Havana.

I took part in the struggle against the dictator, Fulgencio Batista, first in the political field as member of the Orthodox Party, but, on being convinced that this was not the strategy that could lead to a solution, I joined the 26 July Movement, reaching the rank of Major (*Comandante*) of the Rebel Army. During the war against Batista, I led Column 9 which operated in the zone of Santiago de Cuba. When the insurrection triumphed I was named Military Chief of Camagüey, during the year 1959, (but) some months later I resigned from this position and from the Rebel Army. In December of that same year — 1959 — I was sentenced to 20 years in prison, a sentence which I served until the last day of October of the 1979.

The reason for my resignation from my post in the revolutionary government, which took place in October 1959, was the fact that I was in total disagreement with the Marxist parameters which the latter was beginning to apply — a reason which I communicated in writing to Fidel Castro (in a letter a copy of which is attached), at the same time as I presented my resignation, through the regulation channels, to the chief of the army Camilo Cienfuegos.

Two days after my resignation I was arrested, which provoked the resignation of 20 of my officers, as a gesture of disaffection, but neither before nor after my arrest did any of these officers offer any resistance, nor acted as a conspirator.

A mere seven days had elapsed from the time of my arrest when the commander Camilo Cienfuegos disappeared in an aircraft, and with him the best witness I might have had in the trial to which I was submitted in the month of December 1959; because he shared my concern over the Communist infiltration within the ranks of the Rebel Army. Camilo and I had conversed, on different occasions about the Marxist deviation which the revolution was taking; which not all of them could be aware of, but which we perceived because of the ranks we occupied.

On one occasion in which we were together in the Grand Hotel in Camaguey city, Camilo suggested that we should jointly call on Fidel to point out to him the fact that within the Rebel Army could be found, in his own entourage, as chief of that body, individuals who could be acting as "indoctrinators" because they were mere theorists, who, in addition, had not taken part in the campaign, and point out to him the frequency with which pro-Marxist articles appeared in the daily *Verde Olivo*, which circulated within the Armed Forces. During this meeting (he said to me, more or less textually):

> Just imagine what Communism would be for the Cubans, in the first place the United States would not allow it and would invade us, moreover Communism is a retrograde step, it would place the country in a dead-end street, it would negate all possibilities of social and economic development in a democratic framework and would plunge it into a national disaster. Furthermore, the Revolution did not take place in the name of Communism.

His view was that it would be preferable for me alone to talk to Fidel so that I could convey to him quoting him by name, the deep concern which we shared before the possibility of an arrangement with the Soviet Union; for, he told me, "Fidel respects you, whereas at times he treats me like a child."

I wish to make it clear that my resignation was motivated by the fact that there was no sign of any fulfilment of the promise made to the people, during the struggle against the Batista dictatorship, that a democratic government would be established immediately. This pledge was made not only verbally but also in the form of the principal documents which we published, of which the most important ones had been drafted by Castro himself. But once he was in power, the latter permitted and encouraged Communist infiltration in key positions in the government and, in parallel, eliminated anybody who opposed this penetration or the deviation from the democratic projects which had been formulated during the Revolution.

Let us move now to the trial: not only the Tribunal that would pass sentence on me but also the prosecutor who were chosen by Fidel Castro himself, who, in addition, was the principal witness in favour of the accusations against me, which included charges of treason and sedition. For the fact that I had resigned from the Rebel Army was used to sustain the charge of treason. The resignation of my officers was held to justify the charge of sedition. Not one of these accusations could be proved during the trial; Castro therefore tried to demonstrate my guilt by alleging before the Tribunal, in a speech which lasted seven hours, that I had accused the Revolution of having embarked on a Communist course and this false accusation, according to him, was a conclusive proof of my treachery. Such was the emphasis he put on this point that the other charges mentioned were practically invalidated. I now quote a paragraph of Castro's diatribe during the trial which clearly reflected the basis of the accusation against me:

> Huber declared that he opposed Communism. Huber declared that there was Communist infiltration. This means that Huber declared whatever suited the enemies of the Revolution, whatever could serve as a pretext for reaction, whatever used to be argued by Batista, the argument of deserters, the argument of war criminals, the arguments of all the enemies of our Revolution, because they had nothing else to do but to invent and indeed had invented the accusation of Communism; they had nothing else to say and they had brought up this vague thing, they had stirred up this vague fear which is the fear of Communism, the confusion of Communism, accusing a Revolution which they had no right to accuse of being Communist, for two reasons: one because it is a Revolution which has its own characteristics, it is a Revolution which in its essence, in its methods, in its style and in its

idiosyncracies, is a Revolution distinct from other revolutions that have taken place in the world.

There were other witnesses for the Prosecution, to insist on the accusations which they had fabricated: Raúl Castro, Armando Hart, Juan Almeida and nearly a dozen false witnesses. The result of this judicial farce was 20 years of deprivation of liberty.

The treatment which was meted out to me in those 20 years was far below anything deserved by a human, being a brutal treatment, coldly studied with the aim of destabilising me. During the first 10 years, the Castro brothers, through their jailers, tried to send me mad; later they changed their tactics and tried blows to try to intimidate me, moreover the idea of pushing me to suicide was present from the moment of my detention, for example, when they arrested me they took me to a room in the Columbia Encampment with a warder within the enclosure, the latter, believing I was asleep, came near me drawing a 45 pistol from its holster but I anticipated his intentions and asked him what he was doing.

The ensuing days were very difficult, Castro let loose a barrage of insults against my person, using the communication media to present me to the people as a conspirator with the dictator of the Dominican Republic, Trujillo, and with the bailiffs of the Batista dictatorship, which we had just overthrown in Cuba.

From 24 October 1959 until 15 December of that year, the date on which my trial ended, they kept me in a dungeon punishment cell in the ancient fortress of The Moor, which was no more than a window without any more space than the thickness of the wall in which it was embedded, with grills on either side and not even wide enough to stretch my arms. They constantly repeated that they were going to shoot me, they tried, what with the confinement and the threats to intimidate me before the trial, to which I was led without having seen a lawyer and without having been advised of the charges against me, all I knew was that they were going to condemn me to death. However, all this psychological pressure had no effect on me and at no time did I show signs of weakness. Once the judiciary process was concluded, they reunited me with my comrades and, almost as if we were at action stations, and under tremendous pressure, they moved us to the Isle of Pines. I should explain that about 23 persons were implicated in the charges aginst me, who were condemned to seven, three and two years in jail, as part of the attempt to demonstrate that there had been a plot — which would have been impossible if I had been the only one sentenced.

I was immediately submitted to a discipline which made no sense except to humiliate me. I was always placed in the worst spots of the seven or eight prisons in which I was confined. Before each move, they prepared a special place in which they walled up the windows, if there were any, to accommodate me. On the Isle of Pines they installed me, under special vigilance, in a corner apart in which, apparently, was a hospital.

From there they put me in what was simply a concrete box with a hole for natural needs, in a minimum space for survival, without ventilation, where the light of the sun never penetrated; I never even saw the man who checked whether I was there, and the only sign of life he gave was when he tapped on the grills. They kept me in that place for a year.

In 1966, after leaving me alone for some months to make me believe that the ill-treatment belonged to the past, they started a change of method with the aim of unbalancing me; instead of blows and taunts they took me to The Cabin, the most painful aspect of this move was to see my belongings destroyed, including the photos of my family.

During a hunger strike in the year 1968, they transferred me to a cell of G-2. I found myself in appalling conditions, I looked like an inmate in a German Nazi concentration camp, I was a real skeleton, one could feel the roughness of my bones. The strike lasted 165 days, they kept me alive by force-feeding me with a foul-smelling broth, introduced into my stomach by means of a catheter through my nose. After three months of this treatment, on pretext that they were going to arrange the hole which took place of a sanitary service, they left a rope hanging there so that I could hang myself. During another strike, they tortured me and believing me to be unconscious, my eyes being stuck together with pus, I heard one of the warders suggesting that they should cut off my testicles with a surgical knife, but the other one objected, arguing that castration with a surgical knife would leave a scar and that they had not been given permission to mutilate me. He added that the problem was not to kill me but to provoke me into killing myself; they thought to leave me sexually incapable by destroying cavernous bodies with substances which they injected into the genitals. They commented they had received orders "from above" to create conditions so that I should take my own life.

The food was so bad that on more than one occasion we rejected it, demanding that we should be treated like human beings and political prisoners. In one of these strikes, 30 days after I had started it, they took me tied to a bed to the hospital to inject me with serum. Strangely when one starts to eat again one cannot do so the gums having become so soft that it was not possible to masticate solid food.

In the year 1970, together with six or seven companions, they removed me from the prison of Guanajay to the Castle of the Prince and they confined us to a place destined until then for the mentally ill, with permanently sealed windows and watched by a special vigilance group. The bed bugs were so numerous that they could be counted in thousands, so that we had to ask for kerosene to destroy them because they covered the walls and the miserable beds. They took advantage of the change of prison to lead us to the firing squad wall, making us believe that we were about to be shot. I never had access to newspapers; in the 20 years I spent in prison 16 were spent in solitary confinement and punishment, any visits were at the whim of the jailers, for example, during more than seven years I did not see any member of my family or any friends. The tortures and taunts were constant; at times they came in and beat me up without reason, the only explanation seems to be that with unheralded punishments, without any rational explanation, they wanted to turn me into an object full of fear. I remember, specifically, the brutal beating up they subjected me to on 14 May 1973, half my ribs on either side were broken as though they were crumbling biscuits, my rib cage was deformed forever; the articulated muscles of my left arm were stretched in a special form of torture. I needed three years of exercise, perseverance and much pain before the arm, which half adhered to the thorax, could regain its power of movement.

Taken as a whole those 20 years were a very difficult test. The idea was not to hold me prisoner so much as to turn me into a cripple and I, for my part, was in no way disposed to be one. One of the means they used to soften me up was the constant threat of death, they said to me frequently: "We didn't shoot you when we sentenced you because that didn't suit us, but you will have to die in prison, so it had been decided by Fidel and Raúl." They must have taken note of the forms of ill-treatment they had arranged for me, moreover my appearance of ill-health through years without the right to see the sun and with the very worst food, must have made them believe that I was physically finished; always, however, they knew that they had not succeeded in damaging either my will or my morale.

During the 20 years I was a prisoner, and during the experiences I have briefly summarised in the foregoing paragraphs, I witnessed the fulfilment of what I had predicted in my letter of resignation to Castro, and which he had emphatically denied, that is, the betrayal of the Revolution, the oppression of the people of Cuba and the total submission of our country to the Soviet Union.

                                        Huber Matos Benítez

APPENDIX V

J. Michael Waller (IPS case)

The Institute for Policy Studies (IPS) is reputed to have ties to the Cuban Dirección General de Inteligencia (DGI), that country's large and well organized intelligence agency which is funded by and completely subordinated to the KGB.

The DGI, like its parent KGB, invests heavily in political influence operations in the United States. These operations are conducted with the objective of influencing legislation before the United States Congress.

Most of the IPS initiatives on foreign relations, defence and security over the years have coincided with the positions of various Soviet-backed paramilitary organizations, the Cuban government, and the Soviet government.

Council for Inter-American Security Chairman Lt. Gen. Gordon Sumner, an advisor to Secretary of State George Shultz, testified before the Subcommittee on Inter-American Affairs of the Foreign Affairs Committee of the U.S. House of Representatives that individuals working for or affiliated with the IPS during the Carter Administration dealt a severe blow to American interests in the hemisphere. The only beneficiaries were Cuba and the USSR. He said that IPS staff and associates "effectively terminated most of the military relationships and seriously affected political relationships in this hemisphere. Working with like-minded staffers in the Congress, they have done a hatchet job on the long established security apparatus of the Americas that grew out of World War II and was formalized by the Treaty of Rio in 1948".

General Sumner was referring to the Inter-American Treaty of Reciprocal Assistance, signed in Rio de Janeiro, Brazil, in 1947, and therefore often referred to as the Rio Treaty. This pact was an alliance against Soviet penetration of the American hemisphere. After Fidel Castro seized power in Cuba and allowed his country to become a forward base for Soviet military power, he alienated his Latin American neighbours in addition to the United States. Because his government was supporting Marxist-Leninist paramilitary groups attempting to overthrow the government of Venezuela, Cuba was expelled from the Organization of American States (OAS), the offshot of the Rio Treaty.

Since that time, Castro has worked as a tool of the Soviet Union and has sought to undermine the Rio Treaty and the entire OAS Inter-American system. The treaty was designed to evoke a collective response to military aggression by a foreign power against a member state, and has failed to stem covert or paramilitary attacks sponsored by Cuba and the Soviet Union because such warfare was largely alien to Latin America, at the time the treaty was drafted. By using low-intensity warfare against pro-Western governments in Latin America, Cuba and the USSR began attempts to overthrow those governments by "invading" the target countries with ideologically loyal paramilitary groups.

Orlando Letelier: A key figure in the IPS

One of the most prolific figures in the Institute for Policy Studies and its Amsterdam-based Transnational Institute spin off was Orlando Letelier, a former ambassador and defence minister under Chile's communist President Salvador Allende. Letelier was intimately involved in the Allende adminstration's aborted attempt to turn Chile into a Marxist-Leninist state loyal to the Soviet Union.

The American public learned most about Letelier's subversive activities when he was assassinated by agents of the Chilean military government in Washington in 1976. Documents recovered from his briefcase revealed that Letelier had been receiving monthly cash payments from Havana "for his work". These funds were sent from Cuba by Beatriz Allende, daughter of the late Chilean President and wife of a high-ranking Cuban government official. Anderson also disclosed that Letelier was "in close contact" with Julian Torres-Rizo, the director of DGI operations in the United States. As Castro's highest-ranking intelligence officer in the United States, Torres-Rizo was reported in the *New York Times Magazine* to have facilitated Letelier's "transactions" with Cuba via diplomatic pouch at the United Nations. In other words, one of the top officials of the Institute for Policy Studies was receiving cash payments and making transactions with Cuba through the DGI's top officer in the United States.

The evidence about Orlando Letelier and his work at the Institute for Policy Studies indicates:

1. That the IPS was employing a former high-ranking official of a communist-led government as its top expert on Latin America. (Many sceptics euphemistically call Allende and his party "Socialist", when in fact they were ideological communists. Allende's political party is now in exile in East Germany)

2. This former communist official was conducting political activities in Washington and was working with liberal Members of the United States Congress.

3. At the same time, this individual was receiving monthly cash payments from sources in Cuba.

4. Additionally, this individual made his transactions through the Cuban DGI's top operative in the United States.

5. Letelier's activities in Washington were fully consistent with the policies of the government of Cuba, and hence, the Soviet Union, on which Cuba is totally subservient.

Saul Landau and the IPS

Saul Landau, a well-known propagandist for the Castro government and a close friend of Orlando Letelier, is a long-time Fellow of the IPS.

Landau is now considered one of the IPS' top Latin America experts, along with Isabel Letelier. He boasts a career of work for the Cuban regime dating back to the early days of the Castro revolution.

In the late 1960s Landau produced two propaganda films about Castro's Cuba: *Report from Cuba* and *Fidel*. At *Fidel's* premier showing in San Francisco, California in December 1969, Landau permitted the proceeds to go to the Black Panther Defence Fund, for legal aid to the Black Panther terrorist group.

After Letelier's assassination in 1976, Landau succeeded him as head of the IPS Transnational Institute. Landau used Letelier as a courier for messages to Cuba; in a letter that was in Letelier's possession at the time of his death, Landau said, "I think at age forty the time has come to dedicate myself to narrow pursuits, namely making propaganda for American socialism."

Saul Landau considers himself a personal friend of Fidel Castro, and apparently has dedicated his life to promoting Castro's policies in spite of the fact that Castro has long since lost his independent revolutionary goals and is now used as a tool by the Soviet Union.

Apparently, Landau has also put himself at the disposal of the DGI. Landau was one of 34 American radicals who went to Cuba on two separate Cubana airlines flights from Mexico City on 4 and 7 July 1969. The purpose of the trip was to set up the first Venceremos Brigade, which soon served as a cover operation for American Weather Underground terrorist training. Accompanying Landau on his flight was radical writer Richard Rees Fagen and Weather Underground terrorist Bernadine Dohrn. Joining them on 7 July were Teddy Gold and Diana Oughton, among others. The latter two individuals later blew themselves up at their bomb factory in New York City on 6 March 1970.

The Venceremos Brigades attracted hundreds of American radicals, and were used by the DGI as an intelligence-gathering device as well as a training programme for Americans who would return to their country to conduct political and subversive activities in support of Soviet-backed insurgencies and in efforts to undermine the United States government.[1]

IPS strategy for US acceptance of Cuba

After President Jimmy Carter was elected in 1976, the IPS saw a new opportunity to influence public policy.

In the mid-1970's, Roberta Salper was head of the IPS Latin American department when a Latin American Round Table project was begun. This project operated under the auspices of the IPS Transnational Institute.

Salper is known as a firm supporter of the Castro government. She was a member of the U.S. Zone Central Committee of the Puerto Rican Socialist Party (PSP), a Marxist-Leninist party which is considered the political support arm of the *Fuerzas Armadas de Liberacion Nacional*

(FALN), a Puerto Rican terrorist group in receipt of funding and instruction from the DGI.

Salper was head of the Working Group of the Latin American Round Table programme which released its prescription for the Carter Administration in a 22-page report titled *The Southern Connection: Recommendations for a New Approach to Inter-American Relations*. Other members in the Working Group included Michael Locker, a colleague of CIA defector Philip Agee (reputed to be working for the DGI and the KGB); Richard Fagen, a longtime Castro supporter who was with Landau on the 1969 Venceremos Brigade trip to Cuba, and more main-stream scholars like Abraham Lowenthal, Robert Pastor, and Riordan Roett.

The Southern Connection's "recommendations" to the Carter Administration stressed that the United States must accept the presence of Marxist-Leninist revolutionary movements and governments in the Western hemisphere, tolerate the Communist government in Cuba, and lift the economic blockade of Cuba.

While that report was being written, the Soviet bloc was using Cuba as a base from which to infiltrate trained terrorist and guerilla cadres into target nations in Central America and the Caribbean.

Summary

The Institute for Policy Studies/Transnational Institute report made recommendations which would have aided Soviet aims dramatically.

The Southern Connection

1. Ignored the existence of Soviet intelligence and military personnel in Cuba, and ignored Cuba's role as a tool of Soviet subversion and military power projection.

2. Urged the unilateral withdrawal of U.S.military bases from Latin America at a time when Soviet/Cuban-backed paramilitary groups (so-called "national liberation movements") were embarked on a campaign of violence which was aimed at regional destabilisation.

3. Treated the issue of human rights with a double-standard. While Cuba was the most repressive regime in the hemisphere, the IPS report urged that the U.S. lift the economically damaging embargo of

Cuba, while imposing embargoes on anti-communist governments or countries under attack by Cuban-backed paramilitary groups.

IPS Responds to Kissinger Commission Report

When President Regan formed a commission made up of leaders of both the Democrat and Republican political parties to investigate the Central America strife and come up with a bipartisan solution to the poverty and conflict, IPS assembled its own committee to draft a version which would ensure Cuban and Soviet supremacy in that troubled region.

The official bipartisan commission, headed by former Secretary of State Henry Kissinger, was informally known as the "Kissinger Commission". In early 1982, IPS set up its own project called Policy Alternatives for the Caribbean and Central America (PACCA). Two years later, PACCA released a 116-page *Blueprint for Peace in Central America and the Caribbean*, which IPS intended "to be used as an action and organizing document for Congress, the religious community, labour unions, minority and women's groups, community organizations, students," and others.

The political support apparatuses for the principal Marxist-Leninist paramilitary groups battling the governments of Guatemala and El Salvador, which are backed by the Soviet KGB and the DGI, promptly supported this report.

The Committee in Solidarity with the People of El Salvador (CISPES), the political support apparatus for the Soviet-backed FMLN paramilitary organization in El Salvador, gave the IPS/PACCA *Blueprint* wide distribution.

IPS also played a role in helping to set up CISPES, whose resident Fellow Isabel Letelier met with a Salvadoran communist agent and made it possible for him to hold meetings with others interested in his project.

Conclusion

It is clear on the evidence that IPS has a consistent record of support for the policies of the government of Cuba. It is known that the KGB and the DGI have made very aggressive and, by defectors' accounts, very successful attempts to penetrate the United States government, and

the many "think tanks" or foundations which provide so much information on various subjects crucial to government decision making. The
coincidence of positions shared by Cuba and the IPS indicate a very
strong possibility that the Institute for Policy Studies is either infiltrated
by the DGI or is otherwise working with the DGI.

J. Michael Waller
Washington, D.C.
August 3rd 1986

This is an abridged version of a very detailed statement.

Notes

1.   In testimony before the Judiciary Committee of the U.S. Senate
in January 1975, former Weather Underground collaborator Larry
Grathwohl described how the Venceremos Brigades were used to recruit
and train "people that we thought would be more easily susceptible to
political indoctrination".

APPENDIX VI

S. Steven Powell (IPS case)

I, S. Steven Powell, a citizen of the United States, do swear that the following statement is true to the best of my knowledge, and submit it on request of Alasdair Pepper, of Peter Carter-Ruck and Partners, legal counsel for defendant, Mr Brian Crozier, this 25th day of May 1986.

On October 12, 1983, I witnessed one Valeriy Lekarev, a Third Secretary for cultural Exchange at the Soviet Embassy, enter the Institute for Policy Studies (IPS) at 1901 Q St NW, Washington, DC, and attend the talk of IPS Associate Fellow Michael Parenti. Parenti, who frequently writes for Communist Party USA publications, like *Political Affairs*, referred to Valeriy Lekarev as a 'friend from the Soviet Embassy', in a casual conversation with Lekarev following his presentation. I again witnessed Valeriy Lekarev entering IPS on November 28, 1983, where he met with Marcus Raskin. The FBI informed me that Lekarev was under surveillance because of his suspected intelligence activities.

I learned from IPS staffer John Mercer that Lekarev was the chief liaison between IPS and the Soviets in making arrangements for the 'disarmament dialogue' which IPS conducts with the Soviet Institute for the Study of the USA and Canada. According to the FBI Lekarev has been spotted at IPS about two dozen times in 1982 and 1983. Lekarev reports to Sergi Rogov, a First Secretary at the Soviet embassy, who is also under surveillance for his intelligence work. As a senior researcher with the Soviet Institute for the Study of the USA and Canada, Rogov is in charge of the annual disarmament talks with the IPS delegation.

However, it is Lekarev who does most of the liaising with IPS.

It should be noted that the Soviet delegation to the May 1983 Minneapolis, Minnesota 'disarmament dialogue' sponsored by IPS was headed up by one Mikhail Mislteyn, an identified former general in the Soviet military intelligence agency, the GRU.

On December 12, 1983, I met Victor Taltz, an attaché at the Soviet Embassy attending a seminar, 'Report from Nicaragua and Cuba' held by IPS, in which IPS Director Robert Borosage and Senior Fellow Saul Landau recounted their recent meetings with officials from Nicaragua and Cuba. After the lecture Taltz privately approached and spoke to IPS Director Borosage. The FBI later informed me that Taltz is also under surveillance for his alleged intelligence activities. Like Lekarev, Taltz has been seen going in and out of IPS some two dozen times during 1983 and 1984. On February 22, 1984, I met Soviet attaché Taltz once again at an IPS reception being held at the Stuart Mott House at 122 Maryland Avenue in Washington, DC.

I met Rene Mujica, First Secretary of the Cuban Interests Section at the Czechoslovakian Embassy, at IPS on January 19, 1984, following the showing of Saul Landau's laudatory film of Fidel Castro, '*With Fidel*'. In his talk to the audience, Mujica referred to Landau as his 'friend whom he first met when he was in Cuba filming Castro'. Landau makes frequent trips to Cuba.

On April 21, 1984, I met two Soviet officials, Igor Mishchenko, Soviet delegate to the UN and Anatoliy Manakov, New York editor of a Soviet publication *Literary Gazette*, at a seminar, 'Deadly Connections', co-sponsored by Mobilization for Survival and the Riverside Church, an organization headed by Cora Weiss, the wife of IPS Chairman of the Board. The event was held at the 'Cultural Center' of the Communist Party-controlled district 1199 Union of Health Care and Hospital Workers. One of the featured speakers was IPS Fellow Eqbal Ahmad.

On April 27, 1984, I met Margaret Randall, a paid functionary of the Cuban government, at IPS. She gave a talk on Latin America and the Cuban and Nicaraguan revolutions.

On August 16, 1984, I met two Soviets, Pavel Pavlov, First Secretary, and Vladimir I. Strokin, Third Secretary and Vice Consul, at an IPS Seminar, "U.S. Policy in Southern Africa." After the seminar, Strokin approached the panelists Jean Sindab, Executive Director of the

Washington Office on Africa, and Anne Holloway, Staff Director of the U.S. House of Representatives Subcommittee on Africa to arrange dates for future meetings.

On September 13, 1984, I again met Strokin at an IPS seminar, "South Africa and the Media". Again Strokin approached the panelists, Marsha Coleman, director of the Congressional Black Caucus Foundation; and William Minter, member of the editorial board of the Africa News, to attempt to arrange a future meeting.

On February 2, 1985, I again met First Secretary of the Cuban Interests Section Rene Mujica at the Riverside Church in New York, whose political activities are largely guided by IPS funder and wife of IPS chairman of the board, Cora Weiss. Weiss serves as the director of the Riverside Church's Disarmament Program. Mujica gave one of the eulogies at the service being held that day at the Riverside Church to comemorate Communist Party Central Committee member Sandy Pollack, who had died in a plane crash two weeks previously in January 1985 while en route from Havana to Nicaragua. Pollack had served as the International Solidarity Coordinator for the US Peace Council, a Communist Party front formed at the directive of the Moscow-controlled World Peace Council.

Signed this 25th day of May 1986,

S. Steven Powell